Mediterranean Spain

Costas del Sol & Blanca

ROYAL CRUISING CLUB
PILOTAGE FOUNDATION

Revised by John Marchment

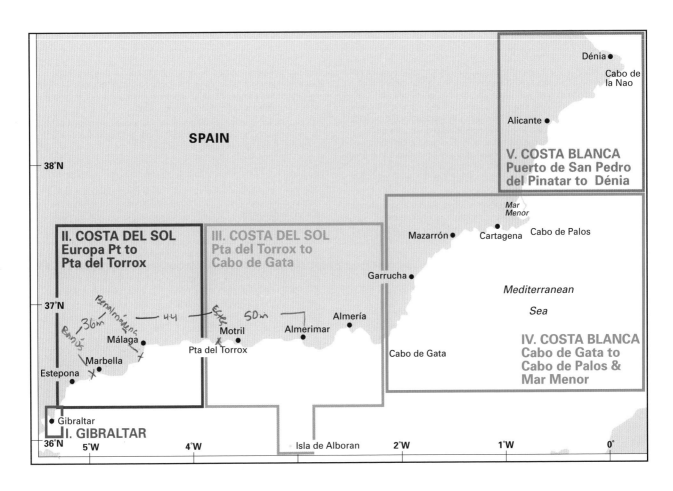

Imray Laurie Norie & Wilson

Published by
Imray Laurie Norie & Wilson Ltd
Wych House The Broadway
St Ives Cambridgeshire PE27 5BT England
☎ +44 (0)1480 462114 *Fax* +44 (0) 1480 496109
email ilnw@imray.com
www.imray.com
2005

1st edition 1989
2nd edition 1995
3rd edition 1998
4th edition 2001
5th edition 2005

ISBN 0 85288 839 2

British Library Cataloguing in Publication Data.
A catalogue record for this title is available from the British Library.

This work, based on surveys over a period of many years, has been corrected to September 2004 from land-based visits to the ports and harbours of the coast, from contributions by visiting yachtsmen and from official notices. The majority of the aerial photographs were taken during September 2004.

Printed in Great Britain at The Bath Press, Glasgow

CORRECTIONAL SUPPLEMENTS

This pilot book may be amended at intervals by the issue of correctional supplements. These are published on the internet at our web site www.imray.com (and also via www.rccpf.org.uk) and may be downloaded free of charge. Printed copies are also available on request from the publishers at the above address. Like this pilot, supplements are selective. Navigators requiring the latest definitive information are advised to refer to official hydrographic office data.

CAUTION

Whilst every care has been taken to ensure that the information contained in this book is accurate, the RCC Pilotage Foundation, the authors and the publishers hereby formally disclaim any and all liability for any personal injury, loss and/or damage howsoever caused, whether by reason of any error, inaccuracy, omission or ambiguity in relation to the contents and/or information contained within this book. The book contains selected information and thus is not definitive. It does not contain all known information on the subject in hand and should not be relied on alone for navigational use: it should only be used in conjunction with official hydrographic data. This is particularly relevant to the plans which should not be used for navigation.

The RCC Pilotage Foundation, the authors and publishers believe that the information which they have included is a useful aid to prudent navigation, but the safety of a vessel depends ultimately on the judgment of the skipper, who should assess all information, published or unpublished.

POSITIONS

All positions in the text have been derived from C-Map electronic charts at WGS 84 datum.
Positions given in the text and on plans are intended purely as an aid to locating the place in question on the chart.

Over the past few years the Spanish Authorities have been updating their charts/documents to WGS 84 datum although many charts in current use will be to European 1950 datum or other. The differences are usually only ±0´.1 (that is 200 yards or 180 metres) but, as always, care must be exercised to work to the datum of the chart in use.

WAYPOINTS

This edition of the Mediterranean Spain pilot includes the introduction of waypoints. The RCC PF consider a waypoint to be a position likely to be helpful for navigation if entered into some form of electronic navigation system for use in conjunction with GPS. In this pilot they have been derived from electronic charts. They must be used with caution. All waypoints are given to datum WGS 84 and every effort has been made to ensure their accuracy. Nevertheless, for each individual vessel, the standard of onboard equipment, aerial position, datum setting, correct entry of data and operator skill all play a part in their effectiveness. In particular it is vital for the navigator to note the datum of the chart in use and apply the necessary correction if plotting a GPS position on the chart.

Our use of the term 'waypoint' does not imply that all vessels can safely sail directly over those positions at all times. Some - as in this pilot - may be linked to form recommended routes under appropriate conditions.

However, skippers should be aware of the risk of collision with another vessel, which is plying the exact reciprocal course. Verification by observation, or use of radar to check the accuracy of a waypoint, may sometimes be advisable and reassuring.

We emphasise that we regard waypoints as an aid to navigation for use as the navigator or skipper decides. We hope that the waypoints in this pilot will help ease that navigational load.

PLANS

The plans in this guide are not to be used for navigation - they are designed to support the text and should always be used together with navigational charts.

It should be borne in mind that the characteristics of lights may be changed during the life of the book, and that in any case notification of such changes is unlikely to be reported immediately. Each light is identified in both the text and where possible on the plans (where it appears in magenta) by its international index number, as used in the *Admiralty List of Lights*, from which the book may be updated.

All bearings are given from seaward and refer to true north. Symbols are based on those used by the British Admiralty - users are referred to *Symbols and Abbreviations (NP 5011)*.

Contents

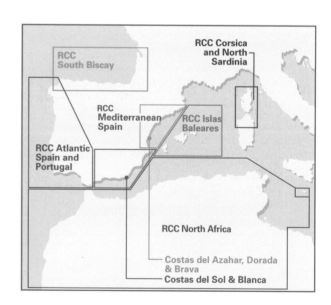

Preface

Foreword to the fifth edition

The origins of this book go back to the late Robin Brandon's *East Spain Pilot*, first produced in 1975. It is one of a family of three – the others being *Mediterranean Spain Costas del Azahar, Dorada and Brava,* and *Islas Baleares*. The RCCPF titles in the Eastern Mediterranean also include *North Africa*, and *Corsica and North Sardinia*.

This coast has become increasingly popular with yachtsmen whether they be passing through or cruising in slow time; or as a good place to keep a yacht in the sun or to overwinter with easy access by land and air. It has become particularly busy in high season, but is still worth visiting.

Since 1975 regular updates and revisions have been made to keep up with the constant development along this Spanish Mediterranean coast. The major work of the 1990s, by Oz Robinson, Claire James and Anne Hammick, has been continued by John Marchment. He has followed his extensive revision in 2001 with yearly supplements and a full visit in 2004. His work, with contributions by other yachtsmen, has led to this edition.

In addition to factual updating we have restructured the fifth Edition to enable more rapid use of information. We have reworked all positions to datum WGS 84 and have included Coastal and Harbour Approach Waypoints. Navigators please note comments on the use of Waypoints under Cautions, the Introduction and Appendix and on heading pages to the main chapters; also note that a book of this nature cannot keep pace with the rapid spread of major fish farms.

This pilot is prepared by yachtsmen for yachtsmen. The Pilotage Foundation warmly thanks John Marchment for his continuing work and also those who have alerted us to changes taking place. We welcome feedback and contributions from those currently sailing the coast so that we may continue to update this book when practicable.

Martin Walker
Director
RCC Pilotage Foundation
April 2005

ACKNOWLEDGEMENTS

This new edition is the result of a couple of visits to the coast but, not unsurprisingly, the inputs from yachtsmen and women have been very limited as this coast fills up with yachts, and people move off to less crowded waters. The last visit, in September 2004, elicited the fact that there are some 20,000 craft awaiting berths on the Spanish Mediterranean coast. Marinas are being built and extended but spaces are very scarce, especially for visitors. The EU regulation that 10% of the spaces of new marinas should be reserved for visitors appears not to be in force.

The majority of the photographs in this new edition were taken in September 2004 by Patrick Roach, although a few are still credited to Anne Hammick from 1997. One can easily see that there are few spaces in any of the marinas and even the hard standings are, in general, crowded even during the season, adding weight to the lack of berth space afloat. Of the 54 or so marinas on this southern half of the coast only three admitted to having room for a 12-metre visitor for a few nights.

There are a number of people that I must thank, firstly Dr Sloma, editor of the Gibraltar *Yacht Scene*, for the permission to use her Straits tidal information and other information on the changes going on in Gibraltar. Secondly I would like to thank Frank Singleton for assisting with the weather information in the introduction and, thirdly, Martin Walker for his assistance with the layout of the volume.

Again I feel I must mention the vast amount of work that the staff at Imray put in to produce this book and, as always, it has been a pleasure to work with them.

John Marchment
April 2005

Introduction

Overview of the Region

This pilot covers Gibraltar and the Mediterranean coast of Spain as far as Denia (which is on the same latitude as Islas Baleares). Millions of tourists are drawn regularly to the area to enjoy the climate and the welcome of the people. The effect is clear to see - high rise and densely packed resorts, strip development along the coast line, packed beaches and the noise of bars, restaurants and discos. However, there are still areas that the developers have yet to reach and much more to Spain than this popular image. The yachtsman has plenty to choose from - both afloat and ashore.

Aside from the sailing, good road communications, and readily available cheap car hire, mean one can easily stop for a day to explore some of the glories and attractions of Southern Spain. West of Costa del Sol lie the sherry bodegas of Jerez. North is the dramatic ravine at Ronda and the white rural villages of Andalucía. Further east is Granada and the wonders of the Alhambra Palace, and easy access to the skiing mountains of the Sierra Nevada. Coastal beaches offer the chance to anchor for a swim or a paella lunch ashore. Costa Blanca provides anchorages north of Cabo de Gata before giving way to the sports playground of La Manga. These costas offer a clear climate, good food, great scenery, and the cultural heritage of the Moors and Christians.

In the Mediterranean, yachts are usually in commission from May to October, the north European holiday season. Whilst there is little chance of a gale in summer, there are few days when there is a good sailing breeze. In winter, whilst it is true that off-shore the Mediterranean can be horrid, there are many days with a good sailing breeze and the weather is warmer and sunnier than the usual summer in the English Channel. Storms and heavy rain do occur but it is feasible to dodge bad weather and slip along shore from harbour to harbour as they are not far apart. In general the climate is mild and, particularly from January to March, very pleasant. A great advantage is that there are no crowds and the local shops and services are freer to serve the winter visitor. Many Clubs Náutico, which have to turn people away in summer, welcome visitors. Local inhabitants can be met, places of interest enjoyed and the empty beaches and coves used in privacy.

Opposite. Images of Andalucia by Graham Hutt. From top left clockwise: The Alhambra in Granada, Almoraima - Costa del Sol, Malaga, apples on the Costa del Sol, Andalucia village scene.

History

There are many traces of prehistoric inhabitants but recorded history starts with a group of unknown origin, the Ligurians, who came from N Africa and established themselves in southern Spain in about the 6th century BC; with the Carthaginians at Málaga and the Phoenicians who had been trading in the area since the 12th century BC and living in various small colonies dotted along the coast.

In 242 BC a force of Carthaginians under Hamilcar Barca, who had previously been driven from Sicily by the Romans, captured and held the south of Spain until 219 BC when the Romans took over occupation, which lasted until the Barbarian invasion in the 5th century AD. This period was one of development and construction when many of the towns were first established. The Barbarians – the Suevi, Vandals and Alans – were, in turn, overrun by the Visigoths who held the area from the 5th to the 8th century AD.

In AD 711 a huge force of Moors and Berbers under Tarik-ibn-Zeyab crossed the Strait of Gibraltar and captured the whole of Spain except for a small enclave in the N. The Moors took over the S and the Berbers the N. By the 10th century AD huge strides had been made in education and development and Cordoba which had become independent was renowned throughout Europe as a seat of learning.

By the 13th century, the Moors and Berbers had been driven out of the country by a long series of wars undertaken by numerous Spanish forces who were supported by the armies of the nobles of France. Granada alone remained under the Moors until 1491 when they were finally driven out by Isabella of Castile and Ferdinand of Aragon who united Spain under one crown.

Then followed a period of world-wide expansion and, when the crown went to the house of Hapsburg in the 16th century, of interference in the affairs of Europe which continued when the house of Bourbon took over in the 18th century.

Over the years the country has been in constant turmoil. Wars and rebellions, victories and defeats, sieges and conquests were common occurrences but none were quite as terrible as the Civil War which started in 1936 and lasted for two-and-a-half years, leaving nearly a million dead. Since then the country has moved away from a dictatorship into the different turmoils of democracy and the European Union, but the Civil War has not been forgotten. Though the country is governed centrally from Madrid, provinces have considerable local autonomy.

Local economy

Along all the coasts tourism is of course a significant factor in the economy but this coastal development is, in a manner of speaking, skin-deep. Inland, agricultural patterns remain though some of them have been drastically developed, for instance by the introduction of hydroponics supported by kilometres of plastic greenhouses. Fishing fleets, inshore and mid-range, work out of many ports and they, together with a supporting boat building industry, help provide the skills on which marinas depend.

Language

The Castilian spoken in Andalucía sounds different to that spoken further north, principally in that the cedilla is not lisped. In Catalunya, Catalan is actively promoted. Though close to Spanish, there are Catalan alternatives for Castilian Spanish, some of which have French overtones, such as: *bondia* – good morning (rather than *buenos días*), *bon tarde* – good afternoon (*buenos tardes*), *s'es plau* – please (*por favor*).

Many local people speak English or German, often learnt from tourists, and French is taught as a second language at school.

Place names appear in the Spanish (i.e. Castilian) form where possible – the spelling normally used on British Admiralty charts – with local alternatives, including Catalan, in brackets.

Currency

The unit of currency is the Euro. Major credit cards are widely accepted, as are Eurocheques. Bank hours are normally 0830 to 1400, Monday to Friday, with a few also open 0830 to 1300 on Saturday. Most banks have automatic telling machines (ATM).

Time zone

Spain keeps Standard European Time (UT+1), advanced one hour in summer to UT+2 hours. Changeover dates are now standardised with the rest of the EU as the last weekends in March and October respectively.

Unless stated otherwise, times quoted are UT.

National holidays and fiestas

There are numerous official and local holidays, the latter often celebrating the local saint's day or some historical event. They usually comprise a religious procession, sometimes by boat, followed by a fiesta in the evening. The Fiesta del Virgen de la Carmen is celebrated in many harbours during mid-July. Dates of other local fiestas are included in the harbour information. Official holidays include:

1 January	*Año Nuevo* (New Year's Day)
6 January	*Reyes Magos* (Epiphany)
19 March	*San José* (St Joseph's Day)
	Viernes Santo (Good Friday)
	Easter Monday
1 May	*Día del Trabajo* (Labour Day)
early/mid-June	*Corpus Christi*
24 June	*Día de San Juan* (St John's Day, the King's name-day)
29 June	*San Pedro y San Pablo* (Sts Peter and Paul)
25 July	*Día de Santiago* (St James' Day)
15 August	*Día del Asunción* (Feast of the Assumption)
11 September	Catalan National Day
12 October	*Día de la Hispanidad* (Day of the Spanish Nation)
1 November	*Todos los Santos* (All Saints)
6 December	*Día de la Constitución* (Constitution Day)
8 December	*Inmaculada Concepción* (Immaculate Conception)
25 December	*Navidad* (Christmas Day)

When a national holiday falls on a Sunday it may be celebrated the following day.

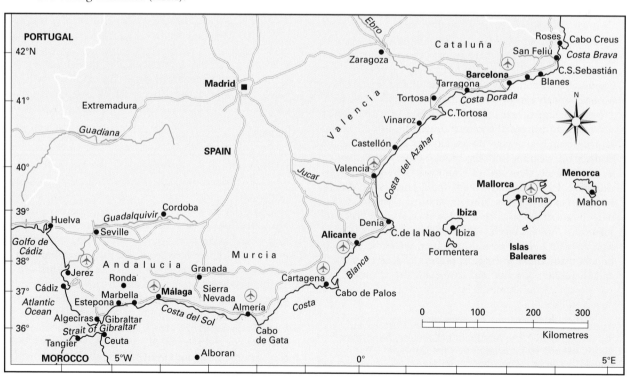

Practicalities

OFFICIAL ADDRESSES

See Appendix VIII

USEFUL WEB PAGES
Junta de Andalucía – www.eppa.es
Describes the marinas and Puerto Deportivos in Andalucía.
Two sites which are really devoted to selling property in
Spain but have some pages devoted to marinas and their
facilities are
http://www.spanish-living.com
http://www.spanishpropertyworld.com

Spanish Tourist Office www.tourspain.co.uk

British Airways www.britishairways.com

Iberia Airlines www.iberia.com

Andalucía www.andalucia.org

Murcia www.murciaturistica.es

Valencia www.comunidadvalenciana.com

Weather web sites on page 15
Port web sites at each port

VAT

Note Value Added Tax (VAT) is called *Impuesto de Valor Agregado* (IVA) and the standard rate is 16%.

Documentation

Spain is a member of the European Union. Other EU nationals may visit the country for up to 90 days with a passport but no visa, as may US citizens. EU citizens wishing to remain in Spain may apply for a *permiso de residencia* once in the country; non-EU nationals can apply for a single 90-day extension, or otherwise obtain a long-term visa from a Spanish embassy or consulate before leaving home.

In practice the requirement to apply for a *permiso de residencia* does not appear to be enforced in the case of cruising yachtsmen, living aboard rather than ashore and frequently on the move. Many yachtsmen have cruised Spanish waters for extended periods with no documentation beyond that normally carried in the UK. If in doubt, check with the authorities before departure.

Under EU regulations, EU registered boats are not required to fly the Q flag on first arrival unless they have non-EU nationals or dutiable goods aboard. Nevertheless, clearance should be sought either through a visit to or from officials or through the offices of the larger marinas or yacht clubs. Passports and the ship's registration papers will be required. A Certificate of Competence (or equivalent) and evidence of VAT status may also be requested - see Appendices IV and VII. Other documents sometimes requested are a crew list with passport details, the radio licence and evidence of insurance. Subsequently, at other ports, clearance need not be sought but the *Guarda Civil* may wish to see papers, particularly passports. Marina officials often ask to see yacht registration documents and the skipper's passport, and sometimes evidence of insurance. Also see Appendix V.

Marine insurance is compulsory in most countries around the Mediterranean and it is essential that territorial cruising limits are extended to cover the planned voyage. The minimum third party insurance

required in Spain is € 1,000,000 and the insurers should provide a letter to this effect written in Spanish. This is usually provided free of cost and should be requested from the insurers if not sent out with the policy.

Temporary import and laying up

A VAT paid or exempt yacht should apply for a *permiso aduanero* on arrival in Spanish waters. This is valid for twelve months and renewable annually, allowing for an almost indefinite stay. Possession of a *permiso aduanero* establishes the status of a vessel and is helpful when importing equipment and spares from other EU countries.

A boat registered outside the EU fiscal area on which VAT has not been paid may be temporarily imported into the EU for a period not exceeding six months in any twelve before VAT is payable. This period may sometimes be extended by prior agreement with the local customs authorities (for instance, some do not count time laid up as part of the six months). While in EU waters the vessel may only be used by its owner, and may not be chartered or even lent to another person, on pain of paying VAT (see Appendix VII for further details). If kept in the EU longer than six months the vessel normally becomes liable for VAT. There are marked differences in the way the rules are applied from one harbour to the next, let alone in different countries - check the local situation on arrival.

See Appendix VII for VAT including information and documentation required and the EU fiscal area. The purely practical side of laying up is covered on page 7.

Chartering

There is a blanket restriction on foreign-owned and/or skippered vessels based in Spain engaging in charter work. See Appendix VI for details.

Light dues

A charge known as *Tarifa G5* is supposedly levied on all vessels. Locally-based pleasure craft (the status of a charter yacht is not clear) pay at the rate of € 5 per square metre per year, area being calculated as LOA x beam. Visiting pleasure craft pay at one tenth of that sum and are not charged again for ten days. Boats of less than 7m LOA and with engines of less than 25hp make a single payment of € 30 per year. In practice this levy appears to be added to the marina or mooring charges on a daily basis.

Charts

See Appendix I. Current British Admiralty information is largely obtained from Spanish sources. The Spanish Hydrographic Office re-issues and corrects its charts periodically, and issues weekly Notices to Mariners. Corrections are repeated by the British Admiralty, generally some months later. Spanish charts tend to be short on compass roses - carry a chart plotter or rule which incorporates a protractor.

Pilot books

Details of principal harbours and some interesting background information appear in the British Admiralty Hydrographic Office's *Mediterranean Pilot Vol 1 (NP 45)*. Harbour descriptions are also to be found in *Guía del Navigante – La Costa de España y el Algarve* (PubliNáutic Rilnvest SL) written in colloquial English with a Spanish translation. Published annually, it carries many potentially useful advertisements for marine-related businesses.

For French speakers, *Votre Livre de Bord – Méditerranée* (Bloc Marine) may be helpful. In German there are *Spanische Gewässer, Lissabon bis Golfe du Lion* (Delius Klasing). See also Appendix II.

Positions and Waypoints

All positions in this pilot are to WGS 84 and have been derived from C-Map electronic charts. If plotting onto paper charts then the navigator is reminded that many source charts of this area remain at European 1950 datum (ED50) and appropriate use of offsets may be necessary.

This pilot includes waypoints: note the caution on page iv. A full list is given in Appendix X.

Coastal waypoints are indicated there in bold and are shown on the plans at the beginning of each chapter. They form a series with which one is able to steer from off Gibraltar to Dénia. The track avoids the main fish farm areas identified in September 2004. However, it is essential to keep a good look out at all times while making a coastal passage in this area.

Waypoints which are not listed in bold, have been selected as close approach waypoints for all but the most minor harbours. The detail is shown in the data section at the beginning of each port and on the associated harbour plan. They have not been proven at sea and should be used with caution. Where scale permits they have been plotted on the harbour plan. The track line from waypoint to harbour mouth has been given on these plans to help orientation. The recommended sector from which to approach these waypoints, and the approximate distance from waypoint to the harbour, is indicated under the heading 'GPS approach'.

The numerical sequence of the waypoint list does not indicate that port waypoints may be grouped together to form a route from one harbour to another. The navigator will need to plot them on a chart in order to plan a hazard-free route.

Magnetic variation

Magnetic variation is noted in the introduction to the coastal sections.

Traffic zones

There are traffic separation zones in the Straits of Gibraltar, off Cabo de Gata, Cabo de Palos and Cabo de la Nao.

Navigation aids

Lights

The four-figure international numbering system has been used to identify lights in the text and on plans – the Mediterranean falls in Group E. As each light has its own four figure number, correcting from *Notices to Mariners* or the annual *List of Lights and Fog Signals*, whether in Spanish or English, is straightforward.

Certain minor lights with a five figure number are listed in the Spanish *Faros y Señales de Niebla Part II* but are not included in the international system.

Positions correspond to the largest scale British Admiralty chart of the area currently available. All bearings are given from seaward and refer to true north. Where a visibility sector is stated this is always expressed in a clockwise direction.

Harbour lights follow the IALA A system and are normally listed in the order in which they become relevant upon approach and entry, working from Gibraltar towards France.

It should be noted that, whilst every effort has been taken to check the lights agree with the documents mentioned above, the responsibility for maintaining the lights appears to rest with the local *capitanía* and, depending on their efficiency, this can mean some lights may be defective or different from the stated characteristics at times.

Buoyage

Buoys follow the IALA A system, based on the direction of the main flood tide. Yellow topped black or red rusty buoys 500m offshore mark raw sewage outlets. Many minor harbours, however, maintain their own buoys to their own systems. Generally, yellow buoys in line mark the seaward side of areas reserved for swimming. Narrow lanes for water-skiing and sailboarding lead out from the shore and are also buoyed.

Hazards

Restricted areas

Restricted areas are outlined in the coastal sections.

Night approaches

Approaches in darkness are often made difficult by the plethora of background lights - fixed, flashing, occulting, interrupted - of all colours. Though there may be exceptions, this applies to nearly all harbours backed by a town of any size. Powerful shore lights make weaker navigation lights difficult to identify and mask unlit features such as exposed rocks or the line of a jetty. If at all possible, avoid closing an unknown harbour in darkness.

Skylines

Individual buildings on the coast – particularly prominent hotel blocks - are built, demolished, duplicated, change colour, change shape, all with amazing rapidity. They are not nearly as reliable as landmarks as might be thought. If a particular building on a chart or in a photograph can be positively identified on the ground, well and good. If not, take care.

Tunny nets and fish farms

During summer and autumn these nets, anchored to the sea bed and up to 6 miles long, are normally laid inshore across the current in depths of 15–40m but may be placed as far as 10 miles offshore. They may be laid in parallel lines. The outer end of a line should be marked by a float or a boat carrying a white flag with an 'A' (in black) by day, and two red or red and white lights by night. There should also be markers along the line of the net.

These nets are capable of stopping a small freighter but should you by accident, and successfully, sail over one, look out for a second within a few hundred metres. If seen, the best action may be to sail parallel to the nets until one end is reached.

Areas where nets are laid are noted in the introduction to the coastal sections.

However, recent reports saw no nets east of Punta Sabinal but many *calas* and bays had fish farms proliferating. These latter are often lit with flashing yellow lights but great care should be taken when entering small *calas* at night.

The positions of some fish farms are indicated on the latest charts but be aware these farms change position frequently. Fish farming is developing along this coast and navigators must be prepared to encounter ones not shown on plans and charts.

Commercial fishing boats

Commercial fishing boats should be given a wide berth. They may be:
- Trawling singly or in pairs with a net between the boats.
- Laying a long net, the top of which is supported by floats.
- Picking up or laying pots either singly or in groups or lines.
- Trolling with one or more lines out astern.
- Drifting, trailing nets to windward.

Do not assume they know, or will observe, the law of the sea – keep well clear on principle.

Small fishing boats

Small fishing boats, including the traditional double-ended *llauds*, either use nets or troll with lines astern and should be avoided as far as possible. At night many *lámparas* put to sea and, using powerful electric or gas lights, attract fish to the surface. When seen from a distance these lights appear to flash as the boat moves up and down in the waves and can at first be mistaken for a lighthouse.

Speed boats etc

Para-gliding, water-skiing, speedboats and jet-skis are all popular, and are sometimes operated by unskilled and thoughtless drivers with small regard to collision risks. In theory they are not allowed to exceed 5 knots within 100m of the coast or within 250m of bathing beaches. Water-skiing is restricted to buoyed areas.

Scuba divers and swimmers

A good watch should be kept for scuba divers and swimmers, with or without snorkel equipment, particularly around harbour entrances. If accompanied by a boat, the presence of divers may be indicated either by International Code Flag A or by a square red flag with a single yellow diagonal, as commonly seen in north America and the Caribbean.

Preparation

THE CREW

Clothing

Summer sunburn is an even more serious hazard at sea, where light is reflected, than on land. Lightweight, patterned cotton clothing is handy in this context – it washes and dries easily and the pattern camouflages the creases! Non-absorbent, heat retaining synthetic materials are best avoided. When swimming wear a T-shirt against the sun and shoes if there are sea-urchins around.

Some kind of headgear, preferably with a wide brim, is essential. A genuine Panama Hat, a *Montecristi*, can be rolled up, shoved in a pocket and doesn't mind getting wet (they come from Ecuador, not Panama, which has hi-jacked the name). A retaining string for the hat, tied either to clothing or around the neck, is a wise precaution whilst on the water.

Footwear at sea is a contentious subject. Many experienced cruisers habitually sail barefoot but while this may be acceptable on a familiar vessel, it would be courting injury on a less intimately known deck and around mid-day bare soles may get burnt. Proper sailing shoes should always be worn for harbour work and anchor handling. Ashore, if wearing sandals the upper part of the foot is the first area to get sunburn.

At the other end of the year, winter weather may be wet and cold. Foul weather gear as well as warm sweaters etc. will be needed.

Shoregoing clothes should be on a par with what one might wear in the UK - beachwear is not often acceptable in restaurants and certainly not on more formal occasions in yacht clubs.

Medical

No inoculations are required. Minor ailments may best be treated by consulting a *farmacia* (often able to dispense drugs which in most other countries would be on prescription), or by contact with an English-speaking doctor (recommended by the *farmacia*, marina staff, a tourist office, the police or possibly a hotel). Specifically prescribed or branded drugs should be bought before setting out in sufficient quantity to cover the duration of the cruise. Medicines are expensive in Spain and often have different brand names from those used abroad.

Apart from precautions against the well recognised hazards of sunburn (high factor sun cream is recommended) and stomach upsets, heat exhaustion (or heat stroke) is most likely to affect newly joined crew not yet acclimatised to Mediterranean temperatures. Carry something such as *Dioralyte* to counteract dehydration. Insect repellents, including mosquito coils, can be obtained locally.

UK citizens should complete a form E111 (see the Department of Health's leaflet *T4 Health Advice for Travellers*, to be found in most travel agents), which provides for free medical treatment under a reciprocal agreement with the National Health Service. Private medical treatment is likely to be expensive and it may be worth taking out medical insurance (which should also provide for an attended flight home should the need arise).

THE YACHT

A yacht properly equipped for cruising in northern waters should need little extra gear, but the following items are worth considering if not already on board.

Radio equipment

In order to receive weather forecasts and navigational warnings from Coast Radio Stations, a radio capable of receiving short and medium wave Single Sideband (SSB) transmissions will be needed. Do not make the mistake of buying a radio capable only of receiving the AM transmissions broadcast by national radio stations, or assume that SSB is only applicable to transmitting radios (transceivers).

Most SSB receivers are capable of receiving either Upper Side Band (USB) or Lower Side Band (LSB) at the flick of a switch. The UK Maritime Mobile Net covering the Eastern Atlantic and Mediterranean uses USB, and again it is not necessary to have either a transceiver or a transmitting licence to listen in, just a receiver. All Coast Radio Stations broadcast on SSB – whether on USB or LSB should be easy to determine by trial and error.

Digital tuning is very desirable, and the radio should be capable of tuning to a minimum of 1kHz and preferably to 0.1kHz.

Ventilation

Modern yachts are, as a rule, better ventilated than their older sisters though seldom better insulated. Consider adding an opening hatch in the main cabin, if not already fitted, and ideally another over the galley. Wind scoops over hatches can be a major benefit.

Awnings

An awning covering at least the cockpit provides much relief for the crew, while an even better combination is a bimini which can be kept rigged whilst sailing, plus a larger 'harbour' awning, preferably at boom height or above and extending forward to the mast.

Fans

Harbours can be hot and windless. The use of 12v fans for all cabins can have a dramatic effect on comfort.

Cockpit tables

It is pleasant to eat civilised meals in the cockpit, particularly while at anchor. If nothing else can be arranged, a small folding table might do.

Refrigerator/ice-box/freezer

If a refrigerator or freezer is not fitted it may be possible to build in an ice-box (a plastic picnic coolbox is a poor substitute), but this will be useless without adequate insulation. An ice-box designed for northern climes will almost certainly benefit from extra insulation, if this can be fitted – 100mm (4in) is a desirable minimum, 150mm (6in) even better. A drain is also essential.

If a refrigerator/freezer is fitted but electricity precious, placing ice inside will help minimise battery drain.

Hose

Carry at least 25 metres. Standpipes tend to have bayonet couplings of a type unavailable in the UK – purchase them on arrival. Plenty of 5 or 10 litre plastic carriers will also be useful.

Deck shower

If no shower is fitted below, a black-backed plastic bag plus rose heats very quickly when hung in the rigging. (At least one proprietary model is available widely).

Mosquito nets

Some advocate fitting screens to all openings leading below. Others find this inconvenient, relying instead on mosquito coils and other insecticides and repellents. For some reason mosquitoes generally seem to bother new arrivals more than old hands, while anchoring well out will often decrease the problem.

Harbours, marinas and anchorages

In spite of the growth in both the number and size of marinas and yacht harbours there is still a chronic shortage of berths. During a visit in September 2004 it was learned that in excess of 20,000 craft are currently awaiting berths on the Spanish Mediterranean coast. One must check in advance whether a berth is available and note that mobile phones are replacing VHF for this function. Only three marinas out of the 50 or so in this volume admitted they had space for 12 to 15 metre craft. Most, however, said they could possibly accommodate an 8 metre shallow draught craft.

Harbour organisation

At local level, the ultimate authority for the workings of a harbour is the *capitán de puerto* whose office is the *capitanía*. In fishing ports there may also be a *guarda de puerto*; in this case the *capitán* looks after the waters of the harbour and delegates berthing arrangements to the *guarda*.

At ports where there is an organised yachting presence, there is almost always a *club náutico*, a marina or both, and arrangements for handling yachts are delegated to them. For the visiting yacht, the first point of reference is the marina if there is one; and if not, the *club náutico*.

Harbour charges

All harbours and marinas charge, at a scale which varies from season to season and usually increases from year to year. May to September are normally 'high season' with charges that are normally nearly double that of the 'low season'. Longer term contracts may work out up to a third cheaper than the daily rate. Some marinas include water, electricity, harbour and light dues, while others charge separately. Published rates rarely include the IVA (at 16%) and sometimes the published information does not always specify all the charges. One should take great care in checking what exactly one is paying for if one is to avoid problems when finally settling up.

With the shortage of berths, mentioned above, and the recent change over to the euro, costs have risen drastically and, with a few exceptions, are now fairly similar along the entire stretch of coast covered by this volume. Charges for a 12 metre craft average around €30 a night (€25 with water and electricity etc. charged separately) in high season and around €20 a night (€15 with water and electricity charged separately) in low season. Departures from these average figures are sometimes great. A further complication is that the newer marinas are beginning to charge by beam times length (or sometimes beam alone). It is not practical either to generalize further on harbour dues or to give detailed charges, let alone give an opinion on value for money but the foregoing may provide some guidance for financial planning. Where a relatively expensive or cheap rate has been found this is noted in the text. *El Mercado Náutico* - the Boat Market, which generally appears every other month during the summer, carries tariffs and is probably the most up-to-date guide to be found.

However, one cannot cruise very long on the Andalucían coast without encountering the string of yacht marinas and sport fishing harbours financed, built and run by the Empresa Publica de Puertos de Andalucía in Seville, ☎ (34)955 00 72 00, *Fax* (34)955 00 72 01, *Email* eppa@eppa.es.

Currently there are eight yacht harbours on the Atlantic side, west of Gibraltar, but only three on the Costa del Sol; Marina de Bajadilla, Caleta de Velez and Villaricos. The Empresa Publica de Puertos de Andalucía maintain a very useful web site at www.puertosdeandalucia.com (versions in both Spanish and English) listing current berthing charges etc. Prices are standard for the entire chain in spite of widely differing facilities and appeal, but it appears that some discretion is allowed when it comes to charging for use of water and electricity. Berthing fees are presently much lower than those of the other marinas and thus the Junta should be supported wherever possible. Visa and other credit cards are accepted throughout the chain

Berthing

Due to the vast numbers of yachts and limited space available, berthing stern-to the quays and pontoons is normal.

For greater privacy berth bows-to. This has the added advantages of keeping the rudder away from possible underwater obstructions near the quay and making the approach a much easier manoeuvre. An anchor may occasionally be needed, but more often a bow (or stern) line will be provided, usually via a lazyline to the pontoon though sometimes buoyed. This line may be both heavy and dirty and gloves will be useful. Either way, have plenty of fenders out and lines ready.

Most cruising skippers will have acquired some expertise at this manoeuvre but if taking over a chartered or otherwise unfamiliar yacht it would be wise both to check handling characteristics and talk the sequence through with the crew before attempting to enter a narrow berth.

Detailed instructions regarding Mediterranean mooring techniques will be found in *Mediterranean Cruising Handbook* by Rod Heikell.

Mooring lines - surge in harbours is common and mooring lines must be both long and strong. It is useful to have an eye made up at the shore end with a loop of chain plus shackles to slip over bollards or through rings. Carry plenty of mooring lines, especially if the boat is to be left unattended for any length of time.

Gangplanks - if a gangplank is not already part of the boat's equipment, a builder's scaffolding plank, with holes drilled at either end to take lines, serves well. As it is cheap and easily replaced it can also be used outside fenders to deal with an awkward lie or ward off an oily quay. A short ladder, possibly the bathing ladder if it can be adapted, is useful if berthing bows-to.

Moorings

Virtually all moorings are privately owned and if one is used it will have to be vacated should the owner return. There are generally no markings to give any indication as to the weight and strength of moorings so they should be used with caution. Lobster pot toggles have been mistaken for moorings.

Laying up

Laying up either afloat or ashore is possible at most marinas, though a few have no hardstanding. Facilities and services provided vary considerably, as does the cost, and it is worth seeking local advice as to the quality of the services and the security of the berth or hardstanding concerned.

In the north of the area, the northwesterly *tramontana* (*maestral*) can be frequent and severe in winter and early spring, and this should be borne in mind when selecting the area and site to lay up. Yachts with wooden decks and varnished brightwork will benefit with protection from the winter sun.

The paperwork associated with temporary import and laying up is detailed on page 3.

Yacht clubs

Most harbours of any size support at least one *club náutico*. However the grander ones in particular are basically social clubs – often with tennis courts, swimming pools and other facilities – and may not welcome the crews of visiting yachts. Often there is both a marina and a club, and unless there are special circumstances the normal first option for a visitor is the marina. That said, many *club náuticos* have pleasant bars and excellent restaurants which appear to be open to all, while a few are notably helpful and friendly to visitors. The standard of dress and behaviour often appears to be somewhat more formal than that expected in a similar club in Britain.

General regulations

Harbour restrictions

All harbours have a speed limit, usually 3 knots. The limits are not noted in the text and none are known which is less than 3 knots. There is a 5 knot speed limit within 100m of coast, extending to 250m off bathing beaches.

In most harbours anchoring is forbidden except in emergency or for a short period while sorting out a berth.

Harbour traffic signals

Traffic signals are rare, and in any case are designed for commercial traffic and seldom apply to yachts.

Storm signals

The signal stations at major ports and harbours may show storm signals, but equally they may not. With minor exceptions they are similar to the International System of Visual Storm Warnings.

Flag etiquette

A yacht in commission in foreign waters is legally required to fly her national maritime flag; for a British registered yacht, this is commonly the Red Ensign. If a special club ensign is worn it must be accompanied by the correct burgee. The courtesy flag of the country visited, which normally is the national maritime flag, should be flown from the starboard signal halliard. The flag for Spain is similar to the Spanish national flag but without the crest in the centre.

Insurance

Many marinas require evidence of insurance cover, though third party only may be sufficient. Many UK companies are willing to extend home waters cover for the Mediterranean, excluding certain areas.

Garbage

It is an international offence to dump garbage at sea and, while the arrangements of local authorities may not be perfect, garbage on land should be dumped in the proper containers. Marinas require the use of their onshore toilet facilities or holding tanks.

Large yachts

Many harbours are too small, or too shallow, for a large yacht, which must anchor outside whilst its crew visit the harbour by tender. It is essential that the skipper of such a yacht wishing to enter a small harbour telephones or radios the harbour authorities well in advance to reserve a berth (if available) and receive necessary instructions.

Scuba diving

Inshore scuba diving is strictly controlled and a licence is required from the *Militar de Marina*. This involves a certificate of competence, a medical certificate, two passport photographs, the passport itself (for inspection), knowledge of the relevant laws and a declaration that they will be obeyed. The simplest approach is to enquire through marina staff. Any attempt to remove archaeological material from the seabed will result in serious trouble.

Spearfishing

Spearfishing while scuba diving or using a snorkel is controlled and, in some places, prohibited.

Water-skiing

There has been a big increase in the use of high powered outboards for water-skiing over the past decade, accompanied by a significant increase in accidents. In most of the main ports and at some beaches it is now controlled and enquiries should be made before skiing. It is essential to have third party insurance and, if possible, a bail bond. If bathing and water-skiing areas are buoyed, yachts are excluded.

Security

Crime afloat is not a major problem in most areas and regrettably much of the theft which does occur can be laid at the door of other yachtsmen. Take sensible precautions – lock up before leaving the yacht, padlock the outboard to the dinghy, and secure the dinghy (particularly if an inflatable) with chain or wire rather than line. Folding bicycles are particularly vulnerable to theft, and should be chained up if left on deck.

Ashore, the situation in the big towns is no worse than in the UK and providing common sense is applied to such matters as how handbags are carried, where not to go after the bars close etc., there should be no problem.

The officials most likely to be seen are the *guardia civil*, who wear grey uniforms and deal with immigration as well as more ordinary police work, the *Aduana* (customs) in navy blue uniforms, and the *Policía*, also in blue uniforms, who deal with traffic rather than criminal matters.

Anchorages

There are a large number of attractive anchorages in *calas* and off beaches, even though many have massive buildings in the background and crowds in the foreground. Previous editions of this guide commented on some of them in the text. In this edition much of that information is presented by photographs. Where known, particular hazards are mentioned but an absence of comment in the text or on the sketch charts does not mean there are no hazards. There are always hazards approaching and anchoring off the shoreline. The plans are derived from limited observation and not from a professional survey; depths, shapes, distances etc. are approximate. Any approach must be made with due care. Skippers are advised that anchorages near hotels and towns may be cordoned off, by small floating buoys, to protect swimmers and therefore not be suitable. It cannot be assumed that anchorages listed in this book are always available for use by cruising yachtsmen.

The weather can change and deteriorate at short notice. During the day the sea breeze can be strong, especially if there is a valley at the head of an anchorage.

Similarly a strong land breeze can flow down a valley in the early hours of the morning. If anchored near the head of a *cala* backed by a river valley, should there be a thunderstorm or heavy downpour in the hills above take precautions against the flood of water and debris which will descend into the *cala*.

Many *cala* anchorages suffer from swell even when not open to its off-shore direction. Swell tends to curl round all but the most prominent headlands. Wash from boats entering and leaving, as well as from larger vessels passing outside, may add to the discomfort. If considering a second anchor or a line ashore in order to hold the yacht into the swell, take into account the swinging room required by yachts on single anchors should the wind change.

In a high-sided *cala* winds are often fluky and a sudden blow, even from the land, may make departure difficult. This type of anchorage should only be used in settled calm weather and left in good time if swell or wind rise.

Whatever the type of *cala*, have ready a plan for clearing out quickly, possibly in darkness. It is unwise to leave an anchored yacht unattended for any length of time.

Choice of anchor

Many popular anchorages are thoroughly ploughed up each year by the hundreds of anchors dropped and weighed. At others the bottom is weed-covered compacted sand. Not without good reason is the four-pronged grab the favourite anchor of local fishermen, though difficult to stow. A conventional fisherman-type anchor is easier to stow and a useful ally. If using a patent anchor - Danforth, CQR, Bruce, Fortress etc. - an anchor weight (or chum) is a worthwhile investment and will encourage the pull to remain horizontal.

Anchoring

Once in a suitable depth of water, if clarity permits look for a weed-free patch to drop the anchor. In rocky or otherwise suspect areas - including those likely to contain wrecks, old chains etc. - use a sinking trip line with a float (an inviting buoy may be picked up by another yacht). Chain scope should be at least four times the maximum depth of water and nylon scope double that. It is always worth setting the anchor by reversing slowly until it holds, but on a hard or compacted bottom this must be done very gently in order to give the anchor a chance to bite - over enthusiasm with the throttle will cause it to skip without digging in.

Supplies and services

Fresh water

In many places drinking water (*agua potable*) is scarce. Expect to pay for it, particularly if supplied by hose, and do not wash sails and decks before checking that it is acceptable to do so. In those harbours where a piped supply is not available for yachts, a public tap can often be found - a good supply of 5 or 10 litre plastic cans will be useful.

Water quality is generally good. However it varies from place to place and year to year. Always check verbally and taste for salinity or over-chlorinating before topping up tanks. If caught out, bottled water is readily available in bars and supermarkets.

Ice

Block ice for an ice-box is widely obtainable - use the largest blocks that will fit; chemical ice is sometimes available in blocks measuring 100 x 20 x 20cms. The latter must not be used in drinks, the former only after inquiring of those who have tried the product. Cube or 'small' ice is obtainable and generally of drinks quality, particularly if bought in a sealed bag. An increasing number of marinas and yacht clubs now have ice machines which are usually as good as the water which is put into them.

Fuel

Diesel (*gasoleo, gasoil* or simply *diesel*) is sold in two forms throughout Spain, *Gasoleo B* which attracts a lower tax and is only available to fishing craft, and *Gasoleo A* which is available to yachts. Not all harbours sell *Gasoleo A*, particularly the smaller fishing harbours. A more limited number also have a pump for petrol (*gasolina*). *Petróleo* is paraffin (kerosene). Credit cards are widely, but not universally, accepted - if in doubt, check first.

Bottled gas

Camping Gaz is widely available from marinas, supermarkets or *ferreterias* (ironmongers), in the 1.9kg bottles identical to those in the UK.

As of 2002 REPSOL/CAMPSOL depots will no longer fill any UK (or any other countries') Calor Gas bottles even with a current test certificate. It is therefore essential to carry the appropriate regulator and fittings to permit the use of Camping Gas bottles. Yachts fitted with propane systems should consult the Calor Gas Customer service agent (☎ 0800 626 626).

Electricity

The marina standard is 220 volt, 50 Hz, generally via a two-pin socket for which an adapter will be needed, though some marinas provide 380 volt supplies to berths for yachts over 20-25m. If using 110 volt 60 Hz equipment seek advice - frequency may be a greater problem than voltage. Even if the yacht is not wired for mains, a 25m length of cable and a trickle charger may be useful.

Food and drink

There are many well stocked stores, supermarkets and hypermarkets in the larger towns and cities and it may be worth doing the occasional major stock-up by taxi. Conversely, some isolated anchorages have nothing. As a rule, availability and choice varies with the size of the town. Even the smallest has something and most older settlements (though not all tourist resorts) have a market with local produce at reasonable prices. Alcohol is cheap by UK standards with, unsurprisingly, good value Spanish wines. Spanish gin and vodka are also good value; Scotch whisky can only come from Scotland but the genuine article is often lower in price than in the U.K. Shop prices generally are noticeably lower away from tourist resorts.

Most shops, other than the largest supermarkets, close for *siesta* between 1400 and 1700 and remain closed on Sunday though some smaller food shops do open on Sunday mornings. In larger towns the produce market may operate from 0800 to 1400, Monday to Saturday; in smaller towns it is more often a weekly affair. An excellent way to sample unfamiliar delicacies in small portions is in the form of bar snacks, *tapas* or the larger *raciónes*. Tapas once came on the house but are now almost invariably charged - sometimes heavily.

Repairs and chandlery

There are many marinas equipped to handle all aspects of yacht maintenance from laying up to changing a washer. Nearly all have travel-hoists and the larger have specialist facilities - GRP work, electronics, sailmaking, stainless welding and so forth. Charges may differ - widely so - if practicable, shop around.

The best equipped chandleries will be found near the larger marinas, where they may equal anything found in the UK (though generally with higher prices). Smaller harbours or marinas are often without a chandlery, though something may be found in the associated town. Basic items can sometimes be found in *ferreterias* (ironmongers).

Telephones and Fax

Telephone kiosks are common, both local and *teléfono internacional*, and most carry instructions in English. Both coins and phonecards, available from tobacconists (*estancos*), are used. If no kiosk is available marina offices have telephones and many have faxes. Most bars and hotels have metered telephones and the latter usually have faxes, though these are seldom metered.

- When calling from within Spain, dial the whole code (beginning with the figure 9) whether or not the number you are calling has the same code. In some areas the number of digits to be dialled is nine, in others eight. To make an international call, dial 00 followed by the relevant country code (44 for the UK). If calling the UK do not dial the first figure of the number if it is 0.

- To reach the international operator dial 025. A telephone number beginning with the figure 6 indicates a mobile telephone which will have no area code and its own code for calling its international operator. The number for information is 1003 and the land based emergency services can be contacted by this route.

- To call Spain from abroad, dial the international access code (00 in the UK) followed by the code for Spain (34), then the area code (which begins with 9 except for mobile phones) followed by the individual number.

Warning Apart from a major re-organisation of area codes, individual numbers in Spain change surprisingly often.

Mail

Letters may be sent *poste restante* to any post office (*oficina de corréos*). They should be addressed with the surname (only) of the recipient followed by *Lista de Corréos* and the town. Do not enter the addressee's initials or title: that is likely to cause misfiling. Collection is a fairly cumbersome procedure and a passport is likely to be needed. Alternatively, most marinas and some *club náuticos* will hold mail for yachts, but it is always wise to check in advance if possible. Uncollected letters are seldom returned.

Mail to and from the UK should be marked 'air mail' (*por avión*) but even so may take up to ten days, so if speed is important communicate by fax or Email. Post boxes are yellow; stamps are available from tobacconists (*estancos*), not from post offices though the latter will accept and frank mail. Almost every town has a post office; ask - *donde esta el Correo?*

Tourist offices

There is at least one tourist office in every major town or resort. Their locations vary from year to year - ask at the port or marina office.

Transport and travel

Every community has some form of public transport, if only one *autobús* a day and many of the coastal towns are served by rail as well.

Taxis are easily found in the tourist resorts though less common outside them, but can always be ordered by telephone. Car hire is simple, but either a full national or international driving licence must be shown and many companies will not lease a car to a driver over 70 years old.

Air - Alicante, Barcelona and Valencia have year round international flights and seasonal charter flights; Gibraltar has year round connections with the U.K. Other airports, Málaga, Murcia, Alicante and Tarragona, have international scheduled and charter flights in summer and year round connections within Spain.

Western Mediterranean weather

The weather pattern in the basin of the western Mediterranean is affected by many different systems. It is largely unpredictable, quick to change and often very different at places only a short distance apart. See Appendix III for Spanish meteorological terms.

WINDS

Winds most frequently blow from the west, northwest, north and east but are considerably altered by the effects of local topography. The Mediterranean is an area of calms and gales and the old saying that in summer there are nine days of light winds followed by a gale is very close to reality. Close to the coast, normal sea and land breezes are experienced on calm days. Along the Costa Brava, northwest, north and northeast winds are most common, especially in winter, though winds from other directions frequently occur. This area is particularly influenced by the weather in the Golfo de León and is in the direct path of the northwesterly *tramontana* (see below), making it particularly important to listen to regular weather forecasts.

The winds in the Mediterranean have been given special names dependent on their direction and characteristics. Those that affect this coast are detailed below.

Northwest – *tramontana*

This wind, also known as the *maestral* near Río Ebro and the *mistral* in France, is a strong, dry wind, cold in winter, which can be dangerous. It is caused by a secondary depression forming in the Golfo de León or the Golfo de Génova on the cold front of a major depression crossing France. The northwesterly airflow generated is compressed between the Alps and the Pyrenees and flows into the Mediterranean basin. In Spain it chiefly affects the coast to the north of Barcelona, the Islas Baleares, and is strongest at the northern end of the Costa Brava.

The *tramontana* can be dangerous in that it can arrive and reach gale force in as little as fifteen minutes on a calm sunny day with virtually no warning. Signs to watch for are brilliant visibility, clear sky – sometimes with cigar-shaped clouds – very dry air and a steady or slightly rising barometer. On rare occasions the sky may be cloudy when the wind first arrives although it clears later. Sometimes the barometer will plunge in normal fashion, rising quickly after the gale has passed. If at sea and some way from land, a line of white on the horizon and a developing swell give a few minutes' warning. The only effective warning that can be obtained is by radio – Marseille (in French) and Monaco (in French and English) are probably the best bet. See page 13 for transmission details.

The *tramontana* normally blows for at least three days but may last for a week or longer. It is frequent in the winter months, blowing for a third of the time and can reach F10 (50 knots) or more. In summer it is neither as strong nor as frequent.

West – *vendaval*

A depression crossing Spain or southern France creates a strong southwest to west wind, the *vendaval* or *poniente*, which funnels through the Strait of Gibraltar and along the south coast of Spain. Though normally confined to the south and southeast coasts, it occasionally blows in the northeast of the area. It is usually short-lived and at its strongest from late autumn to early spring.

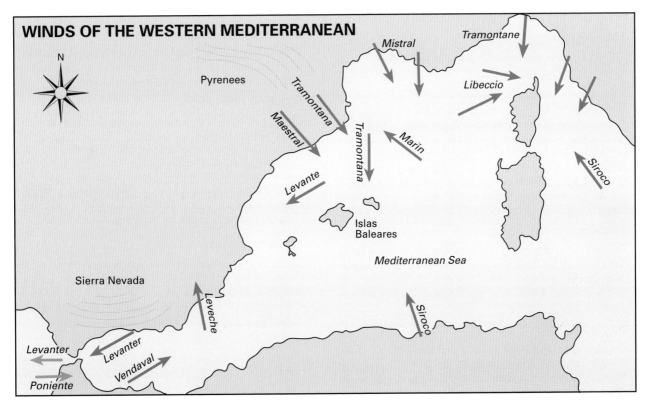

WINDS OF THE WESTERN MEDITERRANEAN

East – *levante*

Encountered from Gibraltar to Valencia and beyond, the *levante*, sometimes called the *llevantade* when it blows at gale force, is caused by a depression located between the Islas Baleares and the North African coast. It is preceded by a heavy swell (*las tascas*), cold damp air, poor visibility and low cloud which forms first around the higher hills. Heavy and prolonged rainfall is more likely in spring and autumn than summer. A *levante* may last for three or four days.

South – *siroco*

The hot wind from the south is created by a depression moving east along or just south of the North African coast. By the time this dry wind reaches Spain it can be very humid, with haze and cloud. If strong it carries dust, and should it rain when the cold front comes through, the water may be red or brown and the dust will set like cement. This wind is sometimes called the *leveche* in southeast Spain. It occurs most frequently in summer, seldom lasting more than one or two days.

Clouds

Cloud cover of between 4/8ths and 5/8ths in the winter months is about double the summer average of 2/8ths. Barcelona, however, seems to manage a year round average of 3/8th to 5/8ths. The cloud is normally cumulus and high level. In strong winds with a southerly component, complete cloud cover can be expected.

Precipitation

Annual rainfall is moderate and decreases towards the north from about 760mm at Gibraltar to 560mm at Barcelona. The rainy seasons predominantly in autumn and winter and in most areas the summer months are virtually dry. The Costa Brava however usually manages about 25mm of rain during each summer month. Most of the rain falls in very heavy showers of 1–2 hours.

Thunderstorms

Thunderstorms are most frequent in the autumn at up to four or five each month, and can be accompanied by hail.

Water spouts

Water spouts occur in the Strait of Gibraltar in winter and spring, usually associated with thunderstorms.

Snow

Snow at sea level is very rare but it falls and remains on the higher mountain ranges inland. Snow on the Sierra Nevada is particularly noticeable from the sea.

Visibility

Fog occurs about four days a month in summer along the Costa de Sol but elsewhere is very rare. Occasionally dust carried by the southerly *siroco* reduces visibility and industrial areas such as Valencia and Barcelona produce haze.

Temperature

Winter temperatures at Gibraltar average 10–15°C, rising steadily after March to average 20–29°C in July and August. Afternoon (maximum) temperatures may reach 30–33°C in these months. At Barcelona, summer temperatures are much the same as at Gibraltar but winter temperatures are lower, 6–13°C.

Humidity

The relative humidity is moderate at around 60% to 80%. With winds from the west, northwest or north, low humidity can be expected; with winds off the sea, high humidity is normal. The relative humidity increases throughout the night and falls by day.

Local variations

In the northeastern area, the common winds blow between northwest and northeast. Gales may be experienced for 10% of the time during the winter, dropping to 2% in July and August, sometimes arriving with little warning and rapidly building to gale force.

The sea

Currents

There is a constant E-going surface current of 1 to 2 knots, passing in to the Mediterranean through the Strait of Gibraltar between the Costa del Sol and the African coast to replace water lost by evaporation. Northeast of Cabo de Gata up to the border with France, a significant inshore counter-eddy runs roughly SSW at 1 to 1½ knots. The shape of the coast produces variations in both direction and strength, especially around promontories.

Tides

Tides should be taken into account at the west end of the Costa del Sol and are noted in the introduction to that section. From Alicante to the border with France, the tide is hardly appreciable.

Swell

Winds between NE and SE can produce a dangerous swell on the E coast. Swell has a nasty capability of going round corners and getting into *calas*.

Scouring and silting

Many harbours and anchorages are located in sandy areas where depths can change dramatically in the course of a storm or a season. Dredging is a common feature but there is no certainty that depths will be maintained. Charts and drawings give no sure guide. When approaching or entering such areas, it is of great importance to sound carefully and to act on the information received.

Sea temperature

Sea temperatures in February are around 14°C on the Costa del Sol and 12°C on the Costa Brava. In summer, along the Costa Blanca it can rise to 20°C. Winds from the south and east tend to raise the temperature and those from the west and north to lower them.

Radio and weather forecasts

Details of coast radio stations, weather forecasts, weatherfax (radio facsimile) Navtex and Inmarsat-C coverage follow. See individual harbour details for port and marina radio information. All times quoted are in UT (universal time) unless otherwise specified. France Inter on LW, 163kHz, France Info on MW and Monaco 3AC on 4363kHx all use local time. Details of frequencies, channel and times are to be found in ALRS Vol 3 (1), RYA Booklet G5 and on the Internet.

Coast radio stations

VHF/MF

Coast radio stations are controlled frj27 om Malaga or Valencia – see diagram p 14. Full details will be found in the Admiralty *List of Radio Signals Vol 1 Part 1 (NP281/1)*.

On receipt of traffic, Spanish coast radio stations will call vessels once on Ch 16; after that the vessel's call sign will be included in scheduled MF traffic lists.

Weather forecasts

Marine VHF and MF

Inshore waters and Sea area forecasts are broadcast in Spanish and English on marine VHF all round Mediterranean Spain and the Balearic Islands. There are also broadcasts of Inshore waters forecasts and actual weather in Spanish only. For details see the tables on page 14.

For local area FM broadcast near Gibraltar see page 21 for details of BFBS and Gibraltar BC.

Sea area forecasts can also be heard in English and Spanish on MF radio (table page 14).

Non-radio weather forecasts

A recorded marine forecast in Spanish is available by telephoning (906) 36 53 71. The 'High Seas' bulletin includes the Islas Baleares.

Spanish television shows a useful synoptic chart with its land weather forecast every evening after the news at approximately 2120 weekdays, 1520 Saturday and 2020 Sunday. Most national and local newspapers also carry some form of forecast.

Nearly all marinas and yacht harbours display a synoptic chart and forecast, generally updated daily (though often posted rather late to be of use).

Rescue and emergency services

In addition to VHF Ch 16 (MAYDAY or PAN PAN as appropriate) the marine emergency services can be contacted by telephone at all times on 900 202 202.

The National Centre for Sea Rescue is based in Madrid but has a string of communications towers. On the spot responsibility for co-ordinating rescues lies with the *Capitanías Marítimas* with support from the Spanish Navy, customs, *guardia civil* etc. Lifeboats are stationed at some of the larger harbours but the majority do not appear to be all-weather boats.

The other emergency services can be contacted by dialling 003 for the operator and asking for policía (police), *bomberos* (fire service) or *Cruz Roja* (Red Cross). Alternatively the police can be contacted direct on 091.

Radio fax and teleprinter

Northwood (RN) broadcasts a full set of UK Met Office charts out to 5 days ahead on 2618.5, 4610, 8040 and 11086.5kHz. (Schedule at 0236, surface analysis at 3 hourly intervals from 0300 to 2100 and 2300.) Deutscher Wetterdienst broadcasts German weather charts on 3855, 7880 and 13882.5kHz. (Schedule at 1111, surface analysis at 0430, 1050, 1600, 2200.)

DWD broadcasts forecasts using RTTY on 4583, 7646 and 10001.8kHz (in English at 0415 and 1610), 11039 and 14467.3kHz (in German at 0535). Note that the 4583 and 14467.3kHz may not be useable in the Mediterranean. The most useful products are forecasts up to 5 days ahead at 12 hourly intervals and up to 2 days ahead at 6 hour intervals. Alternatively, a dedicated receiver 'Weatherman' will record automatically: see www.nasamarine.com.

UK Marine Mobile Net

The Net covering the Eastern Atlantic and the Mediterranean, can be heard daily on 14303kHz USB at 0800 and 1800 UT. On Saturday morning the broadcast sometimes contains a longer period outlook. Forecasts will be a rehash of what the Net leader has gleaned from various sources. No licence is required if a receive-only HF radio is used.

Monaco 3AC

Monaco 3AC broadcasts on 8728 and 8806kHz USB at 0715 and 1830 in French and English. The texts are those broadcast by INMARSAT-C for the western part of METAREA III. Monaco also broadcasts on 4363kHz at 0903 and 1915 LT in French and English and at 1403 in French only. Texts are as the latest Toulon NAVTEX broadcast.

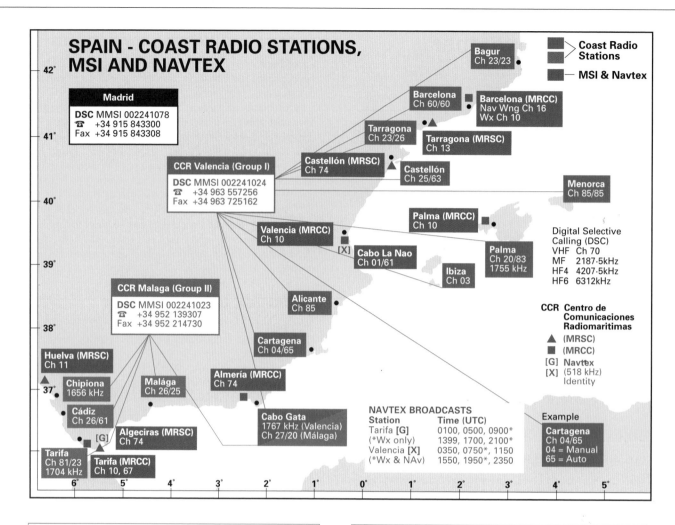

SPAIN - COAST RADIO STATIONS, MSI AND NAVTEX

Coast Radio Stations

MSI & Navtex

Bagur Ch 23/23

Madrid
DSC MMSI 002241078
☎ +34 915 843300
Fax +34 915 843308

Barcelona Ch 60/60

Barcelona (MRCC) Nav Wng Ch 16 Wx Ch 10

Tarragona Ch 23/26

Tarragona (MRSC) Ch 13

CCR Valencia (Group I)
DSC MMSI 002241024
☎ +34 963 557256
Fax +34 963 725162

Castellón (MRSC) Ch 74

Castellón Ch 25/63

Menorca Ch 85/85

Valencia (MRCC) Ch 10

Palma (MRCC) Ch 10

[X] **Cabo La Nao** Ch 01/61

Palma Ch 20/83 1755 kHz

Ibiza Ch 03

Digital Selective Calling (DSC)
VHF   Ch 70
MF   2187·5kHz
HF4   4207·5kHz
HF6   6312kHz

CCR Malaga (Group II)
DSC MMSI 002241023
☎ +34 952 139307
Fax +34 952 214730

Alicante Ch 85

CCR Centro de Comunicaciones Radiomaritimas
▲ (MRSC)
■ (MRCC)
[G] Navtex
[X] (518 kHz) Identity

Cartagena Ch 04/65

Huelva (MRSC) Ch 11

Almería (MRCC) Ch 74

Chipiona 1656 kHz

Malága Ch 26/25

Cádiz Ch 26/61

Cabo Gata 1767 kHz (Valencia) Ch 27/20 (Málaga)

[G] **Algeciras (MRSC)** Ch 74

NAVTEX BROADCASTS
Station	Time (UTC)
Tarifa [G]	0100, 0500, 0900*
(*Wx only)	1399, 1700, 2100*
Valencia [X]	0350, 0750*, 1150
(*Wx & NAv)	1550, 1950*, 2350

Example
Cartagena Ch 04/65
04 = Manual
65 = Auto

Tarifa Ch 81/23 1704 kHz

Tarifa (MRCC) Ch 10, 67

Inshore waters forecasts and reports of actual weather are broadcast in English and Spanish as follows.

MRCC	VHF Ch	Time UT
CZCS Tarifa	10, 67, 73	H2+15
CLCS Algeciras	74	0315, 0515, 0715, 1115, 1515, 1915, 2315
CRCS Almería	10, 67, 73	H1+15
CRCS Barcelona	10	0600, 0900, 1500, 2000
CRCS Valencia	10, 67	H2+15
CLCS Tarragona	13	0533, 0933, 1533, 2033
CRCS Palma	10	0735, 1035, 1535, 2035

H1 = odd hours. H2 = even hours

Sea area forecasts are broadcast in English and Spanish as follows

Station	kHz	Time UT
Chipiona	1656kHz	0733, 1233, 1933
Tarifa	1704kHz	0733, 1233, 1933
Cabo de Gata	1767kHz	0750, 1303, 1950
Palma	1755kHz	0750, 1303, 1950

Sea area and inshore waters forecasts are broadcast in Spanish as follows

MRCC Málaga	VHF Ch	Times UT
Cádiz	26	
Tarifa	81	0833, 1133, 2003
Málaga	26	
Cabo Gata	27	

MRCC Valencia	VHF Ch	Times UT
Cartagena	4	
Alicante	85	
Cabo La Nao	2	
Castellón	25	
Tarragona	23	0910, 1410, 2110
Barcelona	60	
Bagur	23	
Menorca	85	
Palma	20	
Ibiza	3	

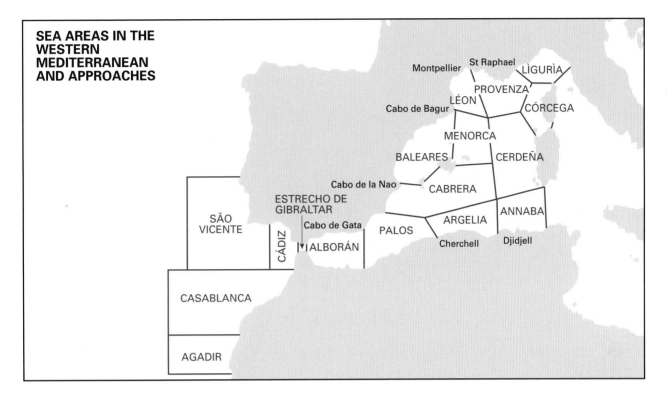

SEA AREAS IN THE WESTERN MEDITERRANEAN AND APPROACHES

The Spanish and French use a common set of sea areas and use the same names although spelling and pronunciation differ at times. The French names for the Mediterranean Sea areas are Alboran, Palos, Alger, Cabrera, Baléares, Minorque, Lion, Provence, Ligure, Corse, Sardaigne, and Annaba. In the approaches to the Mediterranean the French names are identical to the Spanish.

NAVTEX AND INMARSAT-C

NAVTEX and INMARSAT-C are the primary GMDSS modes for transmission of all Marine Safety Information. Broadcast times for weather are as follows

Transmitter	Times (UTC)
Tarifa – G (518kHz)	0900 and 2100
Cabo la Nao – X (Valencia) (518kHz)	0750 and 1950
La Garde – W (Toulon) (518kHz)	1140 and 2340
La Garde – S (Toulon) (490kHz)	0700 and 1900
INMARSAT-C METAREA III	1000 and 2200

Internet

Many sites provide weather information and most, even the official sites, do change from time to time. For a good starting point, the RCCPF recommends Frank Singleton's site at www.franksingleton.clara.net Also see www.rccpf.org.uk under technical matters. Skippers are urged to use the Internet as a supplementary source of information and to ensure that CMDSS forecasts can be obtained on board.

GRIB coded forecasts (Salidocs)

This is a service set up by sailors in the USA. It enables arrow diagram forecasts, for up to 5 days ahead, and other information to be obtained in email form (or by Marine HF and HAM radio). The data are highly compressed so that a great deal of information can be acquired quickly and at low cost – even using a mobile phone connected to a laptop computer. For details email query@saldocs. com subject 'any'. There is no charge for this service. In addition Saildocs can provide the text to any web page stripped of all pictures and dropdowns. This is useful for getting texts of forecasts from the Spanish Met service site from which downloads are very slow.

Key to symbols used on plans

	English	*Spanish*
⚓	harbourmaster/ port office	*capitán de puerto*
	fuel	*gasoil, gasolina*
	yacht chandler	*efectos navales*
	crane	*grua*
	travel-lift	*grua giratoria*
	yacht club	*club náutico*
	showers	*ducha*
i	information	*información*
✉	post office	*correos*
	slipway	*grada*
	anchorage	*fondeadero*
	anchoring prohibited	*fondeadero prohibido*
	yachts	*yates*
⊕	waypoint	

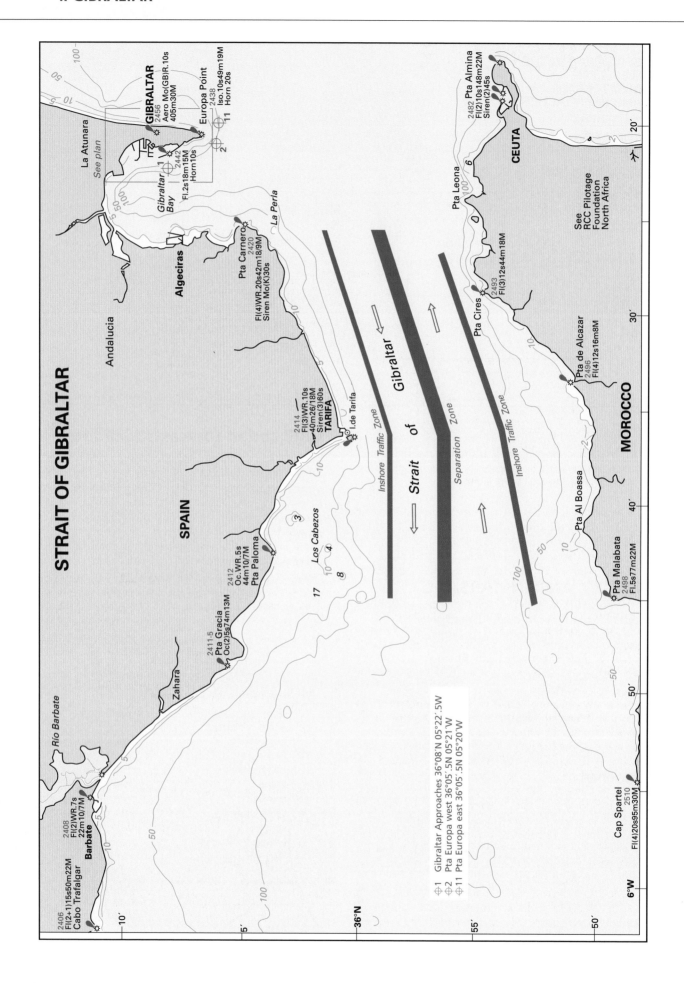

STRAIT OF GIBRALTAR

GIBRALTAR

2456 Aero Mo(GB)R.10s 405m30M

Europa Point
2438 Iso.10s49m19M
Horn 20s

La Atunara

See plan

Gibraltar 1
Bay
2442 Fl.2s18m15M
Horn10s

Algeciras

Pta Carnero
2420
Fl(4)WR.20s42m18/9M
Siren Mo(K)30s

La Perla

Andalucia

SPAIN

TARIFA
2414 I.de Tarifa
Fl(3)WR.10s
40m26/18M
Siren(3)60s

Los Cabezos
3
4
10 8
17

2412
Oc.WR.5s
44m10/7M
Pta Paloma

2411·5
Pta Gracia
Oc(2)5s74m13M

Zahara

Rio Barbate

Barbate
2408
Fl(2)WR.7s
22m10/7M

2406
Fl(2+1)15s50m22M
Cabo Trafalgar

Pta Leona

CEUTA

Pta Almina
2482 Pta Almina
Fl(2)10s148m22M
Siren(2)45s

See
RCC Pilotage
Foundation
North Africa

Pta Cires
2493
Fl(3)12s44m18M

MOROCCO

Pta de Alcazar
2496
Fl(4)12s16m8M

Pta Al Boassa

Pta Malabata
2498
Fl.5s77m22M

Cap Spartel
2510
Fl(4)20s95m30M

Strait of Gibraltar

Inshore Traffic Zone

Separation Zone

Inshore Traffic Zone

100

50

10

5

50

100

5

10

50

100

⊕ 1   Gibraltar Approaches 36°08'N 05°22'·5W
⊕ 2   Pta Europa west 36°05'·5N 05°21'W
⊕ 11 Pta Europa east 36°05'·5N 05°20'W

⊕ 1
⊕ 2
⊕ 11

6°W
10'
5'
36°N
55'
50'

20'
30'
40'
50'

I. GIBRALTAR

Gibraltar

36°09'N 5°22'W

Tides
Gibraltar is a standard port.
Heights in metres

MHWS	MHWN	MLWN	MLWS
1.0	0.7	0.3	0.1

Charts

	Approach	Harbour
British Admiralty	91, 142	145
	773, 3578	144
Spanish	445, 445A	4452
French	7042, 7300	7026
Imray	M11, C19	M11
	C50	C50

Lights
Approach
2420 Punta Carnero
   Fl(4)WR.20s42m18/9M 018°-W-325°-R-018° Siren Mo(K)30s Yellow round tower, green base, silver lantern 19m
2456 Gibraltar Aeromarine
   Mo(GB)R.10s405m30M Obscured on westerly bearings within 2M
2438 Europa Point, Gibraltar
   Iso.10s49m19M Oc.R.10s15M and F.R.15M 042°-vis-067° Horn 20s White round tower, red band 19m

Harbour
2442 South breakwater, north end (A head) Fl.2s18m15M Horn 10s Grey round tower 15m
2445 Detached breakwater, south end (B head) Q.R.9m5M Metal structure on concrete building 11m
2451.2 Queensway Quay Marina, south mole 2F.G(vert)
2451 Queensway Quay Marina, northwest mole 2F.R(vert)
2450.7 Cormorant Camber 2F.R(vert)
2451.5 Coaling Island new mole 2F.G(vert)
2446 Detached breakwater, north end (C head) Q.G.10m5M Metal structure on concrete building 11m
2448 North breakwater, southwest arm (D head) Q.R.18m5M Round tower 17m
2449.2 North breakwater, northwest elbow (E head) F.R.28m5M Tower
Plus other lights in the interior of the harbour and to the north.

Port communications
Radio
Gibraltar VHF Ch 16, 6, 12, 13, 14 (24 hours)
Lloyds radio VHF Ch 8, 12, 14, 16 (24 hours)
Queens Harbourmaster VHF Ch 8 (0800–1600 Mon to Fri)
All marinas VHF Ch 71 (0830–2030 (later in summer))
Telephone
Port Captain ☎ 772 54
Port Operations Room ☎ 781 34/770 04
Marina Bay Office ☎ 743 22 *Fax* 783 73
Pier Office ☎ 733 00 *Fax* 426 56
Sheppards Marina Repair facilities ☎ 768 95, Chandlery ☎ 771 83
Ocean Village ☎ 400 48 *Fax* 400 68
Queensway Quay ☎ 447 00 *Fax* 446 99
Email & web sites
Marina Bay *Email* pieroffice@marinabay.gi
url www.marinabay.gi
Queensway Quay *Email* qqmarina@gibnet.gi
Ocean Village *Email* oceanvillage@hbc.gi
url www.oceanvillagegibraltar.com

'The Rock'

Gibraltar is a safe and convenient stopping point for yachts entering or leaving the Mediterranean, as well as being a duty-free port. All facilities are available for repairs and general maintenance, and both general and ship's stores of every kind can be obtained in Gibraltar or by air from England – it is often cheaper to have equipment exported by air to Gibraltar as 'Ships Stores in Transit' than to buy them off the shelf once there. Both the pound sterling and the Gibraltar pound (at parity) are legal tender.

Long popular with English-speaking yachtsmen, all the marinas are busy and it may be wise to book ahead. Two are close to the airport runway which is convenient for crew changes but noisy. The third, Queensway Quay Marina, is about half a mile further south behind the outer breakwater, in an area previously known as the Auxiliary Camber. All suffer from swell in westerly winds and violent gusting in easterly levanters. Weather forecasts in English are posted daily at all three.

Much land reclamation has taken place over the past few years – the inlet between the Customs Berth and the North Mole has been filled in, as has a large area just off the Varyl Begg Estate.

Unless in a tearing hurry a tour of the Rock itself must be de rigeur and the museum – with displays of Gibraltar in prehistoric, Phoenician and Roman times – is also recommended.

Navigation

Tides and Currents

Gibraltar is a standard port for the Mediterranean where the rise and fall is a mere 0.9m at springs and 0.4m at neaps with a mean level of 0.5m. What is much more interesting for the arriving or departing yachtsman is the tidal current flow in the Straits of Gibraltar itself. There is a permanent flow outward, east to west, from the

Gibraltar from the south

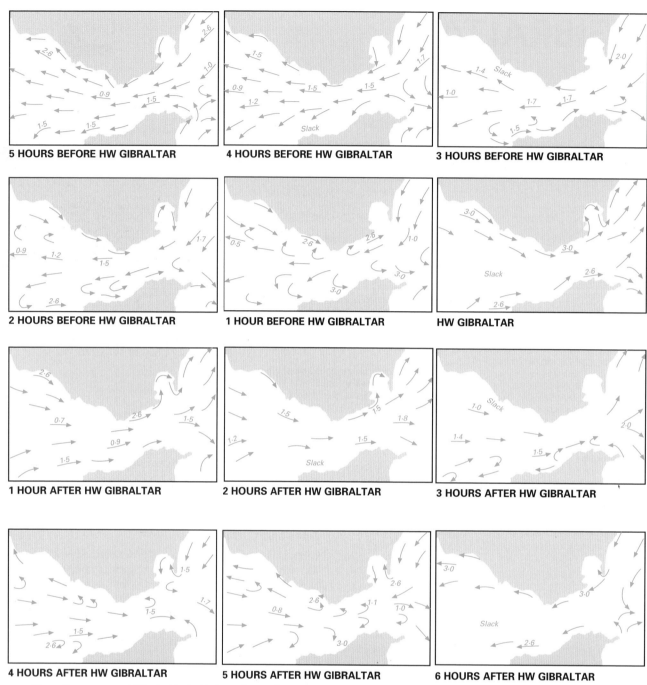

5 HOURS BEFORE HW GIBRALTAR

4 HOURS BEFORE HW GIBRALTAR

3 HOURS BEFORE HW GIBRALTAR

2 HOURS BEFORE HW GIBRALTAR

1 HOUR BEFORE HW GIBRALTAR

HW GIBRALTAR

1 HOUR AFTER HW GIBRALTAR

2 HOURS AFTER HW GIBRALTAR

3 HOURS AFTER HW GIBRALTAR

4 HOURS AFTER HW GIBRALTAR

5 HOURS AFTER HW GIBRALTAR

6 HOURS AFTER HW GIBRALTAR

These diagrams are published with the kind permission of Dr M Sloma, editor of *Yacht Scene*. Under no circumstances will *Yacht Scene* or the Pilotage Foundation be liable for any accident or injury, which may occur to vessels or persons whilst using the above current predictions.

Mediterranean at lower depths, which gives rise to a maximum surface easterly flow of about 4.5 knots and a westerly rate of 2 knots. Under certain conditions of wind and tide, flows can be greater in the narrowest part of the Strait. Where there are shallows near the coast there is distortion of the current and there may be overfalls when wind is against the tide. Prolonged dry periods in the western Mediterranean appear to have an effect on the tidal flow, making the outward flow in the centre of the Strait less than indicated.

Tidal flows for the Straits are difficult to establish with precise accuracy and the diagrams above should be used as approximations. The figures against the arrows indicate the rate in knots at Springs. They give approximate combined values of stream and current in calm weather.

Approach

The massive Rock is visible for many miles, though if approaching from the west it opens fully only after rounding Punta Carnero into Gibraltar Bay. Almost without exception the coastline is steep to, but beware of squalls and sudden windshifts in the bay, particularly during a levanter. Yachts must give way to naval and commercial vessels at all times. There may be tunny nets off La Línea.

GPS approach

Steer for ⊕1 from a southerly quadrant then proceed east of north for the northern 2 marinas or east for Queensway Quay.

Entrance and formalities

If making for the northern two marinas round E Head to starboard and call at the customs and reporting station (Waterport) on the North Mole opposite the end of the runway. At night, after rounding E Head, the row of red lights at the end of the runway mark the north side of the channel leading to the customs berth and marinas.

If heading for Queensway Quay Marina, pass between A and B Heads and steer for the marina entrance 0.4 miles to the east. The reception pontoon is hard round to starboard on entry near the fuel berth. After mooring the skipper must report to Customs at the marina office.

Customs' and immigration formalities.

At present yachts going to the northern two marinas must report to the customs berth, while yachts going to Queensway report to customs in the marina office. They are advised to declare all items they wish to bring in free of duty and failure to do so can result in serious penalties. The reporting procedures for visiting yachts may soon be amended in that yachts will be allowed to radio in their arrival and then proceed to their chosen marina. Each marina will have the relevant forms available for yacht skippers to complete. Officials wishing to attend a yacht will do so at the marina berth. Only in exceptional circumstances will the port insist on a yacht attending the reporting berth before going to their chosen marina.

Immigration is relatively simple. Yachts are required to submit a crew and passenger list in triplicate and to obtain clearance to go ashore; a valid passport and, in some cases, visas are required. Anyone intending to stay ashore must report to the Waterport with the address of the intended stay. Any guest residing aboard or anyone aboard who has employment in Gibraltar must report to the Waterport authorities. Crews must not be paid off or enrolled (regardless of nationality) without permission of the Principal Immigration Officer. The time and date of departure must be given to the Waterport before departure.

Anchorage

Anchoring is permitted (although not encouraged) between the runway and the oil pier to the north. This area has recently been curtailed by the laying of buoys and pontoons for small local craft but space can still be found and the holding is good in 4 to 5 metres on sand. Anchoring is prohibited in line with the runway and on either side of the Rock itself. A better anchorage can be found at La Linea harbour to the NNW.

Marinas

Marina Bay This was the northernmost of the three and largest with about 210 berths (but see Sheppards below). The reception berth is alongside the office towards the outer end of the main pier. Prior booking is advised and proof of insurance is required. On site there

Europa Point

is a bank, chandlery (which can arrange all repairs and caretaking), supermarket, laundry, chemist, bars and restaurants.

Sheppards This company has recently been taken over and the marina has been moved to a new location north of the airport runway. There will be a haul-out and repair facility adjacent to the marina with a scheduled opening of late 2005. It is proposed to have 140 berths of which 40 will be designated for visitors. Other than hauling out, all repair services are now available from Sheppards' temporary workshop facility at Coaling Island (near Queensway Quay marina) ☎ 768 95 *Fax* 717 80. The chandlery shop is still on the Sheppards old site ☎ 771 83 *Fax* 425 35. The old marina is being rebuilt as a part of Ocean Village residential and commercial development. It should open in 2006 as a smarter marina with all modern facilities.

Queensway Quay - this is a modern marina with 120 berths which has been designed with considerable care. Most berths have telephone points and access to pontoons is by security card. It has the advantage over

Gibraltar showing new construction for Sheppards marina north of the runway

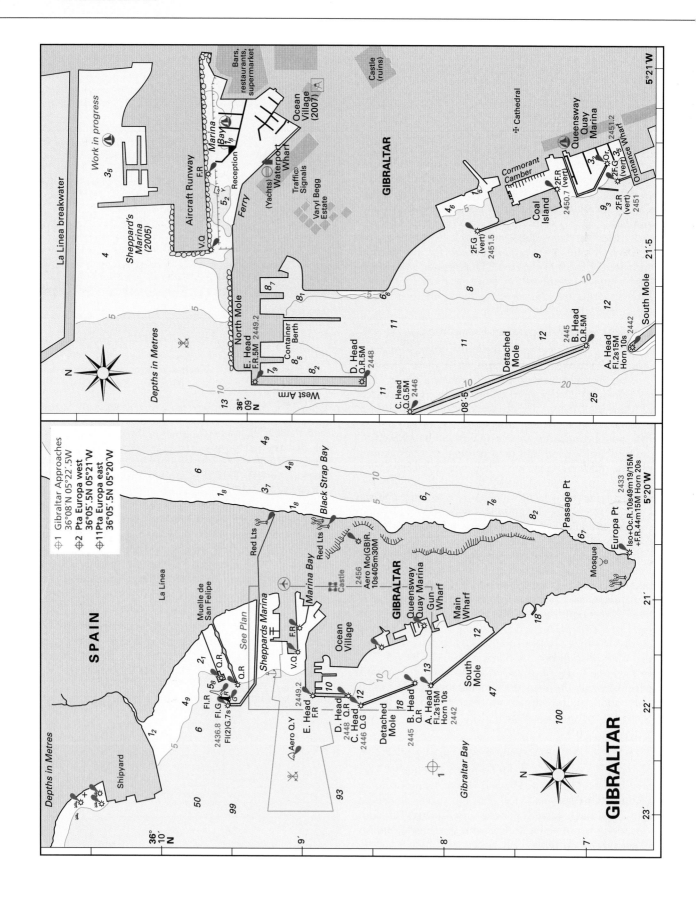

Queensway Quay marina from W

Marina Bay marina (on left) and the old Sheppards Marina which will be moving to N of runway. Space will be renovated for Ocean Village marina

Admiralty charts from the Gibraltar Chart Agency (4 Bayside, Gibraltar. ☎ 76293).

General services include branches of several UK banks with ATM machines and chain stores (including a very large Safeway), shopping of all kinds, English book shops, pubs, restaurants, hotels, hospitals and clinics.

Excellent produce market over the border at La Línea on Wednesday morning. (Crossing the border on foot or by bicycle is quick and easy, crossing by car can entail long delays. In either event a passport is required). The Royal Gibraltar YC, the oldest royal club outside the UK (founded in 1829), welcomes visitors and meals can be booked by phoning the Club Secretary on 78897.

Duty-free stores can be ordered from one of several local suppliers for delivery to the boat on departure. There is also a duty-free shop at the customs berth.

Straits Sailing Handbook Colin Thomas. An annual guide for Chipiona to Benalmadena with part of the Moroccan coast and the tide tables. Available through Imrays or from Straits.sail@gibnynex.gi

A useful directory of local information and services is compiled and published by D M Sloma under the title *Yacht Scene*. It is available at marina offices and chandleries or by air mail orders from P O Box 555, Gibraltar. ☎/Fax +350 79385

Communications

Post office (quick and reliable service to/from the UK – all the marinas will hold mail for yachts). Buses to La Línea, thence a Spanish bus. Taxis and hire cars (which may be taken into Spain). Main line railway at Algeciras. Air services to several UK destinations, Tanger, Casablanca and Marrakesh, but not to Spain. Twice weekly ferry to Tanger. ☎ International code 350.

Wireless broadband Internet connections are available on board your yacht at all Gibraltar marinas. No hardware is required other than a computer with a USB port. Contact Jens Kaersgard, YachtConnect, ☎ +359 5463 7000 (except from Spain); ☎ 9567 5463 7000 (from Spain) or *email* j.kaersgaard@yachtconnect.com

the other two marinas of greater distance from the dust and noise of the airport and is barely five minutes away from the town centre. Proof of insurance is required. Marina trolleys can be borrowed for major restocking at the vast Safeway on the Varyl Begg Estate ten minutes walk to the north.

Note that all marinas charges are reasonable, reductions available in the winter and all have discounted prices for longer stays. Credit cards are accepted.

Other facilities

Diesel and petrol from Shell or Mobil at the fuelling berth inshore of the customs berth. Paraffin from the filling station near Sheppards.

Ice from all filling stations.

Camping Gaz obtainable from Sheppards and from the Shell office at the fuel berth. Calor Gas bottles can no longer be filled, Repsa gas bottles being the only ones available in Spain and Gibraltar.

Sail repairs There is no longer a sailmaker in Gibraltar but J&F Sailmakers, South Pavilion Rd (☎ 41469) will make covers.

Gibraltar weather forecasts

LT	BFBS 1			BFBS2	Gibraltar BC		
	Mon-Fri	Sat	Sun	Mon-Fri	Mon-Fri	Sat	Sun
0530					X	X	
0630					X	X	X
0730					X	X	X
0745	X						
0845	X	X	X				
0945		X	X				
1005	X						
1030					X		
1200				X			
1202		X	X				
1230					X	X	X
1602		X					
1605	X						

Also storm warnings on receipt	1438 AM
93.5 FM 89.4 FM	91.3 FM
97.8 FM 99.5 FM	92.6 FM
Includes high and low water times	100.5 FM

COSTA DEL SOL

Introduction

GENERAL DESCRIPTION

The coast between Gibraltar and Cabo de Gata some 155M to the E is called the Costa del Sol (the Sun Coast). It lives up to its name in that sunshine averages 300 days a year. The three main ports, Gibraltar, Málaga and Almería, are large and can be entered under most conditions; there are 16 smaller harbours.

The section starts with the singular mass of the Rock of Gibraltar which stands high and island-like and can be seen for miles. Behind the Rock is a low, flat and sandy coast backed by high mountain ranges which stretches to Málaga. Beyond Málaga, behind the coastal mountains are the even higher snow-covered ranges of the Sierra Nevada. In many places the mountains reach the sea and form high rocky cliffs and promontories.

The development of the coast for tourism has resulted in many sections supporting rows of tower blocks or flats and hotels. The latest tourists to arrive are the Russians who came with suitcases of dollars to buy up property. The general problem of plastic pollution is compounded by the 100m sheets of polythene discarded from kilometres of greenhouses established on any land suitable for hydroponic cultivation.

Many harbours, now improved by the construction of breakwaters, are based on small fishing harbours originally established in bays where some protection from the winds is available.

At most places the shore may be approached to

COASTAL WAYPOINT LIST

The waypoints listed form a series with which one is able to steer from off Gibraltar to Cabo de Gata. The waypoints are all at WGS 84 datum and although the track avoids the main fish farm areas these farms come and go, seemingly overnight sometimes, and a good lookout must be kept at all times. There are over 50 'official' farms along this section of coast, which are lit and reported in the light lists – however inshore and in various *calas* there are many more farms and these are usually unlit. It is therefore essential to keep a lookout at all times while making a coastal passage in this area.

⊕			
⊕1	Gibraltar Harbour Approaches	36°08′N	05°22′.5W
⊕2	Pta Europa west	36°05′.5N	05°21′W
⊕11	Pta Europa east	36°05′.5N	05°20′W
⊕14	SE of Pta de la Doncella	36°22′.5N	05°08′W
⊕20	Pta de Calaburras	36°29′N	04°38′W
⊕24	Puerto del Candado	36°41′N	04°20′.5W
⊕27	Pta Torrox	36°42′N	03°57′.4W
⊕28	Pta de la Concepción	36°42′.5N	03°44′W
⊕31	Cabo Sacratif	36°41′N	03°28′W
⊕34	SSE of Pta de las Entinas	36°37′.5N	02°46′W
⊕38	S of Pta del Río	36°46′.5N	02°25′.5W
⊕39	Cabo de Gata	36°41′N	02°10′W

100m; headlands with cliffs, for instance Cabo de Gata, may have off-shore rocks or shoals. There are many small river courses, called ramblas, that are dry for most of the year but run in spate when the rare rains fall. Extensive deltas are found at their mouths which are often steep-to.

GALES – HARBOURS OF REFUGE

In the event of onshore gales and heavy seas, Gibraltar, Málaga and Almería are the safest to enter. No attempt should be made to enter small harbours until the seas have subsided.

VISITS INLAND

In addition to the places to visit in the immediate vicinity of each harbour, there are many fascinating places lying some distance inland. Among the many interesting places are the following:

Sevilla, capital of Andalucía and of ancient origin with a wealth of interesting old buildings. In April a famous fair is held here; book very early.

Cordoba, the cordwainers city, developed by the Moors. The cathedral was the second largest mosque in the world, and the site of the oldest synagogue in Spain is in the city.

Granada, with the extraordinary Alhambra, one of the outstanding sites of Europe.

Ronda, a town in a spectacular setting with Roman remains and caves nearby.

Jérez de la Frontera, an intriguing town and centre for the sherry trade which retains strong British connections.

Cádiz, well known to the British since Elizabethan times, retains its seawards fortifications within which the old town plan is largely undisturbed. The Hydrographic Office, where charts may be bought, is just outside the town walls, above the railway line.

Medina Sidonia, an example of the 'white towns' of Andalucia and in a splendid position, was part of the estate of the ill-starred Commander of the Spanish Armada and served as a leading mark into the distant Bay of Cádiz.

If the reader is at the western end of the Costa del Sol, the last three might be combined in a long day's expedition.

Pilotage and navigation

TIDES

The standard port is Gibraltar; secondary ports are Málaga and Almería. From Alicante to the north-east the tide is hardly appreciable. The figures are:

		Heights			Mean
	MHWS	MHWN	MLWS	MLWN	Level
Gibraltar	1.0	0.7	0.3	0.1	0.50
Differences					
HW	LW				
Málaga					
+0005	−0005	−0.3	−0.1	0.0	+0.1	0.45
Almería					
+0010	−0010	−0.5	−0.3	0.0	+0.2	0.40

CURRENTS

There is usually an east going current along the coast. It can be as much as 2–3 knots at the western end and slackens towards the east. It has to be reckoned with when planning a passage and when entering or leaving a harbour.

SOUNDINGS

In most harbours sand builds up at or near the entrance, particularly after a blow, and is periodically dredged. Reported depths are not necessarily accurate and care should be taken to sound whilst approaching and entering harbour.

MAGNETIC VARIATION

Costa del Sol (Málaga) 02°45′W (2005) decreasing 7′ annually.

RESTRICTED AREAS

Anchoring is not permitted in the following areas which should be avoided if possible:
• W and E of the Rock of Gibraltar
• The prolongation of the airstrip at Gibraltar
• An area 2M to E of Estepona
• An area 2M to SW of Málaga
• An area 1M to S of Málaga where passage is also forbidden.

TUNNY NETS

During the summer months, tunny nets may be set between February and October in the following localities:
• Off La Línea
• Off the coast N of Fuerte de Santa Barbara
• Near Marbella
• Near Adra
• Off Punta del Sabinal
• To W of Cabo de Gata.

FISH HAVENS

There are extensive fish havens along this coast.

LANDINGS

The beaches are regularly patrolled by *guardia civil* with a brief to intercept smugglers and drug traffickers. If you wish to land do not be surreptitious.

PLASTIC SHEETS

Gales can dump polythene sheets from the greenhouses into the sea. They may be up to 100m long.

PLANNING GUIDE AND DISTANCE TABLES

See page 45.

II. COSTA DEL SOL Europa Point to Pta del Torrox

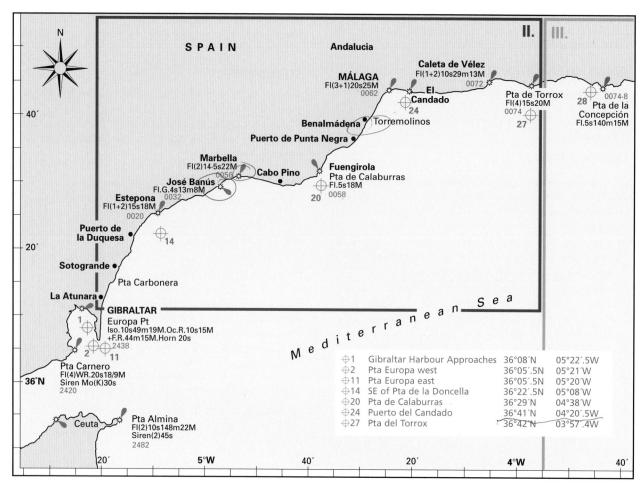

SPAIN

Andalucia

Caleta de Vélez
Fl(1+2)10s29m13M

MÁLAGA
Fl(3+1)20s25M
0062

El
Candado
24

Pta de Torrox
Fl(4)15s20M
0074

28 Pta de la
Concepción
Fl.5s140m15M

0072

0074·8

27

Benalmádena · Torremolinos

Puerto de Punta Negra

Marbella
Fl(2)14·5s22M
0056 · Cabo Pino

Fuengirola
Pta de Calaburras
Fl.5s18M
0058

José Banús
Fl.G.4s13m8M
0032

Estepona
Fl(1+2)15s18M
0020

Puerto de
la Duquesa

14

20

Sotogrande ●

Pta Carbonera

La Atunara ●

GIBRALTAR
Europa Pt
Iso.10s49m19M.Oc.R.10s15M
+F.R.44m15M.Horn 20s
2438

1

2   11

Pta Carnero
Fl(4)WR.20s18/9M
Siren Mo(K)30s
2420

36°N

Mediterranean Sea

Ceuta

Pta Almina
Fl(2)10s148m22M
Siren(2)45s
2482

40′

20′

36°N

20′

5°W

40′

20′

4°W

40′

⊕1	Gibraltar Harbour Approaches	36°08′N	05°22′.5W
⊕2	Pta Europa west	36°05′.5N	05°21′W
⊕11	Pta Europa east	36°05′.5N	05°20′W
⊕14	SE of Pta de la Doncella	36°22′.5N	05°08′W
⊕20	Pta de Calaburras	36°29′N	04°38′W
⊕24	Puerto del Candado	36°41′N	04°20′.5W
⊕27	Pta del Torrox	36°42′N	03°57′.4W

Plan IIA

PORTS
1. La Atunara
2. Puerto de Sotogrande
3. Puerto de la Duquesa
3. Puerto de Estepona
5. Puerto de José Banús
6. Puerto de Marbella
7. Marina de Bajadilla
7. Puerto Cabo Pino
9. Puerto de Fuengirola
10. Puerto de Punta Negra
11. Puerto de Benalmádena
12. Puerto de Málaga
13. Puerto de El Candado
14. Puerto Caleta de Vélez

Europa Point, Gibraltar   Graham Hutt

1. Puerto de La Atunara

36°10′.7N 05°19′.9W

Lights

0008 **Dique de Abrigo head** Fl.G.8s11m5M Green tower
0008.5 **Contadique head** Fl.R.6s8m3M Red tower

Some 5 miles north of Point Europa there has recently been built the small fishing port of La Atunara, a Mediterranean outlet for La Línea. It is solely for the use of commercial fishermen but it could be a possible refuge in storm conditions.

Apart from a fuelling point (for fishing trawlers only) there are no other facilities at the port apart from the normal café. It is a long way from any shops and the port is only included here to inform passing craft of a possible refuge.

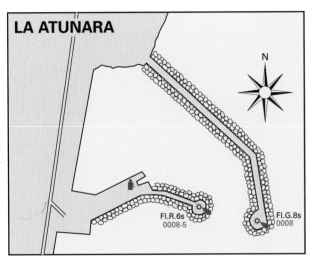

Plan 1

⚓ RÍO GUADIARO

The bar has been impassable in 1997. In the river, holding and depths are variable but, should the situation on the bar change, there was an anchorage in 4m mud between it and the road bridge 300m inland.

Approach

The river has a house with a conical blue roof on its right (SW) bank and training wall of rocks on its opposite bank. There are three dinghy pontoons upriver of the wall. To NNE is the massive development of Puerto de Sotogrande.

Entrance

If there is a channel through the bar, it is usually close to the training wall. The river in spate may reach 4 to 5 knots in the entrance.

2. Puerto de Sotogrande

36°17′N 05°16′W

Charts

British Admiralty *3578, 773*. Imray *M11*
French *4717*. Spanish *453*

⊕12 36°17′N 05°16′.2W

Lights

0016 **Dique Levante S head** Fl(3)G.11s8m4M Masonry
  tower, green top 3m
0016.2 **Dique Levante N head** Q(3)10s8m4M E card (with
  ♦ topmark)
0016.8 **External espigón** Q.R.2m2M Red post 2m
0016.4 **Spur** Q.G.3m2M
0016.6 **Contradique head** Fl(4)R.14s4m2M Red post 2m

Port communications

VHF Ch 9. Port ☎ 956 79 00 00 *Fax* 956 79 01 09
Email puertosotogrande@telefonica.net
url www.puertosotogrande.com

Major marina village

A marina complex close NNE of the Río Guadiaro. It has housing blocks with shops and restaurants around the north side of the harbour. The harbour is easy to approach and enter but in SE-S winds entrance could be difficult and despite additional breakwaters, a swell enters the yacht harbour.

Facilities are good; besides those listed below, there are sandy beaches either side of the harbour, golf, riding, polo, tennis, squash etc.

Yachts ashore may be lived in by special arrangement with the marina manager and winter lay-up prices may be negotiated.

Sotogrande is undergoing a huge development to make use of the lagoon to the west of the present marina. There are now 250 new berths over and above the 550 of the original marina with many more to come in the future.

Approach

From the south Having rounded Europa point follow the coast at 500m in a general NNE direction. Torre Nueva and Torre de Punta Carbonera may be identified. The mass of buildings at Puerto de Sotogrande can be seen from afar.

From the NE Follow the coast at 500m in a general SSW direction. The harbour and breakwaters of José Banús, Estepona and La Duquesa may be seen but caution is needed as there are a number of rocky sand-retaining breakwaters which can be mistaken for harbours.

In the closer approach the anchorage of Cala Sardina with a *torre* on each side and the harbour breakwater and a large red hotel located N of the entrance will be identified. The *torre de control* is a handsome, square, castellated stone tower with cupola and flag-staff.

GPS approach

Steer for ⊕12 from an easterly quadrant and then steer for the end of the breakwater (approx. 0.12M).

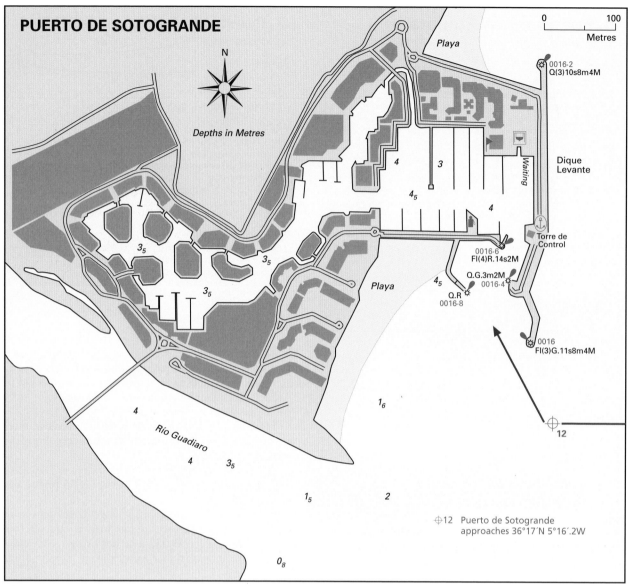

PUERTO DE SOTOGRANDE

N

Depths in Metres

0   100

Metres

Playa

0016·2
Q(3)10s8m4M

4   3

Waiting

Dique
Levante

4₅

4

Torre de
Control

0016·6
Fl(4)R.14s2M

3₅

3₅

Q.G.3m2M
0016·4

3₅

4₅

3₅

Playa

Q.R
0016·8

4

0016
Fl(3)G.11s8m4M

4

Río Guadiaro

1₆

4   3₅

1₅   2

⊕12 Puerto de Sotogrande
approaches 36°17′N 5°16′.2W

⊕12

0₈

Plan 2

Anchorage in the approach

Anchor in 3m sand 300m offshore to N or S of the harbour.

Entrance

Approach S head of the Dique de Abrigo and round it leaving at 15m.

Berths

Secure beneath the *torre de control* and ask there for a berth which will be on one of the yacht harbour pontoons. Two bow lines may be needed.

Formalities

If entering from abroad (e.g. Gibraltar) the office in the *torre* will arrange for customs clearance, should that be required.

Facilities

Maximum length overall: 50m.
Most repair facilities including sailmaker, GRP.
150-tonne travel-lift, large hardstanding, slipways.
Chandlery shop beside the harbour.

Water taps on pontoons and quays.
Shower baths, WCs and sauna at sanitary block.
220v AC and 380v AC on quays and pontoons.
Ice from fuel station.
Gasoleo A, petrol.
Club Marítimo with restaurant.
Launderette near the harbour.
Supermarket and some shops at the harbour, more at Sotogrande 1M away.

Communications

Bus service along the coast. ☎ Area code 956. Taxi
☎ 61 60 78 or 907 59 26 09 (mobile).

⚓ **CALA SARDINA** 36°18′.2N 5°16′.2W

A pleasant anchorage 1.5M N of Sotogrande. Punta de la Chullera is a low sloping point with a conspicuous tower and a few houses in the trees. On the other side of the bay a square fort-like building, Casa Cuartel, is easily seen. Anchor in 3m sand and pebbles about 75m off. There is foul ground 100m off Punta de la Chullera which is sometimes called Punta Europa. The main coast road is behind the beach.

3. Puerto de la Duquesa

36°21´.3N 05°13´.7W

Charts

British Admiralty *3578, 773.* Imray *M11*
French *4717.* Spanish *453*

⊕13 36°21´.1N 05°13´.6W

Lights

0018 **Dique de Levante S head** Fl.G.7s8m5M White
   truncated tower green lantern and base 4m
0018.3 **Dique de Levante N head** Q(3)10s7m3M Yellow
   truncated tower black band 4m
0018.4 **Contradique head** Fl(2)R.7s6m3M White tower
   red top 4m
0018.41 **External espigón head** Fl.R.5s7m3M Metal
   strucure, red top 5m

Port communications

VHF Ch 9. Port ☎ 952 89 01 00 Fax 952 89 01 01
Email duquesa@marinamediterraneo.com
url www.marinamediterraneo.com/duquesa.htm

Puerto de la Duquesa

Useful marina near Gibraltar

A marina surrounded by blocks of apartments and with
good facilities. Approach and entrance are easy and
good shelter is available inside. It is a useful first port of
call after Gibraltar which is less than 20M away. Good
beaches on either side of the harbour.

Approach

From the south Punta de la Chullera, with a tower, has
rocks extending up to 100m offshore. Castillo de la
Duquesa just SSW of the harbour is conspicuous.

From the north Punta de Salto de la Mora with its old
watch tower can be seen. Foul ground extends 200m off
this point. The new buildings around the harbour and
its breakwater are visible during the closer approach.

GPS approach

Steer for ⊕13 from an easterly quadrant and then steer
for the end of the breakwater (approx. 0.13M).

Anchorage

Good anchorage is available to the NE of the harbour,
about 150m offshore in 5m sand.

Entrance

Approach the head of the Dique de Levante on a NW
course, round it and enter on a NE course. Give the
breakwaters a 25m berth; underwater obstructions are
marked by small buoys.

Berths

Secure alongside fuelling berth on the port hand side of
the entrance and ask at the *torre de control* or call on
Ch 9.

Formalities

If entering Spain, the *capitán de puerto* and *aduana's*
offices are in the *torre de control.*

Facilities

Maximum length overall: 20-25m.
Limited workshops on E side of harbour.
75-tonne crane on NE side of harbour.
Water taps on pontoons and quays.
Showers at *torre de control.*
220v AC on pontoons and quays.
Ice on fuel quay.
Gasoleo A and petrol.
Clubhouse with pool.
Local supermarket. Other shops in Manilva village 1½M away
   and Las Sabinilla ½M away.
Washing machine in *torre de control.*

Communications

Bus service. Airfield at Gibraltar. ☎ Area code 95.
Taxi ☎ 280 29 00.

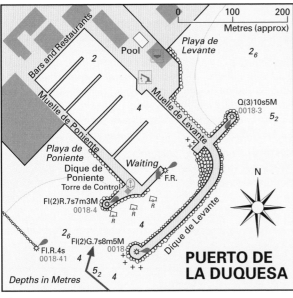

Plan 3

⊕13 Puerto de la Duquesa
   36°21´.1N 5°13´.6W

⚓ FONDEADERO DE LA SABINILLA

A rather open anchorage located just over 1M to NNE of Puerto de la Duquesa, in 3m sand about 100m from the beach. Foul ground exists off Punta de la Salo de la Mora extending out to 200m. The point is not especially conspicuous but the tower and small fort-like buildings on the point can be seen. Main coast road behind beach.

4. Puerto de Estepona

36°24'.8N 5°09'.4W

Charts

British Admiralty *3578*. Imray *M11*
French *4717*. Spanish *453*

⊕15 36°24'.65N 05°09'.6W

Lights

Approach
0020 **Punta de la Doncella LtHo** Fl(1+2)15s32m18M Dark 8-sided tower, grey lantern, white house 21m
Harbour
0022 **Dique de Abrigo spike** Q(6)+LFl.15s9m5M Black tower, yellow top 6m
0022.2 **Dique de Abrigo head** 36°24'.8N 5°09'.4W Fl.G.5s9m5M Green pole 7m
0024 **Dique de Poniente** Fl(2)R.7s9m3M Truncated tower 4m
20990(S) **Buoy** 36°25'.2N 5°08'.4W Q(6)+LFl.15s6m2M ⚐ card

Port communication

VHF Ch 9. Capitanía de Marina ☎ 95 280 18 00
Fax 95 280 24 97 *Email* estepona@eppa.es
Club Náutico de Estepona ☎ 95 280 13 41

Harbour and tourist resort

A town of Roman origin developed from a fishing village into a close-packed tourist resort with restaurants, shops and a supermarket. There is an early morning fishmarket at the harbour. Local holidays are from 24 to 29 June.

Approach

The harbour is backed by four tower blocks of flats. The dark octagonal lighthouse 31m high capped by a grey lantern is to the NE of the harbour entrance. The outer breakwater (Dique de Abrigo) has been extended westwards leaving the old entrance tower in its original position.

GPS approach

Steer for ⊕15 from a SE quadrant and then make for the breakwater head (approx. 0.1M).

Anchorage in the approach

Anchor 200m to the NE of head Dique de Abrigo in 5.5m sand.

Entrance

Approach the head of Dique de Abrigo on a N course, round it at 20m and enter on a NE course.

In a SW gale the entrance could be dangerous. The breakwaters have underwater projections. Dredgers may be in operation as this harbour's mouth frequently silts up. Most harbours along this coast have reported severe reduction in entrance depths in spring due to winter storms.

Berths

Secure to the Muelle de Espera, which is at the end of Pantalan 5, and ask at the *capitanía* which is in a blue building, like a towered wedding cake with white icing, on the north side of the harbour. The *pantalanes* have lockable gates at their shore ends.

Harbour charges

Medium to high.

Facilities

Maximum length overall: 30m.
Repairs (most services) at a shipyard to NE of the harbour.
Sailmaker under the club nautico is Magnusson Sails (Antonio Rodriguez Carrasco) ☎ 952 79 12 41 (the only sailmaker on the west of Costa del Sol. Excellent work has been reported and English is spoken).
80-tonne travel-lift and 3.5-tonne mobile crane.
Yachts up to 25-tonnes may be hauled out on the slipway immediately SW of the *club náutico*.
Hardstandings.
Chandlery in harbour.
Life-raft servicing.
Water taps on quays and pontoons.
Butane: the Marina can arrange refills for 10lb Calor bottles.
220v AC on the Dique de Poniente and pontoons, 380v on berths 20–35m.
Ice from the fish auction building or waiting quay.
Gasoleo A and petrol.
Club Náutico de Estepona has showers, a restaurant and bar and is usually open to non-members.
Provisions from shops in the town about 1M away and from supermarket on N side of the harbour.
Laundry in port, launderettes in the town.

Communications

Bus services. ☎ Area code: 95 Taxi ☎ 280 29 00

⚓ FONDEADERO DE ESTEPONA

An anchorage to the NE of the harbour off the town of Estepona, 500m from the shore in 5m sand. To E of the harbour where five breakwaters were built is a submerged breakwater parallel to the coast and about 400m offshore marked by a S card buoy. The anchorage is somewhat protected by Punta de los Marmoles, a small cliffed headland with a tower surrounded by trees.

Note Further East, anchoring is forbidden between Torre del Padrón and Punta de Guadalmaza because of submarine cables.

Estepona from the south

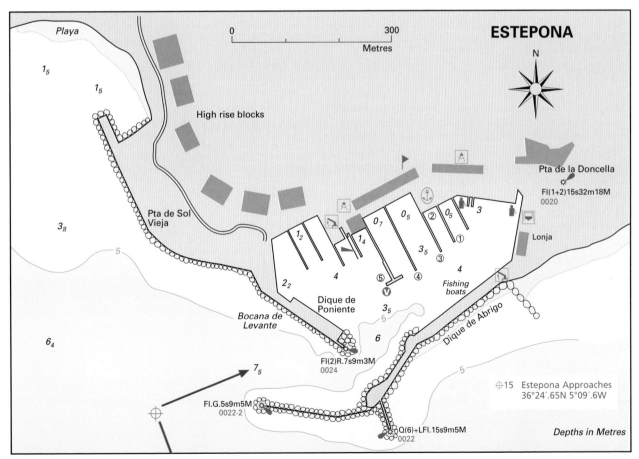

Plan 4

5. Puerto de José Banús

36°29′N 04°57′.2W

Charts

British Admiralty *3578, 773*. Imray *M11*
French *4717*. Spanish *454*

⊕16 36°28′.9N 05°57′.4W

Lights

0030 **Groyne Centre** Q(6)+LFl.15s10m5M Truncated
masonry tower
0031 **Dique de Benabolá elbow** Fl.R.3s7m4M Siren 60s
Truncated masonry tower red lantern 4m
0032 **Dique de Levante W head** 36°29′.1N 04°57′.2W
Fl.G.4s13m8M Truncated masonry tower 9m
0032.2 **E head** Q(6)+LFl.15s10m4M Tower, yellow top 6m

Port communications

VHF Ch 9. *Capitanía* ☎ 952 90 98 00 *Fax* 952 81 08 99
Email torrecontrol@puertobanus.com
url www.puertojosebanus.es

Upmarket marina

An up-market marina handling large and very large yachts, motor and sail, and correspondingly pricey. The enclave also contains apartments, shops boutiques, restaurants, night clubs, casinos and so forth, patrolled by armed security guards and protected from the outside world by automated barriers allowing the passage of selected vehicles. However, it has good repair facilities.

There is a hotel beach and swimming pool to W of the harbour which is available to yachting visitors. Entrance tickets from third floor office of the tower. It is worth escaping to Ronda by taxi.

Approach

The lone rocky-peaked mountain Pico de la Concha in the Sierra Blanca, called Sierra de Marbella on British charts, can be seen from afar. Closer in, some yellow tower blocks 2M to W and the very large Hotel Nueva Andalucía, the bull ring close E and a white flag-poled terrace are conspicuous. The old stone tower with a number of windows at the entrance and the mass of buildings around the harbour are also conspicuous.

GPS approach

Steer to ⊕16 from southerly quadrant and steer for breakwater end (approx. 0.08M).

Anchorage in the approach

200m S of S head of Dique de Levante in 8m sand.

Entrance

Approach the S head of Dique de Levante on a N course, leave it 50m to starboard and enter on an E course.

In a SW gale, the entrance could be difficult except for powerful vessels as it involves turning sharply across the waves in a restricted area of disturbed water.

Berths

Secure alongside E side of Dique de Benabolá near the fuel station for the allocation of a berth from the control tower.

Harbour charges

High.

Facilities

Maximum length overall: 80m.
Two travel-lifts, 50 and 25 tonnes and a 5-tonne mobile crane.
Launching slipway at E of the harbour.
Most shipwright and electronic work possible.
Sailmaker on N side of harbour.
Two chandlers beside the harbour.
Water points on quays and pontoons.
Showers by the tower.
220v AC to berths and 380v AC to berths over 15m.
Petrol.
Ice from fuelling point or slipway.
Yacht Club: Club Náutico Internacional Nueva Andalucia.
Supermarket at the harbour but fresh food has to be obtained from Marbella, 15 minutes away by bus or taxi, or from San Pedro.
Laundry in port and launderette behind the house on Dique de Riberea.

Communications

Bus service. ☎ Area code 95. Taxi ☎ 278 38 39.

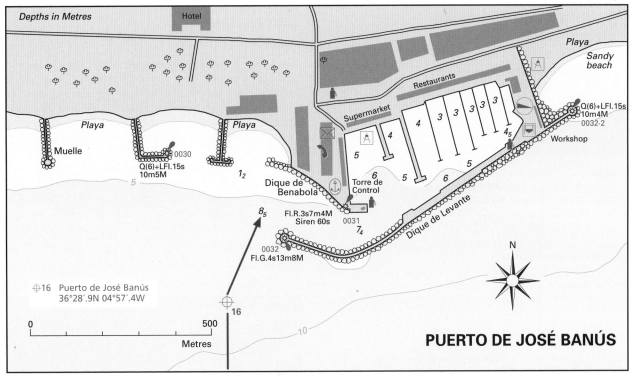

Depths in Metres

Hotel

Playa

Playa

Muelle

Q(6)+LFl.15s
10m5M

0030

1₂

Dique de
Benabola

8₅

0032
Fl.G.4s13m8M

Torre de
Control

Fl.R.3s7m4M
Siren 60s

0031

7₄

Restaurants

Supermarket

Dique de Levante

Playa
Sandy
beach

Q(6)+LFl.15s
10m4M
0032·2

Workshop

N

⊕16   Puerto de José Banús
       36°28'.9N 04°57'.4W

0   500

Metres

16

PUERTO DE JOSÉ BANÚS

Plan 5

Puerto de José Banús

6. Puerto de Marbella

36°30'.3N 04°53'.4W

Charts

British Admiralty *3578, 773*. Imray *M11*
French *4717*. Spanish *454*

⊕17 36°30'.25N 04°53'.55W

Lights

Approach
0056 **Marbella LtHo** Fl(2)14·5s35m22M White round
tower 29m
Marina
0056·2 **Dique de Levante** Fl(2)G.7s7m4M Green tower 3m
0056·6 **Dique de Poniente** Fl.R.5s6m2M Red tower 3m
Note There may be several fish farms off this harbour
which normally have 4 buoys, Fl.Y.5s marking their
extent

Port communications

VHF Ch 09. *Capitanía* ☎ 95 277 57 00 *Fax* 95 282 44 62.
Club Marítimo ☎ 95 277 25 04.

Noisy tourist town

One of the original tourist towns on this coast, a mass
of high rise blocks. There are two small harbours, the
one to the W being for yachts, the other for fishing
craft. The approach and entrance to the marina are easy
but could be dangerous in strong SW-W winds. Strong
winds from that quarter as well as from the East
produce a serious surge in the harbour which may
become untenable. If sitting out a blow, use your own
gear and double up on the lines.

The harbour is noisy at night during the high season
and during the day the long sandy beaches on either
side of the harbour are often crowded.

The local holidays are 10-18 June, Ferias de San

Bernabé. 18-24 August, Semana del Sol. 18 October, San
Pedro de Alcantara.

Approach

The mass of skyscraper apartments and hotels along the
seafront and the high Sierra Blanca mountain range
behind make the whereabouts of the marina easy to
locate. The marina itself is immediately S of Marbella
light; in day time the lighthouse is difficult to spot as it
is the middle of a group of high-rise buildings. Do not
be confused by a number of rocky jetties between the
marina and the fishing harbour, built as breakwaters to
retain sand for bathing beaches, and look out for a
fishing platform at 36°30'.0N 04°52'.4W, about half a
mile off the fishing harbour. The marina breakwater has
been heightened to give extra protection within.

GPS approach

Steer to ⊕17 from southerly quadrant and steer for
breakwater end (approx. 0.04M).

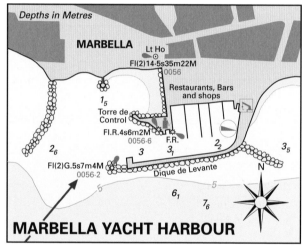

Plan 6b

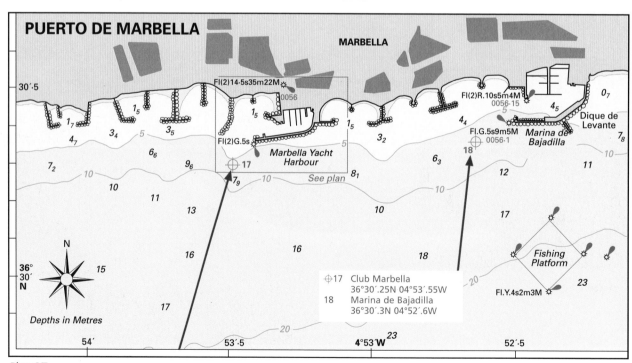

Plan 6/7

Anchorage in the approach

Anchor in 5m sand anywhere 200m to SW of the entrance to the yacht harbour.

Entrance

Give the jetty heads a good berth as they are not vertical at the foot. Line of small red can buoys on the north side of the entrance and a wreck on the south side, leave to port and starboard respectively.

Berths

Secure to the fuelling station on the port side of the entrance and ask at the *capitanía*, behind the fuel station.

Facilities

Maximum length overall: 15–20m.
A fork-lift type hoist on a tractor, rated at 16 tonnes.
A small slipway in NE corner of the harbour and a slipway on the W side of the harbour.
Small hardstanding.
Chandlery shop in the town.
Water from club marítimo and on pontoons and quays.
125v, 220v AC on quayside and pontoons and 380v on berths of 20m.
Gasoleo A and petrol.
Ice from factory 100m NE of the club marítimo.
Club Marítimo de Marbella is really a high quality hotel and restaurant with showers and other services in the basement.
There is a market about 1M to N of the club marítimo. Buy food from shops in back streets, they have better quality provisions and are cheaper.
Several launderettes in town.

Communications

Bus service along the coast. ☎ Area code 95.
Taxi ☎ 277 44 88.

Marbella

7. Marina de Bajadilla

36°30'.4N 04°52'.5W

Lights

0056.1 **Dique de Levante head** 36°30'.4N 04°52'.5W
Fl.G.5s9m5M White tower, green top 4m
0056.15 **Dique de Poniente head** Fl(2)R.10s5m4M Grey tower, red top 3m

⊕18   36°30'.3N 4°52'.6W

Port Communications

VHF Ch 9. *Capitanía* ☎ 952 85 84 01 *Fax* 952 85 84 26. *Email* marbella@eppa.es

Fishing harbour turned marina

This used to be the fishing harbour where yachts were definitely not welcome but recently it has been developed into a 260-berth marina with all the usual facilities. The entrance is quite straightforward but the harbour is subjected to swell from W and SW.

GPS approach

Steer to ⊕18 from southerly quadrant and steer for breakwater end (approx. 0.07M).

Approach

Marbella with its line of high-rise buildings can be seen from afar but the tall (35m) Marbella lighthouse is difficult to spot amongst them. Close the coast aiming at the east end of the high-rise buildings until the breakwater and/or the lighthouse can be identified. The marina is just over half a mile east of the lighthouse.

Berths

Moor to the fuel berth, at the end of the Dique de Poniente immediately to port on entering and obtain a berth at the *capitanía* which is at the very NE corner of the harbour.

Facilities

Maximum LOA 15m.
Crane, travel-lift, hardstanding etc.
Water and electricity on pontoons.
Showers etc at base of main pier.
Restaurant in marina.
Shops in town.

Marina de Bajadilla

8. Puerto Cabo Pino

36°29′N 04°44′.4W

Charts

British Admiralty *3578, 773.* Imray *M11*
French *4717.* Spanish *454*

⊕19   36°28′.8N 04°44′.5W

Lights

0057.4 **Espigón Antiarena** Q(6)+LFl.15s3M ⚐ black and
   yellow post
0057.6 **Dique de Levante head** Fl(4)G.10s7m4M White
   round tower 4m
Note 3F.R vertical means port closed.
0057.8 **Muelle de Poniente head** Fl(2)R.5s7m4M White
   tower 4m
To the east
0058 **Punta de Calaburras** Fl.5s46m18M White tower,
   house with red roof, 25m

Port communications

VHF Ch 9. Port manager ☎ 952 83 19 75 *Fax* 952 83 02
37. Peter Holmer, the manager, has good English.
Email marinacabopino@eppa.es

Small private harbour

An attractive small private harbour with houses built in
the local style; it is one of the less oppressive in terms
of not being surrounded by high rise buildings and
boutiques. The approach and entrance may be
problematic – see below – but there is good protection
once inside. Facilities are good and there are beaches on
either side of the harbour.

Approach and entrance

Cabo Pino lies 8M to the E of Marbella and 4M to
WSW of Punta Calaburras lighthouse, both of which are
easily recognised. The high white apartment blocks and
harbour breakwater can be seen from afar. The partly
ruined square, Torre de Cala Honda, located just to W
of the harbour will be seen closer in.

The approach and entrance silt and are dredged by
the marina to a least depth of 1.5m though there is
usually more water than that and yachts drawing 2m
and more have entered without difficulty. Enter on the
flood, sounding, and pass the Dique de Levante at about
one third the distance between it and the Espigón
Antiarena; sand builds up off the head of the Dique de
Levante. Care is particularly necessary in strong SW-W
winds or swell which may effectively reduce depths. If
in doubt, call the marina and inquire about depths.

GPS approach

Steer to ⊕19 from southerly quadrant and steer for
breakwater end (approx. 0.14M).

Puerto Cabo Pino

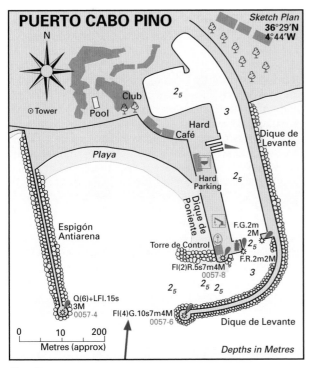

PUERTO CABO PINO

Sketch Plan
36°29'N
4°44'W

N

⊙ Tower

Pool

Club

2₅

3

Hard Café

Dique de Levante

Playa

Hard Parking

2₅

Espigón Antiarena

Dique de Poniente

F.G.2m 2M

Torre de Control

2₅

F.R.2m2M

Fl(2)R.5s7m4M
0057·8

3

Q(6)+LFl.15s
3M
0057·4

2₅

2₅ 2₅

Fl(4)G.10s7m4M
0057·6

Dique de Levante

0   10   200
Metres (approx)

Depths in Metres

Plan 8

⊕19   Puerto Cabo Pino approaches
36°28'.8N 04°44'.5W

Punta de Calaburras

Anchorages

The sea floor near the harbour is mainly stony with poor holding, particularly on the E side, though some sandy patches may be found.

In the approach

Cala Moral 36°29`.8N 04°40`.7W 2M to ENE has a sandy bottom. Anchor between Torre Pesetas on Punta de la Torre Nueva and Torre de Cala Moral 200m from the shore in 3m sand.

Berths

Secure to the fuel berth which is just inside the harbour to port and near the F.R light and ask at the *torre de control* for berthing instructions.

Harbour charges

High.

Facilities

Maximum length overall: 16m (4 berths only).
Small yard which can pressure clean and apply anti foul.
8-tonne crane and 26-tonne travel-lift.
Slipway on W side of the harbour.
Engine mechanics.
Water points on all quays.
Showers at *torre de control*.
220v AC points on all quays. Some at 380v by the larger berths.
Gasoleo A and petrol.
Ice from the bars or from fuel quay.
Supermarket behind the harbour.
Launderettes near harbour.

Communications

Bus along the coast. ☎ Area code 95.
Taxi ☎ 277 44 88.

9. Puerto de Fuengirola

36°32´.5N 04°36´.9W

Charts

British Admiralty *3578, 773*. Imray *M11*
French *4717*. Spanish *455, 454*

⊕21 36°32´.6N 04 36°65´W

Lights

0059 **Dique de Abrigo** 36°32´.6N 04°36´.8W
 Fl(4)R.12s10m4M Red metal pyramidal tower 4m
0059.4 **Contradique** Fl(2)G.7s6m3M Green truncated
 pyramidal tower 4m
0058.5 **Espigón S head** 36°32´.8N 04°36´.7W Fl.G.5s5m5M
 Green tower 4m (on submerged groyne to the north
 of entrance)
To the west
0058 **Punta de Calaburras** 36°30´.5N 04°38´.3W
 Fl.5s46m18M White tower, house with red roof, 25m

Port communications

VHF Ch 9. Port ☎ 952 46 80 00 *Fax* 952 46 99 89
Email fuengirola@terra.es

Harbour with good shelter and facilities

Planned as a harbour in two parts, only the western side
has been built. It has good shelter and facilities. All
necessary provisions may be bought from large modern
tourist town nearby. Usually the approach and entrance
are easy but could be difficult with strong NE–E winds
and/or swell. In these conditions parts of the harbour
are uncomfortable.

The town is very busy and noisy in the season. There
are good beaches each side of the port but they are
crowded in summer. Local holidays: three days in August
and 7–10 October for their Patron Saint.

Approach

From the SW The low headland of Punta Calaburras
with its conspicuous lighthouse and a mast 6.2M to N,
is about 2M SW of Fuengirola. An old castle on a small
hill lies halfway between this point and the harbour. The
town of Fuengirola with its high-rise hotels and
apartments is easily seen.

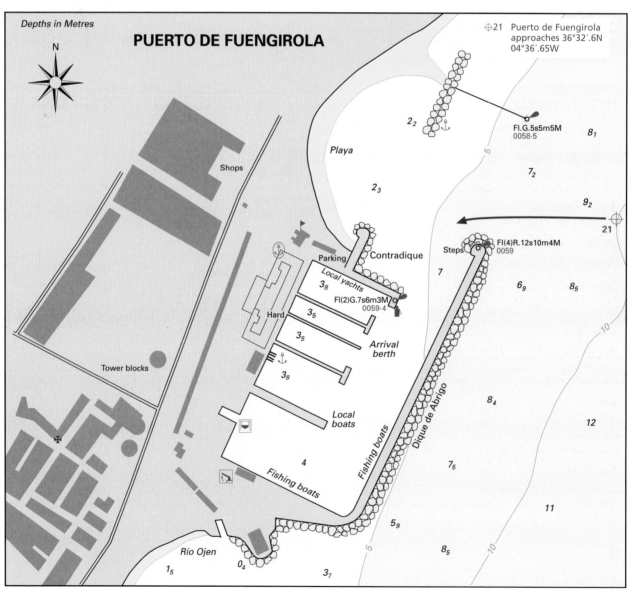

Plan 9

Fuengirola. Note submerged breakwater running SE from groynes to NE

From the NE The massive high-rise tourist development around Torremolinos continues with minor interruptions along the coast as far as Fuengirola after which it peters out.

The four minarets of the marina, although they do not compete in altitude with the buildings in the background, are conspicuous and catch the sun.

GPS approach

Steer to ⊕21 from easterly quadrant and steer for breakwater end (approx. 0.13M).

Anchorage in the approach

Anchor 200m to N of the head of the breakwater in 3m sand. An alternative deeper anchorage lies 500m to SE of the harbour in 15m sand.

Entrance

Approach the head of the Dique de Abrigo on a NW course and round it. A shallow area has developed on the starboard side of the entrance; keep in mid-channel.

Berths

Pick up a mooring line and go bows- or stern-to one of the new concrete pontoons and check with the office near SW corner of the port.

Facilities

Maximum length overall: 20m.
Repairs – limited; there is a small yard to the SW of the harbour.
35-tonne travel-lift and 6-tonne crane.
Chandlery.
Water taps on quay and pontoons.
220v AC on pontoons and quays.
Gasoleo A and petrol.
Ice at the SW end of the harbour.

Club náutico – inquire about using its facilities.
Shop in the town for provisions.
A market near the centre of town and an open market on Tuesdays.
Launderettes in the town.

Communications

Rail and bus service. Airport at Málaga. ☎ Area code 95. Taxi ☎ 247 10 00.

The minarets at Fuengirola

10. Puerto de Punta Negra

36°34′.7N 04°32′.43W
For charts, lights etc. see Fuengirola page 36.

Small private harbour

This very small private harbour for small yachts and runabouts is part of the casino complex.

Approach

The harbour lies 4M to NE of Fuengirola and ½M to SW of Puerto Principe at Torremolinos. The casino building is conspicuous.

Anchorage in the approach

Anchor 200m to S of the entrance in 7m sand.

Entrance

Approach the casino building heading NNW and identify the entrance in the centre of the harbour breakwater. Go in to either basin. Depths believed to be 2m or less.

Puerto de Punta Negra

11. Puerto de Benalmádena

36°35′.7N 04°30′.7W

Charts

British Admiralty *773*. Imray *M11*
French *4717*. Spanish *455*, *455A*

⊕22   36°35′.5N 04°30′.5W

Lights

0060·3 **Laja de Bermeja** Q(3)10s7m5M ♦ E card post 4m
0060.4 **Dique Sur SW head** Fl.G.5s9m10M White tower, with green bands 5m
0060.5 **Dique Sur NE corner** Q(3)10s9m4M ♦ Truncated conical masonry tower 5m
0060.7 **Dique Sur inner head** Fl(3)G.10s4m4M White tower, green bands 2m
0060.6 **Dique del Oeste head** Fl.R.5s4m4M Truncated conical masonry, red bands 2m
There is a 20m spur projecting northnortheastwards from the inside of the Dique Sur head. It is not visible until the head is almost rounded. There is a small tower with green band and a green light of unknown characteristics.

Port communications

VHF Ch 9. *Capitanía* ☎ 952 57 70 22, *Fax* 952 44 13 44
Email: info@puertobenalmadena.org
url www.puertobenalmadena.org

Huge yacht harbour

This is a huge artificial yacht harbour enclosing 150,000 square metres of water located at the SW end of Torremolinos. The area near the harbour is a mass of soulless high-rise buildings and as it is very difficult to find a berth in Málaga, Benalmádena is a good alternative. Good beaches on each side of the harbour.

Approach

The approach requires care to avoid the shoal, Laja de Bermeja (see below) which breaks in heavy weather. The entrance is easy and good protection is offered once inside though there is some swell in outer harbour with W gale.

From the west The prominent walls of Benalmádena can be seen when passing the large casino building and small harbour of Punta Negra. Keep over ½M off the coast to pass south of the Laja de Bermeja and make for a position where the S end of the harbour is due W.

From the east Passage is forbidden through the area of an oil terminal located 1M to S of Puerto de Málaga. This area is about ½M square and lies ¾M off the coast. From Puerto de Málaga keep ½M off coast and pass inside prohibited area. Pay attention to an exposed wreck in the area. The mass of high rise blocks of flats at Torremolinos ends shortly before Benalmádena. Keep well to the east of Laja de Bermeja.

GPS approach

Steer to ⊕22 from easterly quadrant and steer for breakwater end, leaving the Laja de Bermeja post well to port (approx. 0.3M).

Anchorage in the approach

Anchor 200m to the NE of the E end of the Dique Sur in 5m sand.

Entrance

The Laja de Bermeja (2.5m), lying some 250m S of Dique Sur head light, is the easterly outlier of a large rock strewn and shallow area to the west of the actual rock. The E cardinal post marks this large shallow area (although to the west of the actual Laja de Bermeja!)

From a position ½M out and where the S end of the harbour is due W, approach on this course leaving the Laja de Bermeja post well to port. Follow the Dique Sur to its head then round it, keeping at least 30 metres clear and pass the new spur close to starboard and enter on an ENE'ly course.

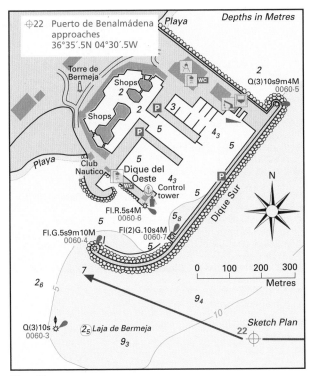

Plan 11

Berths

Go to the fuelling point and ask at the control tower for a berth. (There may be significant swell on outer wall.)

Benalmádena

Facilities

Maximum length overall: 30m.
Most yacht maintenance services including sailmaker.
Slipway in the E corner of the harbour.
50-tonne travel-hoist and 5-tonne crane.
Chandleries inside and outside the port.
Water taps on all quays.
Showers.
220v AC and 380v AC on berths between 18–30m.
Gasoleo A and petrol pumps by the control tower.
Ice on fuel quay.
Supermarket in port.
Shops and supermarkets in Benalmádena Costa and Torremolinos, 1M away. Good shops and market (Friday) at Arroya del Miel 1½M inland.
Laundry collected within the port and launderettes in the town.
Diving school.

Communications

Bus and rail services to most parts of Spain, bus stop on main road near the marina. Airport at Málaga.
☎ Area code 95. Taxi ☎ 244 15 45.

⚓ FONDEADERO DE TORREMOLINOS

Anchor off Torremolinos, 1M to NE of Puerto de Benalmádena, 250m from the shore in 6 to 7m sand

⚓ LA CARIHUELA

Anchor to the S of the old castle.

12. Puerto de Málaga

36°43′N 04°25′W

Tides

Time differencesr
based on Gibraltar   *Height difference*   *Mean*
HW   LW   MHWS MHWN MLWS MLWN   *level*
+0005 −0005   −0.3   −0.1   0.0   +0.1   0.45

⊕23 36°41′.7N 04°25′.0W

Currents

Offshore these are normally E-going but a counter-current sometimes runs off the entrance. The tidal streams up to 0.5 knots run NE and SW in the entrance.

Charts

British Admiralty *1850, 1851*. Imray *M11*
French *4717, 7294*. Spanish *455, 455A, 4551*

Lights

Approach

0062 **Málaga LtHo**
Fl(3+1)20s38m25M 243°-vis-047° White truncated conical tower on white two-storey building 33m

Harbour

0064 **Dique del Este head** Fl(2)G.7s13m3M 000°-vis-200° Conical masonry tower 7m

0064.5 **New Dique de Levante N head** Q(3)10s12m3M Black tower, yellow band 2m

0065 **New Dique de Levante S head** Fl.G.5s7m5M Green tower 4m

0065.3 **Submerged breakwater head** Q(6)+LFl.15s3M ⬇ cardinal post 4m

0065·5 **Contradique SW corner** Q(6)+LFl.15s3M ⬇ card. post 4m

0065.7 **Contradique E head** Fl.R.5s5M Red pyramid 5m.

0066 **Dique del Oeste head** Fl(2)R.6s13m4M 374°-vis-231° Conical masonry tower 7m

0067 **Puerto Pesquero Espigón Sur** Q.R.4m2M Conical stone tower 3m

0067.5 **Puerto Pesquero Espigón Norte** Q.G.5m2M Conical stone tower 3m

0068 **Dique Transversal del Este head** SE corner Fl(2)G.7s6m2M Conical masonry tower 5m

0070 **Muelle Transversal del Oeste head** Fl(2+1)R.12s7m2M Tower with red top 4m

0070.2 **Muelle de Romero Robledo** Fl(4)R.11s7m2M Tower with red top 4m

0069 **Small craft basin. Dique Norte** Fl(3)R.9s6m2M Red metal column

0069.2 **Small craft basin. Dique Sur head** Fl(3)G.8s6m2M Green metal column

0069.4 **Muelle Canovas del Castillo head** Fl(2+1)G.12s7m2M Tower with green top 4m

Port communications

Port VHF Ch 9, 11, 12, 13, 14, 16
☎ 952 21 05 90
Real Club Mediterraneo VHF Ch 9
☎ 952 22 85 41 *Fax.* 952 21 63 11
Email cbotes@realclubmediterraneo.com
url www.realclubmediterraneo.com

Storm signals

Storm signals may be displayed at the signal station.

Puerto de Málaga

Jose Banus

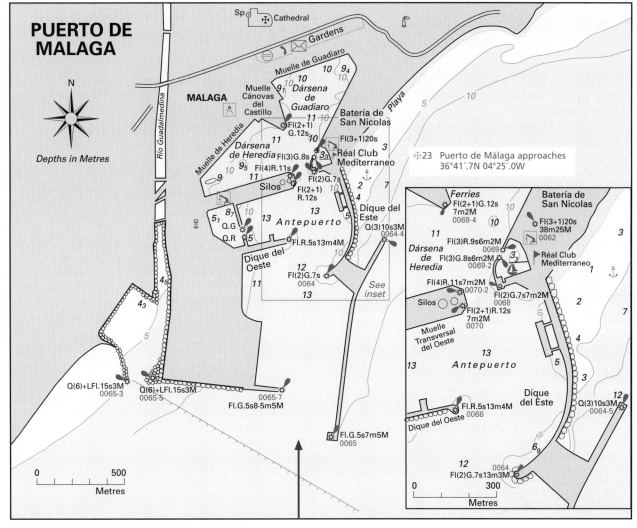

Plan 12

Major working port

This is a port to be avoided unless prior arrangements have been made for a berth especially now with the extensive works going on in the harbour. A new Dique de Levante and a new *contradique* have been constructed and much work is still going on in the harbour. It is the major commercial and fishing port of the Costa del Sol without special provision for yachts and there is very limited room at the Real Club Mediterráneo de Málaga which is an exclusive club. Yachts are turned away from Málaga by the harbour authorities and sent to Benalmádena and it has been reported that even in difficult conditions this applies as there is now, effectively, no room for pleasure craft in Málaga.

Local holidays 27 August for 10 days. Fair, August 1 to 9.

Approach by day

From the west The line of high-rise apartments and hotels at Torremolinos and Puerto de Benalmádena are conspicuous, as are the round storage tanks and the power station with two very tall chimneys 1.5M to SW of the port. Keep within ½M of the shore or more than 1½M off-shore to avoid the Passage Prohibited Area. Pay attention to the exposed wreck in the area.

From the east A grey cement factory about 4 miles to E of the port is identifiable and the wide flat valley between high ranges of mountains where the port and city are located can be seen from afar. Avoid the prohibited area.

GPS approach

Steer to ⊕23 from a south easterly quadrant and steer for breakwater end (approx. 0.2M).

Prohibited area

There are a number of mooring buoys and yellow lit buoys 1½M S of the port, opposite the oil terminal, about 1M offshore and surrounding an oil pipeline terminal. Passage is forbidden through these buoys. Pass inside within ½M of the shore or more than 1½M offshore.

Anchorage in the approach

Anchor to E of port with lighthouse about 300m to NW in 6m sand.

Entrance

Enter on a NE course between breakwater heads. Then on a N course between the inner two quays, the port hand quay being very low.

Berths

The Real Club Mediterráneo de Málaga is on the E side of Darséna de Heredia.

Try the E side of the quay that separates the Puerto Pesquero from the Ante Puerto or stern to quay with anchor from the bow in SW corner of Dársena de Heredia either side of the large floating dock; use an anchor trip line and before heaving it up, make sure the deck wash is working. Larger yachts are sometimes allowed alongside the N side of the Dique Transversal del Oeste while on other occasions yachts have been directed to the NE corner of the Dársena del Guadiaro where the quay wall is high.

Harbour charges

Very high.

Formalities

Check with the harbour authorities on VHF Ch 9.

Facilities

Geared towards large commercial vessels. There are points for electricity and water (contact Obras de Puerto, office at the main gate), cranes (no travel hoist), a slipway, ice etc. all something of a hassle to organise.

Chandleries, shops, supermarkets in town but the harbour is enclosed and only the main gate (which has to be negotiated) is open at night.

Spanish chart agency at the Comandancia de Marina near the lighthouse.

Communications

Málaga airport is halfway between Málaga and Benalmádena and has year-round international services. Ship ferry service to Tanger, Barcelona, Canary Islands, Genoa and Marseille. Rail and bus services. Railway. ☎ Area code 95.
British Consulate Málaga
Edificio Eurocom, Calle Mauricio Moro Pareto 2-2°, 29006 Málaga ☎ 95 235 23 00 *Fax* 95 235 92 11.

RC Málaga

The coast between Málaga and Candado

There are several bathing beaches along this stretch of the coast which are protected by breakwaters. From the sea they may appear to be harbours. They are not.

13. Puerto de El Candado

36°42´.8N 04°20´.8W

Charts

British Admiralty *773*. Imray *M11*
French *4717, 7294, 6569*. Spanish *455*
⊕25 36°42´.8N 04°20´.9W

Lights

0071 **Head of Dique de Levante** Oc.G.3s7m4M
    White truncated cone tower green lantern 4m
0071.2 **Head of Dique de Poniente** Iso.R.2s7m3M
    Masonry tower red lantern 4m

Port communications

Club náutico VHF Ch 9 ☎ 952 29 60 97 Fax 952 29 58 04
Email clubcandado@portalmalaga.com

Small shallow harbour

A very small harbour some 3½M to E of Málaga. Only suitable for yachts and vessels drawing 2m or less – and there is not much room for manoeuvre. The narrow entrance tends to silt up and is occasionally dredged to 4m. It is open to W. It would be uncomfortable to remain there in strong SW-W winds and difficult to enter or leave in those conditions. As of January 2002 it is understood that this port is to be used in daylight hours only and there is also a draught restriction of 2m on entering craft.

Approach

There is a large, grey cement factory just to the E of the harbour.

GPS approach

Steer to ⊕25 from a southerly quadrant and steer for breakwater end.

Anchorage in the approach

Anchor 200m to SW of entrance in 10m sand.

Entrance

Approach a point 200m to NW of the entrance of the harbour, sounding continuously. Leave three small red buoys to port and four small green buoys to starboard. Leave the head of the Dique de Levante 10m to starboard.

Berths

Berth stern-to the quay or pontoon with anchor or mooring buoy from the bow.

Harbour charges

Low.

Facilities

Maximum length overall: 10m.

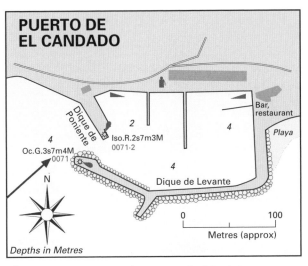

PUERTO DE
EL CANDADO

Iso.R.2s7m3M
0071·2

Oc.G.3s7m4M
0071

Dique de Poniente

2

4

4

Bar,
restaurant

Playa

Dique de Levante

N

0   100

Metres (approx)

Depths in Metres

Plan 13

⊕25 Puerto de El Candado
approaches 36°42'.8N 04°20'.9W

Puerto de El Candado

A hard in the corner of the harbour.
Water and Electricity (220v AC) on the pontoons and quays.
Chandlery to N of harbour.
Club náutico with bar, showers.

Communications

Bus service. ☎ Area code 95.

⚓ FONDEADERO DE VÉLEZ-MÁLAGA

An open anchorage off the town of Torre del Mar. Anchor in 6m sand 100m offshore, E of the lighthouse (0072 Fl(1+2).10s30m13M White tower 28m)or further NE. Everyday supplies from the town which has a *club náutico*. The new Puerto Caleta de Vélez lies 1½M to NE.

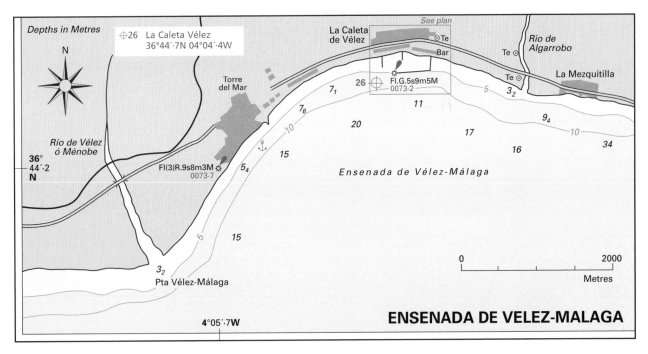

Depths in Metres

⊕26 La Caleta Vélez
36°44'·7N 04°04'·4W

La Caleta
de Vélez

See plan

⊙Te

Bar

Te ⊙

Rio de
Algarrobo

Te ⊙

La Mezquitilla

Torre
del Mar

7₁

26 ⊕

Fl.G.5s9m5M
0073·2

5

3₂

7₆

11

10

20

17

9₄

10

34

Río de Vélez
ó Ménobe

16

15

36°
44'·2
N

Fl(3)R.9s8m3M ✲
0073·7

5₄

15

Ensenada de Vélez-Málaga

5

15

3₂
Pta Vélez-Málaga

0   2000

Metres

4°05'·7W

ENSENADA DE VELEZ-MALAGA

Plan 14

14. Puerto Caleta de Vélez

36°44´.8N 04°04´W

Charts

British Admiralty *773*. Imray *M11*
French *6569*. Spanish *455*

⊕26 36°44´.7N 04°04´.4W

Lights

To the west
0072 **Torre del Mar (Torre de Vélez)** Fl(1+2)10s30m13M
White round tower 28m
Harbour
0073.2 **Dique de Abrigo head** Fl.G.5s9m5M White
truncated conical tower, green top 4m
0073.6 **Contradique** Fl(2)R.7s4m3M White post, red band
2m
0073.7 **Espigón head** Fl.R.4s8m3M Red tower 4m
To the east
0074 **Punta de Torrox** Fl(4)15s29m20M White tower and
building 23m

Port communications

VHF Ch 10. *Capitanía* ☎ 952 51 13 90 and
Fax 952 55 05 26. *Email* caleta@eppa.es *url* www.eppa.es

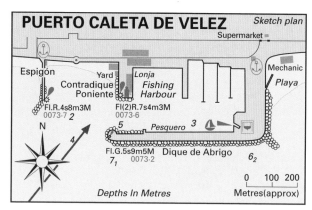

Plan 14a

⊕26 Puerto Caleta de Vélez
36°44´.7N 04°04´.4W

Quiet fishing harbour

A quiet, in terms of it not being full of tourists, fishing harbour at the head of the Ensenada de Vélez Málaga. It is one of eleven yacht harbours run by the *Junta de Andalucía*. It is easy to approach and enter though care is necessary with heavy onshore wind and/or swell. Facilities for yachts are limited but it is a useful place to spend a day or two on passage between Málaga and Motril. Sand and pebble beaches either side of the harbour.

Puerto Caleta de Vélez

Approach

From the west The sandy coast from Málaga eastward is relatively featureless, lined with small housing estates. Punta de Vélez Málaga, which is the delta of a river, is not prominent. Only after rounding it, will Torre del Mar light become plain among the houses and flats of the town. A factory chimney to its NE is conspicuous.

From the east Punta de Torrox is on a low, flat sandy delta which itself is not prominent. The lighthouse is conspicuous. The large block of flats at La Mezquitilla, 1M to the E of the harbour, and the road bridge over the Río del Algarrobo will also be seen. In the closer approach the harbour walls are conspicuous.

GPS approach

Steer to $\oplus26$ from a southerly quadrant and steer for breakwater end (approx. 0.1M).

Anchorage in the approach

Anchor 200m offshore in 5m sand either side of the harbour.

Entrance

Approach the W end of the breakwater on a northerly course and round the head of the Dique de Levante, giving it a berth of at least 30m. This is to avoid a small partly submerged espigón running NNE from the head of the dique. Also keep a look out for fishing craft leaving at speed as they can be obscured by the high dique.

Berths

Secure stern to the quay or pontoon at the E end of the harbour. There are mooring buoys but they are private.

Harbour charges

Medium.

Facilities

Maximum length overall: 20m.
45-tonnes hoist. The whole E side of the harbour is hard.
Electricity and water on the quay.
Gasoleo A, petrol 0900–1230, 1600–2000hrs.
Supermarket 100m from the port, more in Torre del Mar and a hypermarket about 3km from the port towards Torre del Mar.

Communications

Bus service along the coast. ☎ Area code 95.

Planning guide and distances

⚓ Anchorage

Miles	Harbours & Anchorages	Headlands
	— **Gibraltar** page 17	Europa Point
8M	**1. La Atunara** page 25	
7M	⚓ *Río Guadiaro*	
	2. Puerto de Sotogrande page 25	
5M	⚓ *Cala Sardina*	Punta de la Chullera, Punta de la Salo de la Mora
	3. Puerto de la Duquesa page 27	
5M	⚓ *Fondeadero de la Sabinilla*	
	4. Puerto de Estepona page 28	
11M	⚓ *Fondeadero de Estepona*	
4M	**5. Puerto de José Banús** page 30	
1M	**6. Puerto de Marbella** page 32	
7M	**7. Marina de Bajadilla** page 33	Punta Calaburras
9M	**8. Puerto Cabo Pino** page 34	
4M	**9. Puerto de Fuengirola** page 36	
12M	**10. Puerto de Punta Negra** page 38	
	11. Puerto de Benalmádena page 38	
9M	⚓ *Fondeadero de Torremolinos*	
	⚓ *La Carihuela*	
	12. Puerto de Málaga page 40	
4M	**13. Puerto de El Candado** page 42	
14M	⚓ *Fondeadero de Vélez-Málaga*	
	14. Puerto Caleta de Vélez page 44	Punta de Torrox
	⚓ *Fondadero de Nerja*	
	⚓ *Cala de la Miel*	
17M	⚓ *Cala de los Cañuelos*	
	⚓ *Ensenada de la Herradura*	
	15. Marina del Este page 48	Punta de la Concepción
	⚓ *Ensenada de los Berengueles*	

Miles	Harbours & Anchorages	Headlandss
	⚓ *Punta San Cristóbal and Almuñecar*	
	⚓ *Fondeadero de Almuñecar*	
	⚓ *Ensenada de Belilla*	
10M	⚓ *Ensenada de Robaina*	
	⚓ *Surgidero de Salobreña*	
	16. Puerto de Motril page 50	
	⚓ *Anchorage east of Cabo Sacratif*	Cabo Sacratif
	⚓ *Cala Honda*	
	⚓ *Anchorages to Castell de Ferro*	
26M	⚓ *Fondeadero de Castell de Ferro*	
	⚓ *Anchorages in La Rábita*	Punta Negra
	17. Puerto de Adra page 54	
	⚓ *Balerma*	
	⚓ *Punta de los Baños*	Punta de los Baños
12M	⚓ *Ensenada de las Entinas*	
14M	**18. Puerto de Almerimar** page 57	
	19. Puerto de Roquetas del Mar page 59	
4M	**20. Puerto de Aguadulce** page 60	
4M	**21. Puerto de Almería** page 61	
60M	⚓ *Cabo de Gata anchorages* Cabo de Gata	Punta del Río
	22. Isla de Alborán page 65	

III. Costa del Sol
Pta del Torrox to Cabo de Gata and Isla del Alboran

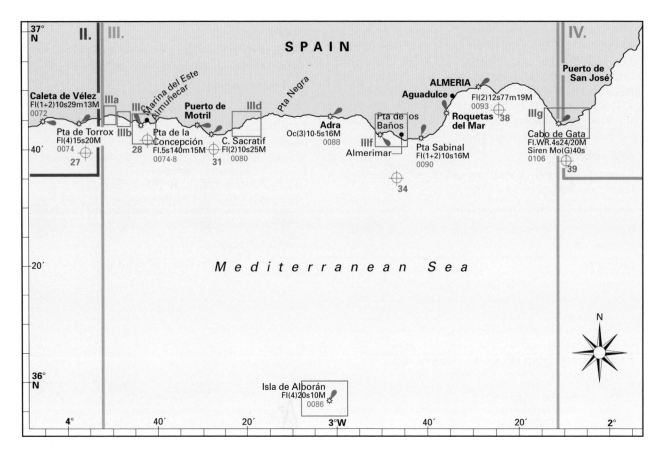

COASTAL WAYPOINT LIST

The waypoints listed form a series with which one is able to steer from off Gibraltar to Cabo de Gata. It is essential to keep a lookout at all times while making a coastal passage in this area.

⊕27	Pta del Torrox	36°42′N	03°57′.4W
⊕28	Pta de la Concepción	36°42′.5N	03°44′W
⊕31	Cabo Sacratif	36°41′N	03°28′W
⊕34	SSE of Pta de las Entinas	36°37′.5N	02°46′W
⊕38	S of Pta del Río	36°46′.5N	02°25′.5W
⊕39	Cabo de Gata	36°41′N	02°10′W

Punta del Torrox

PORTS

15. Marina del Este Puerto de la Mona
16. Puerto de Motrol
17. Puerto de Adra
18. Puerto de Almerimar
19. Puerto de Roquetas del Mar
20. Puerto de Aguadulce
21. Puerto de Almería
22. Isla de Alborán

Anchorages between Pta de Torrox and Motril

⚓ FONDEADERO DE NERJA

A pleasant anchorage just E of Nerja where everyday supplies are available. Anchor 100m from the Playa de Barranja in 5m, sand, or 400m off in 18m, stones.

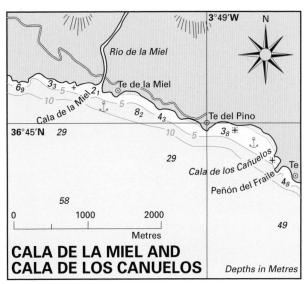

Plan 111b

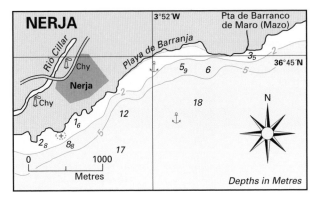

Plan 111a

⚓ CALA DE LA MIEL

An interesting and attractive open anchorage with a stony beach and a track to the main road on the cliffs behind. Anchor in 5m sand and pebbles. Conspicuous ruined tower on cliff to W of bay with three small disused houses. There is a freshwater spring.

⚓ CALA DE LOS CAÑUELOS

Anchor in 5m sand and pebble off the centre of the shingle beach which has isolated rocks at either end of the beach. The track leads to the main road.

⚓ ENSENADA DE LA HERRADURA

A bay a mile wide between Puntas Cerro Gordo and de la Mona. Anchor in 5m sand 100m from the beach or 200m out in 11m mud. Additonal shelter at either end but beware rocks. Everyday supplies from the town.

Cañuelos

Ensenada de la Herradura west and, opposite, east

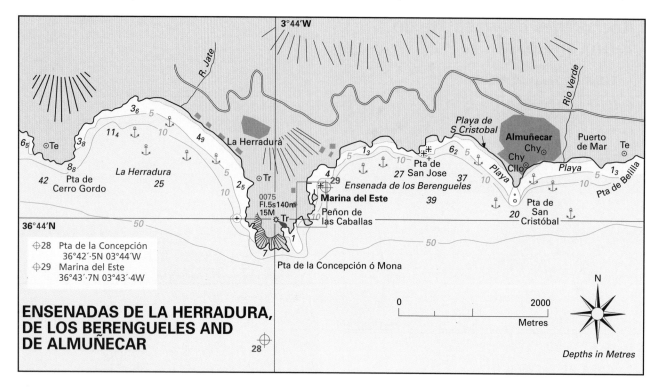

ENSENADAS DE LA HERRADURA,
DE LOS BERENGUELES AND
DE ALMUÑECAR

⊕28 Pta de la Concepción
      36°42'·5N 03°44'W
⊕29 Marina del Este
      36°43'·7N 03°43'·4W

Pta de la Concepción ó Mona

Plan IIIc

15. Marina del Este
Puerto de la Mona

36°43'.7N 03°43'.5W

Charts

British Admiralty *773*. Imray *M11*
French *4717*, *6569*. Spanish *456*

⊕29 36°43'.7N 03°43'.4W

Lights

To the south
0074.8 **Punta de la Mona** Fl.5s140m15M Masonry tower
  14m
Harbour
0075 **Dique de Abrigo** Fl.R.5s13m4M Red tower 5m
0075.2 **Contradique** Fl(2)G.6s5m3M Green tower 3m
To the east
0080 **Cabo Sacratif** Fl(2)10s98m25M White tower and
  building 17m

Port communications

VHF Ch 9. ☎ 958 82 70 18 *Fax* 958 82 72 40.
Email capitania@marinadeleste.es
url www.marinadeleste.es/puerto/

Small harbour in beautiful area

A small artificial yacht harbour which is part of a huge
housing development in a beautiful area. The approach
and entrance are easy and good protection is provided
especially from the W. Some swell is experienced with
NE-E winds and is sometimes unpleasant due to
deflected waves. Basic facilities are provided. This
harbour together with the Puerto Caleta de Vélez (Torre
del Mar) form useful stopping places between Málaga
and Motril, but prices are high. A small beach near the
harbour, pool at yacht club.

The prehistoric caves at Nerja, the old villages in the
hills and the famous city of Granada can all be visited.
The mountains of Sierra Nevada lying inland are very
beautiful.

Approach

From the west Nerja and the Punta de Cerro Gordo are
easily recognised. The high prominent Punta de Mona
(Concepción) is unmistakable; the harbour lies round
the corner.

From the east After passing the delta of Río Guadalfeo
the coast becomes hilly. Almuñecar with an old fort
above it is conspicuous at the beginning of the
Ensenada de los Berengueles. The harbour lies on the W
side of this Ensenada, about half-way along the ridge
leading to Punta de la Mona.

GPS approach

Steer to ⊕29 from a easterly quadrant and steer for
breakwater end (approx. 0.06M).

Anchorage in the approach

Anchor 100m off the beach in 5m sand in the NW
corner of the Ensenada de Berengueles.

Entrance

Approach the W side of the Ensenada de los
Berengueles keeping 400m from the coast, due to off-
lying rocks, until the N end of the harbour bears W then
approach and round the head of the breakwater leaving
it 25m to port and enter on a S course.

Berths

Secure to fuel berth on the starboard side on entering
and ask at control tower.

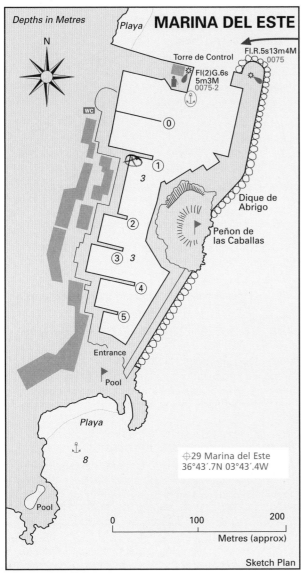

Depths in Metres

Playa **MARINA DEL ESTE**

N

Torre de Control

Fl.R.5s13m4M
0075

Fl(2)G.6s
5m3M
0075·2

WC

⓪

①

3

②

Dique de Abrigo

③ 3

Peñon de las Caballas

④

⑤

Entrance

Pool

Playa

8

⊕29 Marina del Este
36°43´.7N 03°43´.4W

Pool

0   100   200

Metres (approx)

Sketch Plan

Plan 15

Harbour charges

High in summer.

Facilities

Maximum length overall: 30m.
30-tonnes travel-lift and a 3.3-tonne crane.
A large hard for laid-up yachts.
Limited repair facilities. The marine engineer and chandler can find specialists.
Water points on the quays and pontoons.
Showers at yacht club.
220v AC points on the quays and pontoons, 380v on large berths.
Gasoleo A and petrol.
Ice near the fuel quay.
Small supermarket and laundry in the marina. Other shops in Herradura 2M over the hill.

Communications

Bus service on the main road 1M away – a long, steep climb.
☎ Area code 958. Taxi ☎ 63 00 17.

⚓ ENSENADA DE LOS BERENGUELES
(See plan IIIc)

Another large anchorage on the E side of Punta de la Mona in attractive surroundings. There are several places where anchorage is possible – 100m off the Playa de San Cristóbal that lies to the W of Almuñecar in 5m sand or off the two beaches in the NW corner of the bay. All normal facilities from the town of Almuñecar and some repairs possible. Almuñecar fort is conspicuous.

⚓ PUNTA DE SAN CRISTÓBAL AND FONDEADERO DE ALMUÑECAR
(See plan IIIc)

Anchor 200m off the beach in 5m sand or 400m out in 20m stones. Punta de San Cristóbal gives protection from the west. Almuñecar has a conspicuous fort. Everyday supplies in the town.

Marina del Este

Almuñecar

⚓ **ENSENADA DE BELILLA** (See plan IIIc)

An anchorage 150m off the Playa de Belilla in 5m clay and sand, or further out in 30m stones. Modern holiday development along the coast where everyday supplies may be found.

⚓ **ENSENADA DE ROBAINA** 36°44′.5N 03°39′.4W

A pleasant small anchorage 50m off a small pair of sand and pebble beaches in 5m sand. A conspicuous small fort is located on Punta de Jesus o del Tesorillo and a large block of flats behind the W beach.

⚓ **SURGIDERO DE SALOBREÑA**
36°44′.1N 03°35′.7W

Peñón and Surgidero de Salobreña: anchor either side of the conspicuous peñon, 100m off the coast in 5m, sand and pebbles, or 400m out in 25m, mud. The Moorish castle above the town of Salobreña is easily seen.

Salobreña

16. Puerto de Motril

36°43′.4N 03°31′.7W

Charts

British Admiralty *773, 774.* Imray *M11*
French *4717, 6569.* Spanish *4571, 457*

⊕30 36°42′.7N 03°30′.07W

Lights

To the west
0074.8 **Punta de la Mona** Fl.5s140m15M Masonry tower 14m
Harbour
0077 **Dique de Poniente head** Fl(2)R.6s11m10M Red truncated conical tower 5m
0077.5 **Dique del Este** Fl(2)G.4.5s9m5M Metal post 4m
0079 **Nuevo Dique de Levante elbow** Fl(3)G.12s6m5M Green truncated conical tower 4m
0079.2 **Nuevo Dique de Levante head** Fl.G.5s6m2M Green truncated conical tower 5m
0078 **Dique de Levante head** Fl(2+1)G.12s6m5M Green tower, red band 5m
0078.4 **Espigón head** Fl.R.5s6m2M Red truncated conical tower 5m
To the east
0080 **Cabo Sacratif** Fl(2)10s98m25M White tower and building 17m

Port communications

VHF Port Ch 12 (Tugs), 13. Marina Ch 9. ☎ 958 60 00 37 *Fax* 958 60 12 47 *Email* cnauticomotril@radiovision.es *url* www.motril.org

Primarily a commercial harbour

A small fishing harbour that has developed into a commercial harbour which has recently been doubled in size. It has an easy approach and entrance but rather poor facilities for yachtsmen. The harbour is uncomfortable in strong easterly winds but some shelter can now be found behind the huge new *contradique*.

Puerto de Motril from SE

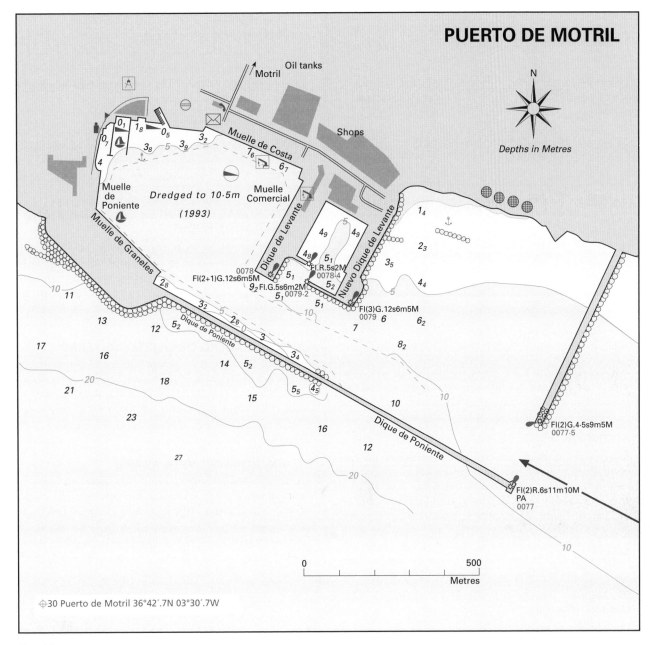

PUERTO DE MOTRIL

N

Depths in Metres

Plan 16

The little village near the harbour can provide basic needs but there are many more shops in Motril itself, two miles away. Local holidays occur on 15 August and 15 October.

Approach

From the west The flat open plain of the delta of the Río Guadalfeo and the cranes, buildings and tall silos just to the W of Cabo Sacratif show the location of this harbour. Several large blocks of flats line the coast just to the W of this harbour. The town of Motril 2M inland shows in the closer approach.

From the east Cabo Sacratif, a distinctive headland with an isolated conspicuous lighthouse at its summit can easily be recognised from afar. There are two white radar domes on the mountain Sierra do Pelaos 4M to NE of this cape.

The new *contradique* has 4 large columns and a crane at its end (Sep 2004). Further work is going on at the end but the columns and immense length of the new Dique de Poniente make the entrance unmistakable.

GPS approach

Steer to ⊕30 from a southerly quadrant and steer for breakwater end (approx. 0.27M).

Entrance

Approach the new head of the Dique de Poniente on a N course. Round it and enter between the heads, and steer parallel to the *dique* up the harbour on a WNW course.

Berths

If there is space, go stern-to on the pontoons at the *club*

Puerto de Motril Club Náutico from S

náutico in the NW corner of the harbour. Otherwise go stern-to either side but clear of the diesel pumps on the Muelle de Poniente on the west side of the harbour. In strong SE or E winds, lie alongside the Muelle Comercial with permission of the *capitanía*.

Anchorage

Along with most of the commercial harbours on this coast anchoring in the port is frowned on, if not expressly forbidden. However rumour has it that another marina was to be constructed SE of the root of the Nuevo Dique de Levante (I wonder what they are going to call the newer *dique*!). Some work seems to have been done and there is a small groyne built just offshore in the vicinity of the oil tanks. Yachts were anchored behind this in comparative quiet during the Sept 2004 visit.

Harbour charges

Low. Yachts at anchor may escape charges.

Facilities

Maximum length overall (*club náutico*): 20m.
Slipways at the yard in the NW corner of the main harbour and in the Puerto Pesquero can handle up to 100 tonnes.
Cranes up to 2.5 tonnes.
Engine and mechanical workshops outside the harbour.
A small chandlery shop in the village.
Water from points on quays and pontoons. For water hose, contact a harbour official if using water from quays.
220v AC points on quays and pontoons.
Gasoleo A on west side of harbour.
Ice from the ice factory in the village or from restaurant.
Club Náutico de Motril has bars, lounge, terrace and restaurants, also showers and a pool. Visiting yachtsmen are welcomed.
Supermarket just outside harbour area. Market and many more shops in Motril.

Communications

Frequent bus service to Motril. Buses to Granada and back (a long day's outing). ☎ Area code 958. Taxi ☎ 60 18 54.

⚓ ANCHORAGE E OF CABO SACRATIF
36°41′.5N 03°28′W

An open coastal anchorage tucked under the E end of the rocky cliffed Cabo Sacratif. Anchor 100m offshore in 5m sand and pebbles. The main road runs a little way inland.

⚓ CALAHONDA 36°42′.1N 03°24′.7W

There are now yellow swimmers buoys all along the beach and the available area for anchoring is in 20+ metres of water. The village, which has a church tower like a lighthouse, has everyday supplies.

⚓ ANCHORAGES BETWEEN CALAHONDA AND CASTELL DE FERRO

This 3M stretch of high, rocky cliffed coast is broken into several deep bays. It is possible for experienced navigators to anchor at the heads of these bays in good conditions providing the water is clear enough to see the odd isolated rock. The coast road runs along the top of the cliff.

⚓ FONDEADERO DE CASTELL DE FERRO
(Plan IIIe)

Anchor in the corner of the bay near Punta del Melonar (at the left of the photograph), 100m from the shingle beach, 5m sand and mud or further out in 10m, mud. Good protection from the west. Everyday supplies in the village.

⚓ ANCHORAGES IN LA RÁBITA
36°44′.7N 03°10′.5W

A useful coastal anchorage at the W end of a gravel beach. Anchor 100m offshore in 5m sand and stones. The small village is readily recognised by the small blocks of flats 'hung' on a cliff face behind the village with a tower nearby. There is a small fort to the E of the tower. Everyday supplies from the village. Another possible anchorage is small bay to E of Punta Negra.

Calahonda

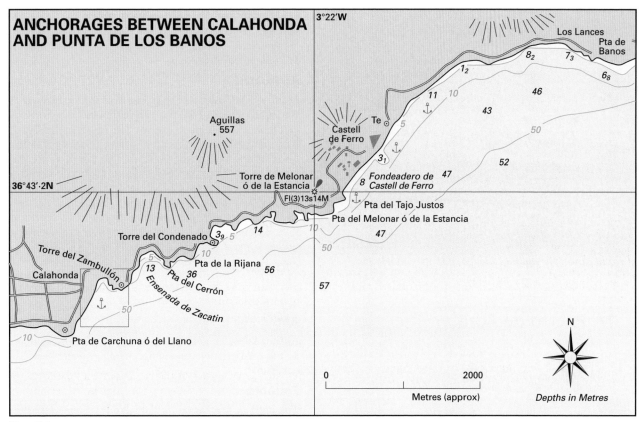

ANCHORAGES BETWEEN CALAHONDA AND PUNTA DE LOS BANOS

Plan IIId

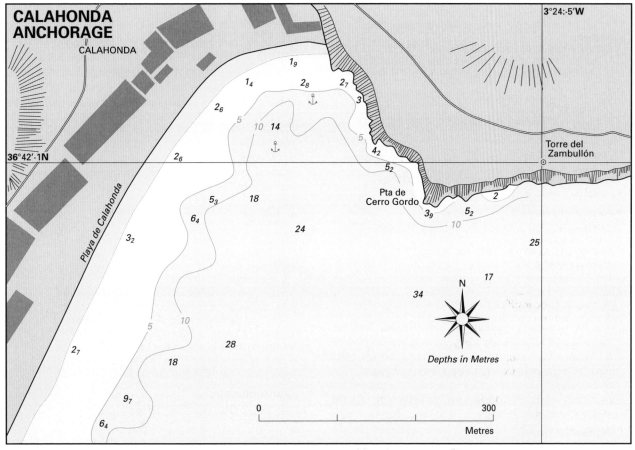

CALAHONDA ANCHORAGE

Plan IIIe

Fondeadero de Castell de Ferro

17. Puerto de Adra

36°44′.7N 03°01′.2W

Charts

British Admiralty *773, 774*. Imray *M11*
French *4717, 6569*. Spanish *457, 458*

⊕32 36°44′.25N 03°01′W

Lights

To the west
0082 **Castell de Ferro** Fl(3)13s237m14M White tower 12m
0088 **Adra lighthouse** 36°44′.9N 03°01′.8W
  Oc(3)10.5s49m16M White tower, red bands 26m
Harbour
0088.4 **Dique de Poniente head N end** 36°44′.6N
  03°01′.1W Fl(2)R.6s8m5M Red masonry tower 6m
0088.6 **Inner breakwater head** Fl(3)R.10s5m2M Red post
  3m
0089 **Dique de Levante head** Fl(2)G.10s8m3M Green
  masonry tower 5m
0089.2 **Inner breakwater head** Fl(3)G.10s5m2M Green
  post 3m
To the east
0089.5 **Punta de los Baños** Fl(4)11s22m11M Rectangular
  white tower 21m
0090 **Punta Sabinal** Fl(1+2)10s34m16M Tower above
  white houses 32m

Port communications

Capitanía VHF Ch 9. ☎ 950 40 10 53 *Fax* 950 56 05 93
Email adra@eppa.es
Club náutico ☎ 950 40 14 17 *Fax* 950 40 07 12
Email adra@eppa.es

A working harbour

A rather desolate commercial and fishing harbour, established by the Phoenicians, who called it Abdera, and in use ever since. It has accommodation for small motor boats but is less suitable for keeled yachts. The approach and entrance is easy in normal conditions but in strong winds, especially those from the E, the entrance can be dangerous and the harbour very uncomfortable. The harbour is also disturbed by the constant movement of fishing boats. Facilities for yachtsmen are poor but there are sandy beaches on either side of the harbour. The town is small and without much tourist development. Local holidays September 6 to 10 in honour of Our Lady of the Sea and St Nicholas of Tolentino.

Approach

From either direction the harbour can be identified by the lighthouse and by the very large and tall Torre de Perdigones which has windows. The upper half is brown brick and the lower painted white. A smaller similar tower is located further inland. There is a deep grey sandy beach along the SW side of Dique de Poniente which makes identification somewhat difficult from seaward as it merges into the shore line. However there is a sand elevator and other machinery and blocks of flats. A conspicuous factory with a pair of grey chimneys stands some 2M to W of the harbour.

GPS approach

Steer to ⊕32 from a southerly quadrant and steer for breakwater end (approx. 0.28M).

Anchorage in the approach

Anchor 200m to E of Dique de Levante in 5m sand and pebbles. Alternative anchorage in deep water S of the harbour.

Entrance

The head of the Dique de Poniente is T-shaped and the NE spur extends about 30m in that direction from the light. Give it a good berth and pass between the two inner moles. The depths in the entrance and harbour frequently change and are sometimes dredged; depths are approximate.

Berths

Alongside or stern-to the off-shore end of the Dique de Levante. The *club náutico* is crowded with small boats. It has four visitors berths but check to see if you will fit.

Harbour charges

High.
Anchorage
Anchor in 3m mud near centre of harbour using an anchor with a trip line. Anchor light and shape are necessary.

Facilities

Maximum length overall: 20m for berthing.
Shipyards geared towards fishing boats.
150-tonnes travel hoist and hardstanding in fishing harbour.
5-tonnes crane.
Several slipways which will take the largest yachts.
Chandlers shop in town.
Water from points on quay or from *club náutico*.
125v and 220v AC supply point near water point.
Ice factory on NE side of the harbour.
Club náutico with a bar and restaurant.
Supermarket and shops in the village.

Communications

Bus service along the coast. ☎ Area code 950.

Puerto de Adra

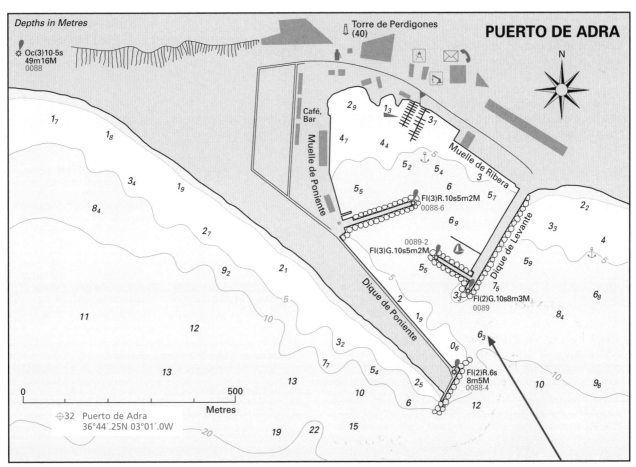

Plan 17

⚓ **BALERMA** 36°43′.6N 02°53′.7W

An open coastal anchorage some 100m off the beach in 5m sand and pebbles, opposite the low Torre de Balerma which has a few buildings around and a factory to NE. A somewhat unattractive flat coast with plastic-covered greenhouses stretching for miles.

⚓ **PUNTA DE LOS BAÑOS** 36°41′.6N 02°51′.2W

An extraordinary and rather exposed anchorage between the double spurs of a point. Anchor about 50m from the coast in 3m sand and stones. The very conspicuous Castillo de Guardias Viejas stands on a small hill just within the double point and Punta de Los Baños light is on the eastern side. There are a few buildings and shacks in the area but the nearest small village is about 2M away.

⚓ **ENSENADA DE LAS ENTINAS**
36°41′.8N 02°49′.0W

Spanish chart 3550. A wide bay where anchorage is possible anywhere along the coast in 3 to 5m and 50 to 100m offshore. The shore is flat and the whole area covered with plastic greenhouses. The Castillo de Guardias Viejas on Punta de los Baños and the high-rise flats and buildings around the Puerto de Almerimar near Punta Entinas are both very conspicuous. Supplies from the Puerto de Almerimar.

Balerma

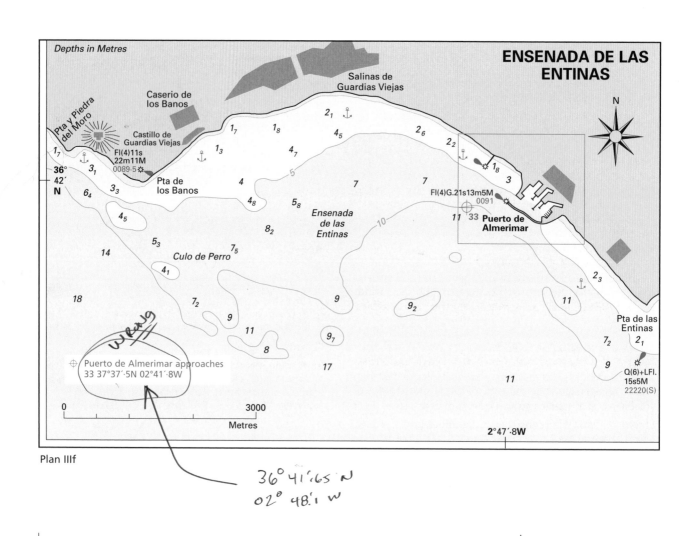

Plan IIIf

18. Puerto de Almerimar

36°41´.7N 02°47´.6W

Winter 2007-08

Charts
British Admiralty *774*. Imray *M11*
French *6569*. Spanish *45B*

⊕33 36°41´.65N 02°48´.1W

Lights
To the west
0089.5 **Punta de los Baños** Fl(4)11s22m11M Rectangular white tower 21m
Harbour
22187(S) **Red port hand buoy** Fl.R.7.5s2M
0091.6 **Espigón** Fl(4)R.11s3m3M Post on red turret 1m
0091 **Dique Sur head** Fl(4)G.21s13m5M Green tower 8m
0091.3 **Dique Sur Middle** LFl.G.9.5s2m2M Green turret 1m
0091.35 **Contradique head** Fl(2)R.9.5s2m2M Red tower 1m
0091.4 **Ldg Lts** *Front* Iso.10s3m2M White tower, winged top 2m
0091.41 *Rear* Oc.10s4m2M White tower, winged top 3m
To the east
22220(S) **Bajo Punta de las Entinas** Q(6)+LFl.15s5M ⚑ card buoy
0090 **Punta Sabinal** Fl(1+2)10s34m16M Tower on white buildings 32m
Buoys There may be 5 or 6 small yellow buoys marking the starboard and port hand of the entrance channel as the leading lines are sometimes difficult to make out.

Port communications
VHF Ch 9. Port Control ☎ 950 60 77 55, 950 49 73 50
Fax 950 49 73 53 *Email:*info@marina-almerimar.com
url www.marina-almerimar.com

Welcoming good yacht harbour

This artificial yacht harbour is very pleasant. Much of the hinterland is a sheet of plastic under which a major proportion of north Europe's winter vegetables are grown. The marina is built to an ambitious plan and not only provides good facilities for yachts but also for crews. Approach and entrance are easy except in strong SW winds which sometimes send a swell into the harbour. Very secure with good shelter from easterly gales. Rates, which are on the low side, can be examined on the internet web-site.

Winter liveboard community.

Almería and the Alcazaba are worth a visit. There are beaches on either side of the harbour. Fishing, wind surfing, diving, golf, tennis and horse riding are possible.

Approach

From the west The coast from Adra is low and flat, Puerto de Adra and the Castillo de Guardias Viejas which is on a small hill near Punta de los Baños are easily recognised while the high blocks of flats to the E of Puerto Almerimar can be seen from afar.

From the east The conspicuous lighthouse on the low flat Punta del Sabinal will be seen and also the blocks of flats mentioned above.

GPS approach

Steer to ⊕33 from a southwesterly quadrant and steer for breakwater end (approx. 0.17M).

Anchorage in the approach

It is possible to anchor either side of the harbour about 100m to 150m from the coast in 5m sand.

Entrance

The harbour entrance silts but is frequently dredged to 6m. In spite of frequent dredging it has been reported that there is a shallow patch running out along the breakwater. Exercise care and watch the echo-sounder on entry, giving the hooked end of the breakwater a reasonable berth (50 metres or so). Leave the red buoy to port and enter between two lines of small yellow buoys or pick up the leading lines at night.

Berths

Secure to fuel berth and ask at the control tower.

Note the 4 pontoons shown at the east of the harbour are being refurbished (Nov 2000) for the 2001 season and will be available for small craft only. However this will free up a lot of space in the deeper areas of the harbour and there should be more room available for transiting craft.

Harbour charges

Medium.

Facilities

Maximum length overall: 60m.
Most repair and maintenance facilities.
Volvo dealer and servicing.
110 and 60-tonne travel-lift.
5-tonne crane.
Slipways on the E side of the harbour.
Large hardstanding.
Two chandlers in the port plus other useful shops.
Water points on all quays and pontoons – potable but taste before filling tanks.
Showers in the service block and in the port.
220v AC points on all quays and pontoons. 380v AC on the larger berths.
Gasoleo A and petrol.
Ice available from control tower and bars.
Club náutico.
A small supermarket at the west end of the harbour and a well-stocked one near the boatyard.
Launderettes.
An active Live-Aboard Club has a small club room near the boatyard.
A hypermarket is on the bus route to the town of El Ejido. Restrictions 2004. Yachtsmen may not work on their boats.

Communications

Regular bus service to El Ejido whence further buses. Airport at Almería, year round services to Barcelona, Madrid and Melilla, summer charter flights from other European countries. ☎ Area code 950. Taxi ☎ 57 06 11, 48 00 63.

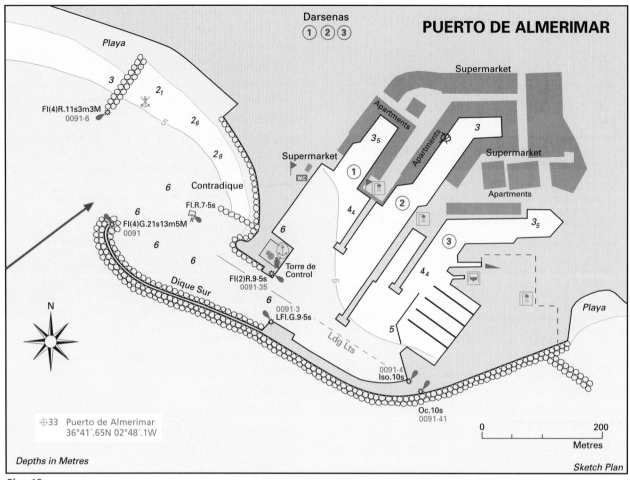

Darsenas
①②③

PUERTO DE ALMERIMAR

Supermarket

Playa

3

2₁

Fl(4)R.11s3m3M
0091·6

2₆

2₈

6 *Contradique*

Fl.R.7·5s

6

Fl(4)G.21s13m5M
0091

6

6

6

6

6

Dique Sur

Fl(2)R.9·5s
0091·35

Torre de Control

6

0091·3
LFl.G.9·5s

Ldg Lts

Apartments

3₅

Supermarket

WC

①

4₄

②

Apartments

3

Supermarket

Apartments

3₅

③

4₄

5

Playa

N

0091·4
Iso.10s

Oc.10s
0091·41

0   200
Metres

⊕33   Puerto de Almerimar
       36°41′.65N 02°48′.1W

Depths in Metres

Sketch Plan

Plan 18

Puerto de Almerimar

19. Puerto de Roquetas del Mar

36°45′.4N 02°36′.3W

Charts

British Admiralty *774*. Imray *M11*
French *4718, 6569*. Spanish *459*

⊕35 36°45′.5N 02°36′.15W

Lights

To the west
0090 **Punta Sabinal** Fl(1+2)10s34m16M Tower on white
 buildings 32m
Harbour
0092 **Dique Sur head** Fl(3)R.9s10m5M Round concrete
 tower 4m
0092.4 **Dique Norte head** Fl(3)G.9s6m3M Round tower on
 square base 3m
0092·5 **Interior Quay** Fl(4)G.8s6m2M Green post 5m
To the east
0106 **Cabo de Gata** Fl.WR.4s55m24/20M 356°-W-316°-R-
 356° Siren Mo(G)40s White tower, grey lantern 19m

Port communications

Capitanía VHF Ch 9 ☎/Fax 950 32 08 90
Email roquetas@eppa.es
Club náutico ☎ 950 32 07 89 *Fax* 950 32 01 44

Primarily for fishing boats

A small harbour for sardine fishing boats and a few
yachts. Easy to approach and enter but would be
uncomfortable in heavy weather between SE and NE.
Attractive in a simple way but tourist development is
taking place around this area. There are a few facilities,
some basic shops near the harbour and other, better,
shops in the village about 2 miles away.

The fuel point on the Dique Sur is for fishing vessels
only. The yachts' fuel point is on the NW corner quay
but it is very shallow there and fuel can only really be
obtained with jerrycans.

Fine beaches each side of the harbour. Local holidays
7 and 8 October in honour of the Virgen del Rosario.

Approach

From the SW The low flat-topped headland of Punta
Sabinal which has an isolated lighthouse and tower with
radomes. A large tourist complex of high-rise buildings
is located between this headland and the port. The old
disused yellow lighthouse and small castle just S of the
harbour are recognisable.

From the NE From Almería the cliffs reach within 4M
of Roquetas which is at the edge of a plain covered with
plastic greenhouses. There are buildings and blocks of
flats behind the harbour.

GPS approach

Steer to ⊕35 from an easterly quadrant and steer for
breakwater end (approx. 0.05M).

Entrance

Straight-forward between *dique* heads which have small
stone towers. Give Dique Sur head a reasonable berth in
case sand has built up off the end. The entrance is
dredged and depths vary.

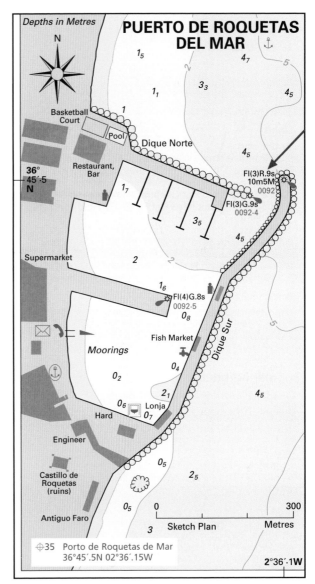

Depths in Metres

PUERTO DE ROQUETAS DEL MAR

⊕35 Porto de Roquetas de Mar
36°45′.5N 02°36′.15W

Plan 19

Berths

Bow or stern to pontoons on the north side of the
entrance but make up wherever possible in the outer
harbour and ask at the *club náutico*. Due to the shallow
harbour, keel yachts should only attempt to berth at the
easternmost pontoon. The harbour becomes crowded
when the fishing fleet returns.

Harbour charges

Low.

Facilities

Maximum length overall: 15m.
50-tonnes travel hoist and 8-tonnes crane.
220v and 380v AC points on quays.
Water on the quays.
Club náutico with restaurant and bar.
Several small shops and a supermarket in the village. A market
 and some other shops 2M away.

Communications

Bus service to Almería. ☎ Area code 950.

20. Puerto de Aguadulce

36°48′.9N 02°33′.7W

Charts

British Admiralty *774*. Imray *M11*
French *4718*. Spanish *459*

⊕36 36°48′.7N 02°33′.8W

Lights

To the west
0090 **Punta Sabinal** Fl(1+2)10s34m16M Tower on white
    buildings 32m
Harbour
0092.6 **Dique head** Fl(2)G.6s5m5M Green pyramid 4m
0092.8 **Contradique head** Fl(2)R.7s6m3M Red concrete
    tower 4m
To the east
0093 **San Telmo LtHo** Fl(2)12s77m19M White square
    tower oblong black stripes 7m
0106 **Cabo de Gata** Fl.WR.4s55m24/20M 356°-W-316°-R-
    356° Siren Mo(G)40s White tower, grey lantern 19m

Port communications

Capitanía/club náutico VHF Ch 9 ☎ 950 34 31 15
Fax 950 34 31 64 *Email* pdeporti@cajamar.es

Popular harbour

Aguadulce provides a useful alternative to Puerto de
Almería. It harbour is easy to enter and provides good
shelter except in strong ESE winds when some swell
enters making it uncomfortable. Facilities are good. The
Alcazaba at Almería should be visited. Long sandy
beaches to SW. Popular for winter liveaboards.

Local holidays: The ten days before the last Sunday
in August and the first two weeks in January.

Approach

From the SW Round the low headland of Punta del
Sabinal with its conspicuous white, round lighthouse
tower. Follow the low featureless coast dotted with
various housing estates in a NE direction until Puerto de
Roquetas del Mar which has a disused lighthouse, a
small square fort and a breakwater, has been passed.
Puerto de Aguadulce is located just beyond the point
where a range of rocky hills reaches down to the coast.
The rocky breakwaters, *torre de control* and low blocks
of flats will be seen in the close approach.

From the east Round the unmistakable Cabo de Gata
and cross the Golfo de Almería on a WNW course. The
mass of buildings of Almería surmounted by the
Alcazaba castle and fronted by the harbour breakwater
are all conspicuous. The S cardinal light buoy
(Q(6)+LFl) off Punta del Río may also be seen. This
harbour is located near where the rocky range of coastal
hills drops back and the low flat coast commences.

GPS approach

Steer to ⊕36 from a southeasterly quadrant and steer
for breakwater end (approx. 0.09M).

Puerto de Aguadulce

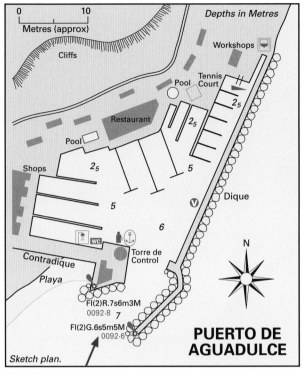

Plan 20

⊕36 Puerto de Aguadulce
36°48´.7N 02°33´.8W

Entrance

Approach the head of the *dique* on a course between SW and N, round it and then the head of the *contradique* to port.

Berths

Secure to the quay by the *torre de control* and report to the office for allocation of a berth.

Facilities

Maximum length overall: 25m.
Workshops at N end of harbour for mechanical, electrical and hull repairs; maintenance, painting etc. Work on own boat permitted.
50-tonnes travel-lift.
Slipway at N end of the harbour.
Hardstanding at N end of the harbour; additional space for 100 yachts under cover.
Sailmaking.
Water taps on quays and pontoons.
Showers.
220v AC on quays and pontoons.
Gasoleo A and petrol.
Ice at fuel quay.
Club náutico with good facilities.
Many shops and a large market at Almería about 5M away.
Swimming pool beside the harbour.

Communications

Bus to Almería on road behind the harbour. Airport (11 miles) and rail (5 miles) at Almería. ☎ Area code 950. Taxi ☎ 34 05 46.

21. Puerto de Almería

36°49´.8N 02°27´.9W

Tides

Time differences
based on HW Gibraltar   Height difference   Mean

HW	LW	MHWS	MHWN	MLWS	MLWN	*level*
+0010	–0010	0.5	0.4	0.3	+0.3	0.40

Current

There is a constant E-going current across the mouth of the bay.

Charts

British Admiralty *1515, 774.* Imray *M11*
French *7504, 4718.* Spanish *4591, 459*

⊕37 36°49 25N 02°27 75W

Lights

To the west
0093 **San Telmo LtHo** Fl(2)12s77m19M White square tower oblong black stripes 7m
Puerto Pesquero
0094 **Dique del Oeste head** Fl(3)R.9s10m4M Red tower 5m
0095 **Dique Sur head** Fl(4)G.10·5s10m3M Green tower 5m
0095·5 **Interior mole head** Fl(4)R.11s5m1M Red tower 3m
Main harbour
0096 **Dique de Poniente head** Fl.R.5s19m7M White 8-sided tower, red top and base 12m
0102 **Cargadero No.2 head** Fl.G.5s8m4M Green metal structure 3m
0101 **Cargadero No.1 head** Fl.R.3s7m1M
0101.5 **Corner** Fl.Y.5s5m1M Yellow concrete tower
0101.4 **Club de Mar del Almería Dique de Abrigo** Fl(2)G.10s4m1M Green inclined concrete tower 3m
0101.6 **Club de Mar del Almería Contradique** Fl(2)R.10s4m1M Red inclined concrete tower
0099 **Muelle de Poniente o Comercial E corner** Fl(2)R.7s5m1M Red concrete structure 3m
0098 **Dique de Levante head** Fl(2+1)G.21s4m2M Green structure, red band 10m
0103 **Power station wharf head** Q(9)15s11m4M ⌁ on yellow metal framework tower, black band 9m F.R on building 360m E
To the east
0106 **Cabo de Gata** Fl.WR.4s55m24/20M 356°-W-316°-R-356° Siren Mo(G)40s White tower, grey lantern 19m
DGPS
Cabo de Gata Lt 298.5kHz 40M (Planned)
Buoys
Black and yellow S card lightbuoy Q(6)+LFl ⌁ topmark off Punta del Río de Almería

Port communications

Port VHF Ch 12, 14 and 16. Club de mar VHF Ch 9
☎ 950 23 07 80 *Fax* 950 26 11 47
Email cma@clubdemaralmeria.com
url www.clubdemaralmeria.com/index.html

Useful commercial harbour

A commercial and fishing port with an old and interesting town and castle nearby. Approach and entrance can be made in almost any conditions and good shelter obtained but winds from the E cause an uncomfortable swell inside the harbour. The town, which is the capital of the province of the same name has good shops and markets. Yachts use the Club de Mar del Almería, outside the Dique de Levante; they are not welcome in the main harbour.

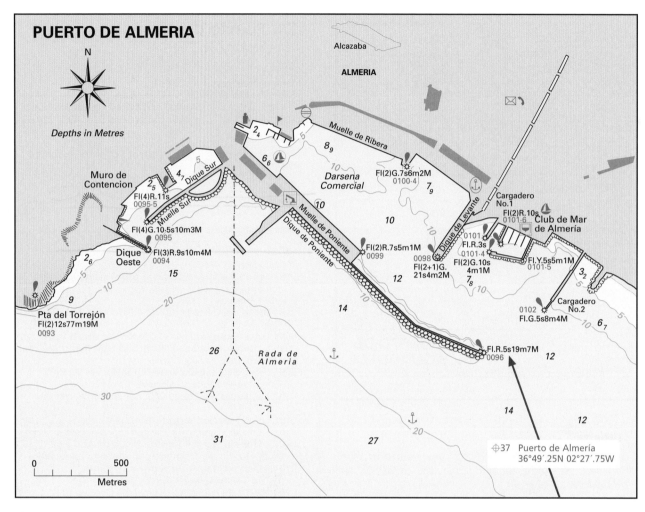

PUERTO DE ALMERIA

N

Depths in Metres

Alcazaba

ALMERIA

Muro de Contencion

Dique Sur

Muelle de Ribera

Darsena Comercial

Fl(2)G.7s6m2M
0100·4

Dique de Levante

Cargadero No.1
Fl(2)R.10s
0101·6

Club de Mar de Almería

Muelle Sur

Fl(4)R.11s
0095·5

Fl(4)G.10·5s10m3M
0095

Muelle de Poniente

Dique de Poniente

Fl(2)R.7s5m1M
0099

Fl(2)G.10s 4m1M

Fl.R.3s
0101
0101·4

Fl.Y.5s5m1M
0101·5

Dique Oeste

Fl(3)R.9s10m4M
0094

Fl(2+1)G. 21s4m2M

Fl(2)G.10s 4m1M

Cargadero No.2
Fl.G.5s8m4M

Pta del Torrejón
Fl(2)12s77m19M
0093

0102

Fl.R.5s19m7M
0096

Rada de Almeria

⊕37 Puerto de Almería
36°49′.25N 02°27′.75W

0   500
Metres

Plan 21

Note that the fishing port has its own separate harbour to the west of the main harbour. In 2004 there was construction work beginning outside the root of the Dique de Poniente. Unfortunately no official was available to confirm (or deny) the local rumour that it was for another yacht harbour.

The Moorish Alcazaba (castle) is most impressive and attractive and should be visited. There are four interesting churches, many old buildings and an archaeological museum. Miles of beaches to the E of the harbour.

Local holidays: the ten days before the last Sunday in August and the first two weeks in January.

Approach

From the SW Almería lies at the head of a wide bay at the foot of the mountains. The low flat headland of Punta del Sabinal with its isolated lighthouse is recognisable 10M to SW. The Alcazaba (castle) on a hill near the town is conspicuous at a distance but is dwarfed by tower blocks of flats to E. The town buildings and the long Dique de Poniente are seen in the closer approach.

From the east After Cabo de Gata, a rugged high promontory, the coast is low and flat. The town and harbour are visible from afar; there are a pair of power station chimneys about a mile to the E of the harbour entrance and three loading piers along the coast SE of the entrance.

GPS approach

Steer to ⊕37 from a southerly quadrant and steer for breakwater end (approx. 0.35M).

Anchorage in the approach

Anchor to SW of Dique de Poniente.

Entrance

Straight-forward but keep a lookout for commercial and fishing vessels leaving, sometimes at speed. Inside the harbour there are a number of unlit mooring buoys.

Berths

Go to the Club de Mar de Almería: otherwise try stern-to or alongside near the root of Muelle Comercial in the W corner of the port. Berths are sometimes available alongside the quay in the NE corner of the harbour, on the pontoons at the *club náutico* at the west end of the harbour or alongside the Anden de Costa. Swell is prevalent at these berths.

Moorings

Apply to the *capitán de puerto* or *club de mar* for any mooring buoys which may be available.

Almería

Anchorage

Anchor in 6m sand and mud 150m S of club de mar, clear of moorings. Show anchor light and shape.

Harbour charges

High.

Facilities

Maximum length overall: 15m in the *club de mar*.

Shipyards geared to fishing boats beside the slipway and also at the W end of Puerto Pesquero.

Slipways in both the main of the harbour and the Puerto Pesquero.

Cranes 4–12 tonnes in the harbour and a 4-tonne crane at the *club de mar*.

Several engineering workshops in town and one on the quay on Muelle Sur.

Chandlers and Engineers in the NW corner of the main harbour.

Water and 220v AC on all berths at *club de mar*.

Gasoleo A and petrol at *club de mar*.

Ice from ice factory between Puerto Pesquero and Dársena Comercial.

The Club de Mar del Almería is a tennis and yachting club with a bar, restaurant, showers and terrace. Visitors should first contact the secretary for permission to use the facilities.

A number of small shops and a small market near the port.

Many large and varied shops and a large market about 1M away in the town.

Several launderettes in the town.

Communications

Airport with summer charter flights from Europe and year-round services to Madrid or Barcelona. Railway. Occasional service by boat to Marseille, Algeria, Canary Isles and South America. ☎ Area code 950. Taxis ☎ 25 11 11.

Club de Mar del Almería

⚓ CABO DE GATA ANCHORAGES

Anchor off the village of San Miguel de Cabo de Gata and its conspicuous tower in 5m of sand some 200m off the coast. One can also anchor 100m off Playa de los Corrales further to the SE in sand, well sheltered from N and E. There is a sheltered anchorage 150m NW of Cabo de Gata light in 5m sand and stone, or about 400m offshore in 10m. There is a small settlement and conspicuous church by the saltworks on the road to San Miguel de Gata. Tunny nets are sometimes laid in this area.

NOTES ON ROUNDING CABO DE GATA

1. Stay close inshore or 1.0M offshore to avoid Laja de Cabo de Gata shoal (3m) which breaks in heavy weather
2. Winds tend to increase around this cape
3. Current is normally east-going and can be very strong.

Cabo de Gata from the west

Cabo de Gata from the east

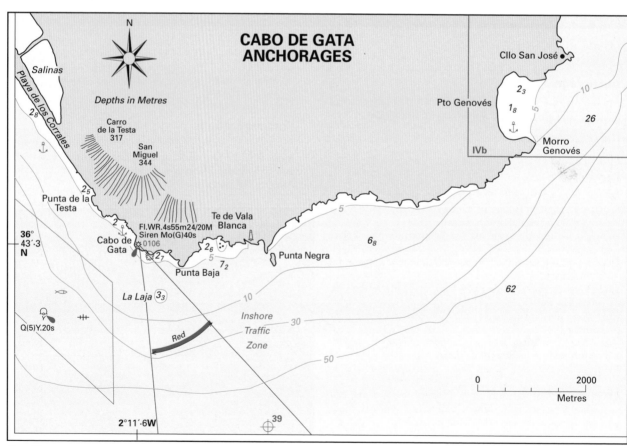

Plan IIIg

22. Isla de Alborán

35°56´.3N 03°02´.1W

Current

A permanent current of up to 3 knots runs past the island on an E and SE-going direction.

Charts

British Admiralty *774*. Imray *M11*
French *5864, 6569*. Spanish *4351, 435*

Lights

0086 **Alborán lighthouse** Fl(4)20s40m10M Grey conical tower and house 20m

0087 **Puerto refugio E wharf head** Q.R.3s4m3M Red square column 3m

0087.1 **Dique de Abrigo head** Q.G.4m3M Green square column 3m

Isolated island S of Puerto de Adra

This small island lies some 49M to S of Puerto de Adra and about 30M from the African coast. It is a bare, low, reddish-cliffed island 700m long and 300m wide with two small landing jetties and several anchorages. The sole inhabitants are the staff for the lighthouse and a military detachment.

Facilities are non-existent and, officially, in order to visit, permission must be obtained from the Naval Commander in Almería. If you arrive without permission you may or may not be allowed to stay for a short visit depending on the officer on duty.

Approach

The island can be approached from any direction but as it is low, it will not be seen until within 10M. There are a number of sunken rocks extending in places to 200m from the coast.

Entrance

Approach the E jetty on a W course with the jetty in line with the lighthouse. Approach the W jetty on an ESE approach. In both cases keep a sharp lookout for submerged rocks during the last 200m of the approach.

Anchorages

There are several anchorages to suit the prevalent wind direction in about 6m sand and stone.

Formalities

Call on the military commander.

Facilities

In an emergency, water and food might be obtained from the garrison.

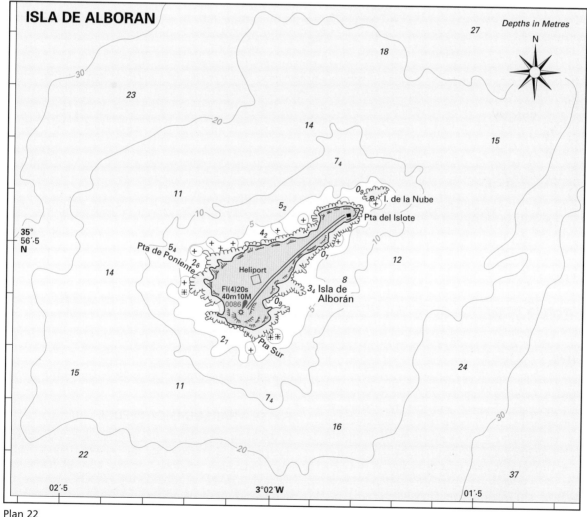

Plan 22

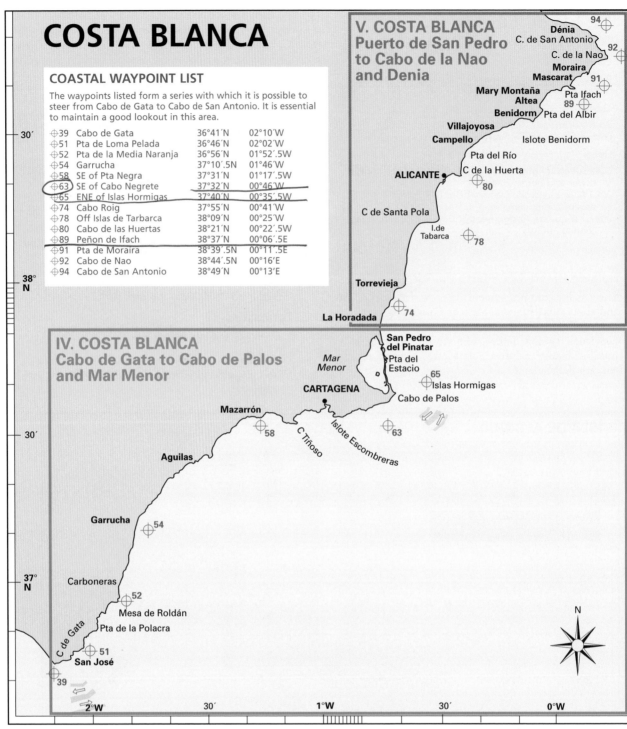

COSTA BLANCA

COASTAL WAYPOINT LIST

The waypoints listed form a series with which it is possible to steer from Cabo de Gata to Cabo de San Antonio. It is essential to maintain a good lookout in this area.

39	Cabo de Gata	36°41'N	02°10'W
51	Pta de Loma Pelada	36°46'N	02°02'W
52	Pta de la Media Naranja	36°56'N	01°52'.5W
54	Garrucha	37°10'.5N	01°46'W
58	SE of Pta Negra	37°31'N	01°17'.5W
63	SE of Cabo Negrete	37°32'N	00°46'W
65	ENE of Islas Hormigas	37°40'N	00°35'.5W
74	Cabo Roig	37°55'N	00°41'W
78	Off Islas de Tarbarca	38°09'N	00°25'W
80	Cabo de las Huertas	38°21'N	00°22'.5W
89	Peñon de Ifach	38°37'N	00°06'.5E
91	Pta de Moraira	38°39'.5N	00°11'.5E
92	Cabo de Nao	38°44'.5N	00°16'E
94	Cabo de San Antonio	38°49'N	00°13'E

V. COSTA BLANCA
Puerto de San Pedro to Cabo de la Nao and Denia

IV. COSTA BLANCA
Cabo de Gata to Cabo de Palos and Mar Menor

Plan IV

CURRENTS

Along this coast the current is reasonably consistent and is not discussed under each port. Off Cabo de Gata the current is normally E-going and can be strong. It changes its direction to NE-going and becomes weaker along the coast, although it is stronger off Cabo de Palos. In the summer and autumn months this NE and ENE-going current is felt as far as Cabo de San Antonio but in the other months it is usually SW-going between Cabo de Palos and Cabo de San Antonio.

TIDES

Maximum spring range is less than 1m and its effects are small.

GALES – HARBOURS OF REFUGE

In the event of onshore gales and heavy seas, Cartagena, Torrevieja and Alicante are the safest to enter. Shelter may sometimes be found where a small harbour is located behind a promontory which protects the entrance from the wind and swell.

COSTA BLANCA

Introduction

GENERAL DESCRIPTION

This 195M stretch of coast between Cabo de Gata to just beyond Cabo de San Antonio is called Costa Blanca (the White Coast). Much of the coastal rock is a light grey which appears white in the bright sunlight. There has been much development in the past two decades. Communications and services have been much improved, many harbours have been built and old harbours adapted for yachts but the discovery of the Costa Blanca by the developers has resulted in many of the once deserted *calas* becoming surrounded by holiday homes and, in some cases, high-rise buildings for package tourists.

However, some sections remain comparatively deserted and with isolated anchorages. By no means all anchorages are noted here and the cruising yacht should be able to find unlisted spots where there is peace and quiet.

The section begins with the impressive promontory of Cabo de Gata which has several white patches of rock on its E side. The high coastal cliffs are broken by many valleys and small coves with good anchorages. The major promontories are high with steep cliffs; Punta de la Media Naranja (half an orange!), Cabo Cope and Cabo Tiñoso are examples.

Beyond Cartagena, which is one of the few natural harbours, lies the long, low sand bar that separates the Mar Menor from the sea, now looking more like a high-rise breakwater. From here to Alicante and beyond, the coast is made up of low rolling hills coming down to broken cliffs with long sandy beaches. Inland ranges of higher hills can be seen and these mountainous features reach the sea in places such as Cabo de La Huerta, Sierra Helada, Cabo de la Nao and Cabo de San Antonio.

Outlying dangers are the small islands; Isla de los Terreros near Aguilas, Isla Grosa and some smaller islets off the Mar Menor, Isla de Tabarca off Cabo de Santa Pola, Islote de Benidorm off Benidorm and the Isla de Portichol. In general, deep water can be carried quite close to the coast with the exception of some areas bordering the Mar Menor.

VISITS INLAND

Apart from places mentioned in the text, there are many interesting places to visit and things to see further inland which may be reached by taxi, bus or, in some cases, by rail. The narrow gauge FEVE runs from the north station of Alicante to Dénia and puts on the 'Lemon Express' for tourists during summer – an expedition which includes a bottle of 'champagne'. Suggestions for other expeditions can be obtained from the various information offices but the following are worth considering: Lorca, a very picturesque old town; Murcia, the capital city of the province of the same name, which has interesting churches, museums and art galleries; Orihuela, with an old church and valuable paintings; Jijona, where the nougat-like sweet turrón is made and with a ruined Moorish castle; and Alcoy, an old Visigoth town with many ancient remains.

Pilotage and navigation

TUNNY NETS

In spring, summer and autumn tunny nets may be laid at the places listed below (see the Introduction, page 4).
- Off San José
- Near Punta del Esparto
- Off Punta de la Polacra
- In Cala de San Pedro
- 2M to SW of Punta de la Media Naranja
- 1½M to N of Villaricos
- 3M to SW of Isla de los Terreros
- ½M to N of Isla de los Terreros
- 2M and 1M to SW and 1M to E of Aguilas
- In Cala Bardina
- S of Cabo Cope
- 1M to NE of Punta de Calnegre
- 5, 3 and 1M to W of Punta Negra
- Off Punta de la Azohía
- Centre and E end of Ensenada de Mazarrón
- N of Cabo Tiñoso
- Off Puerto de Portmán
- Off Cap de Palos
- N of Cabo de las Huertas
- In the Ensenada de Benidorm
- W of the Peñón de Ifach
- Ensenada de Moraira

FISH HAVENS

There are extensive fish havens along this coast.

RESTRICTED AREAS

In Cartagena there are areas reserved for the Spanish navy which may not be entered by yachts. Submarines exercise in areas from Cabo de Gata to Cabo San Sebastian and there is a firing area S of Cartagena. Anchoring is prohibited in an area to the S of Puerto de Jávea where there are underwater cables.

MAGNETIC VARIATION

Costa Blanca (Cartegena) 01°25′W (2005) decreasing 7′ annually.

PLANNING GUIDE AND DISTANCE TABLES

See page 107.

IV. COSTA BLANCA Cabo de Gata to Cabo de Palos and Mar Menor

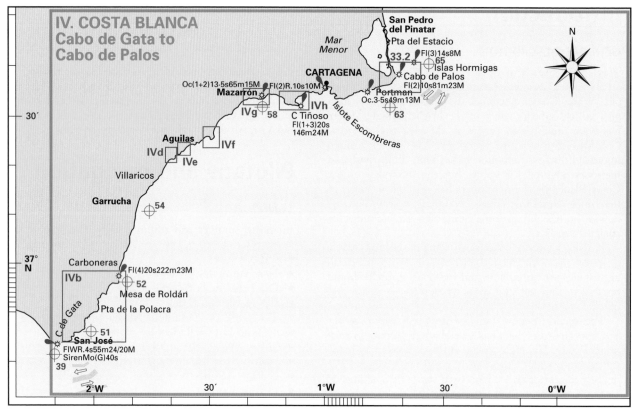

Plan IVa

PORTS

23. Puerto de San José
24. Puertos de Carboneras
25. Puerto de Garrucha
26. Puerto de Villaricos
27. Puerto de Esperanza
28. Puertos de Aguilas y del Hornillo
29. Puerto Deportivo de Mazarrón
30. Puerto de Mazarrón
31. Puerto de Cartagena
32. Puerto de Portmán
33. Puerto de Cabo de Palos (Cala Avellán)

The ports of Mar Menor

34. Puerto de Tomás Maestre
35. Puerto de Dos Mares
36. Puerto de la Manga
37. Puerto de Mar de Cristal
38. Puerto de los Islas Menores
39. Puerto de Los Nietos
40. Puerto de los Urrutias
41. Puerto de los Alcázares
42. Puerto de Lo Pagan

COASTAL WAYPOINT LIST

The waypoints listed form a series with which it is possible to steer from Cabo de Gata to off Cabo de Palos. It is essential to maintain a good lookout in this area.

⊕39	Cabo de Gata	36°41′N	02°10′W
⊕51	Pta de Loma Pelada	36°46′N	02°02′W
⊕52	Pta de la Media Naranja	36°56′N	01°52′.5W
⊕54	Garrucha	37°10′.5N	01°46′W
⊕58	SE of Pta Negra	37°31′N	01°17′.5W
⊕63	SE of Cabo Negrete	37°32′N	00°46′W
⊕65	ENE of Islas Hormigas	37°40′N	00°35′.5W

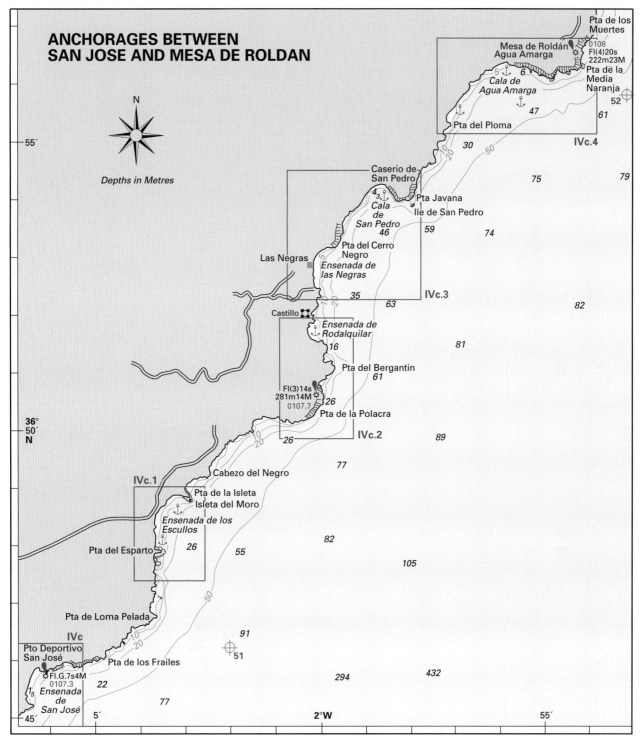

ANCHORAGES BETWEEN
SAN JOSE AND MESA DE ROLDAN

N

Depths in Metres

Pta de los
Muertes
0108
Fl(4)20s
222m23M
Mesa de Roldán
Agua Amarga
Pta de la
Media
Naranja
52
Cala de
Agua Amarga
5
6
47
61
Pta del Ploma
30
50
IVc.4

Caserio de
San Pedro
75
79
Pta Javana
Cala
de
San Pedro
Ile de San Pedro
46
59
74
Pta del Cerro
Negro
Las Negras
Ensenada de
las Negras
82
35
63
IVc.3

Castillo
Ensenada de
Rodalquilar
16
81
Pta del Bergantin
61
Fl(3)14s
281m14M
0107.7
26
89
Pta de la Polacra
IVc.2
26
77

IVc.1
Cabezo del Negro
82
Pta de la Isleta
Isleta del Moro
Ensenada de los
Escullos
105
Pta del Esparto
26
55

Pta de Loma Pelada
91
IVc
10
20
Pto Deportivo
San José
51
Pta de los Frailes
Fl.G.7s4M
0107.3
22
294
432
Ensenada
de
San José
1.5
5
50
77
45′
5′
2°W
55′

55′

36°
50′
N

Plan IVb

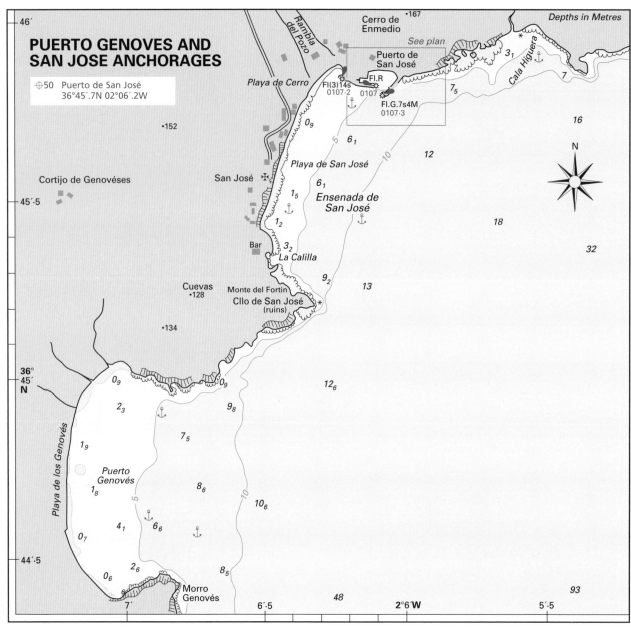

**PUERTO GENOVES AND
SAN JOSE ANCHORAGES**

⊕50   Puerto de San José
      36°45′.7N 02°06′.2W

Cerro de
Enmedio

•167

Depths in Metres

See plan

Rambla del Pozo

Puerto de
San José

Cala Higuera

Playa de Cerro

Fl(3)14s
0107·2

Fl.R

0107

Fl.G.7s4M
0107·3

•152

3_1

0_9

6_1

5

7_5

7

10

12

16

Playa de San José

Cortijo de Genovéses

San José ⌖

6_1

1_5

Ensenada de
San José

18

1_2

3_2

13

32

Bar

La Calilla

9_2

Cuevas
•128

Monte del Fortin

Cllo de San José
(ruins)

•134

N

0_9

0_9

2_3

9_8

12_6

7_5

Playa de los Genovés

1_9

Puerto
Genovés

8_6

10_6

5

1_8

4_1

6_6

0_7

0_6

2_6

8_5

Morro
Genovés

7

6′·5

48

2°6′W

5′·5

93

Plan IVc

Puerto Genovés. The word 'Puerto' covers both an enclosed harbour and a bay with some shelter

⚓ PUERTO GENOVÉS

A bay with a gently sloping sandy bottom. Open between NE and SE with good protection from other winds especially close inshore at N and S sides of bay. Anchor to suit wind in 5m, sand and mud.

Note that there are rocks to the SE of Morro Genovese so do not pass too close to the cliffs on entering bay from the south.

⚓ ENSENADA DE SAN JOSÉ/CALA HIGUERA

Similar open bay to Puerto Genovés but with sandy and rocky beach with developments. A small village now exists with a road to Almería. Protection from N–NE winds at NE end of bay under cliffs.

In strong S to SW winds the swell curls round the headland into this ensenada and Porto Genovés is quieter and should be used in these conditions.

23. Puerto de San José

36°46′N 02°06′W

Charts

British Admiralty *774*. Imray *M11*
French *4718*. Spanish *461*

⊕50 30°45′.7N 02°06′.2W

Lights

To the southwest
0106 **Cabo de Gata** Fl.WR.4s55m24/20M 356°-W-316°-R-
356° Siren Mo(G)40s White tower, grey lantern 19m
Harbour
0107.3 **Dique Este head** Fl.G.7s8m4M Green ▲ on
truncated tower 3m
0107 **Dique Sur E head** Fl.R.6s7m3M Red ■ on truncated
tower 3m
0107.2 **Dique Sur W head** Fl(3)14s4m2M White masonry
tower 1m
To the northeast
0108 **Mesa de Roldán** Fl(4)20s222m23M White octagonal
tower 18m

Port communications

Capitanía VHF Ch 9. ☎/Fax 950 38 00 41
Email c.n.sanjose@terra.es

Attractive small harbour

A small yacht harbour in attractive surroundings which
is a useful break in the 50M stretch of coast between
Almería and Garrucha. The harbour is subject to swell
from E-SE but is otherwise well protected. A small
village nearby can supply basic requirements. There are
walks in empty country, fine views from the hills, caves
near top of Monte del Fortin and excellent sandy
beaches.

Approach

From the south Round the prominent Cabo de Gata
(344m), either close inshore or 1M offshore to avoid the
Laja de Cabo de Gata shoal (3.3m) which breaks in
heavy weather. It lies 1300m SSE of Cabo de Gata light
and in its red sector. 1M to E of the lighthouse there are
some conspicuous white rock patches on the dark cliff
face which, seen from afar, resemble sails. Keep ½M
offshore rounding onto a NE course after the Morro
Genovés which is conically shaped and lies at the S side
of Puerto Genovés, a deep bay with a sandy beach. The
Monte del Fortin, which has a ruined fort, separates
Puerto Genovés from Ensenada de San José. This bay is
lined with houses and the harbour lies in the N corner

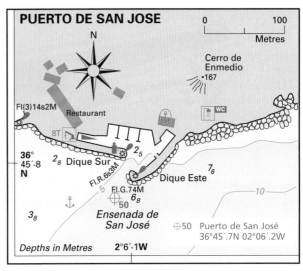

Plan 23

San José

under a small white rock patch.

From the north The Mesa de Roldán is a high plateau
(221m). The lighthouse is on Punta de la Media Naranja
and can be seen from afar. Agua Amarga is just to the
west of Media Naranja. These features can easily be
identified. To the SW Punta Javana has a small island,
Isla de San Pedro, off its point. Punta de la Polacra
(263m) with a tower on its summit and Punta de Loma
Pelada which has the high Cerro de los Frailes
(489-444m) inland should be recognised. San José lies
SW of this high ground. Keep over ¼M offshore.

GPS approach

Steer to ⊕50 from a southeasterly quadrant and steer
for breakwater end.

Anchorage in the approach

The whole of the Ensenada de San José is suitable for
anchorage - 200m to SW of the harbour entrance in 5m
sand is recommended. If wind is strong from N an
alternative is in a small bay off Playa de Cala Higuera,
just under ½M E of the harbour.

Entrance

Approach the harbour heading N and give the head of
Dique Sur 10m clearance.

Berths

Secure to starboard-hand quay or fuel berth to port and
ask at the *capitanía* for a berth.

Charges

High.

Facilities

Maximum length overall: 14m.
Slipway.
8-tonne crane.
A few taps on pontoons but water may be salty.
220v AC.
Gasoleo A and petrol.
Shops in village.

Communications

Bus service to Almería. ☎ Area code 950.

⚓ ENSENADA DE LOS ESCULLOS
36°48′.2N 02°03′.2W

An open bay anchorage with sloping sandy bottom, some sandy beaches. Coast road, some development. The ruined castle, *guardia civil* barracks and a point with a white, skull-shaped rock, lie near the centre of the bay. The bay is wide open to E but some protection from NE in N corner of the bay is possible under Punta de la Isleta.

⚓ ENSENADA DE RODALQUILAR
36°51′.6N 02°00′W

The holding is reportedly poor in places. Open between NE and SE.

Punta de la Isleta

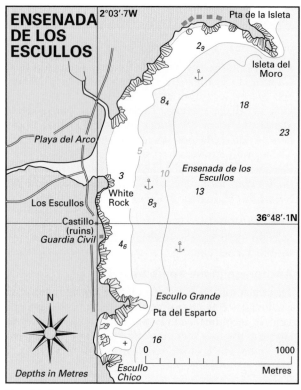

Plan IVc.1

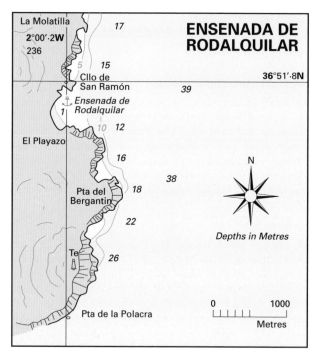

Plan IVc.2

Los Escullos

Rodalquilar

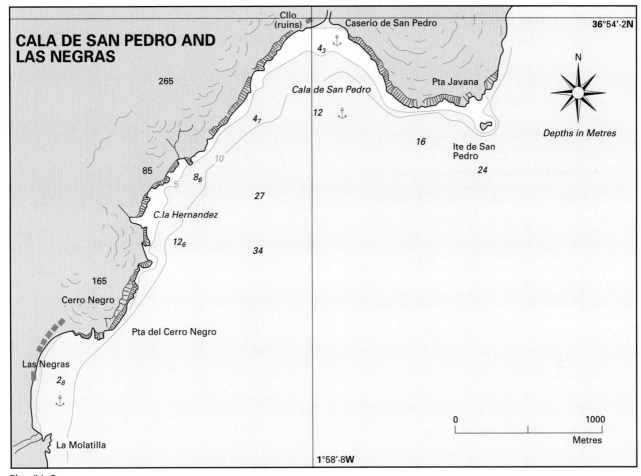

CALA DE SAN PEDRO AND LAS NEGRAS

265

4₃

Cllo (ruins)

Caserio de San Pedro

36°54′·2N

Cala de San Pedro

Pta Javana

N

12

Depths in Metres

4₇

16

Ite de San Pedro

10

24

85

8₆

5

27

C.la Hernandez

12₆

34

165

Cerro Negro

Pta del Cerro Negro

Las Negras

2₈

La Molatilla

0   1000

Metres

1°58′·8W

Plan IVc.3

San Pedro

⚓ **LAS NEGRAS** 36°52′.6N 01°59′.9W

Anchor in 3m sand and weed off the village. Open between NE and SE. The beach is sand and rock. The village has some shops.

⚓ **CALA DE SAN PEDRO** 36°53′.9N 01°58′.7W

An imposing anchorage where fluky and strong gusts may be expected. Anchor to suit draught in sand and weed.

⚓ **ENSENADA DE AGUA AMARGA (BITTER WATER BAY)** 36°56′.0N 01°56′.0W

Anchor outside the small boat moorings in 6 to 8 metres of water. Excellent shelter from the NE winds but open between E and S. Alternative anchorages lie off the hamlet of El Ploma 2M to SW or off a small cove 1M to SW of Agua Amarga. Use these with care.

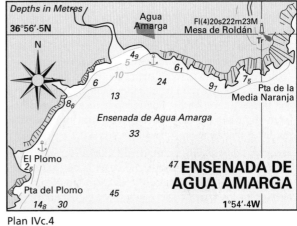

Depths in Metres

36°56′·5N

N

Agua Amarga

Fl(4)20s222m23M
Mesa de Roldán

Tr

4₉

5

6₁

6

10

24

9₇

7₅

8₆

13

Pta de la Media Naranja

Ensenada de Agua Amarga

33

El Plomo

2₅

⁴⁷**ENSENADA DE AGUA AMARGA**

Pta del Plomo

14₈   30

45

1°54′·4W

Plan IVc.4

24. Puertos de Carboneras

36°59′.3N 01°53′.8W

Charts

British Admiralty *1515, 774.* Imray *M12*
French *4718.* Spanish *4621, 462*

⊕53 36°59′.2N 01°53′.5W

Lights

South Harbour (Puerto de Hornos Ibéricos SA)
0109 **Dique Este head** Fl(2)G.10s12m5M Green round
    tower 3m
0109.2 **Dique Este elbow** Q(3)10s14m3M ♦ card BYB
    tower 3m
0109.3 **Dique Oeste head** Fl(2)R.10s7m3M Red round
    tower 3m
**Middle harbour (PUCARSA – Puerto de Generar
Electricidad)**
0109.4 **Dique de Abrigo** 36°58′.5N 01°53′.6W
    Fl.G.10s14m5M Green metal post 4m
0109.5 **Dique auxiliar N head** Fl(2)R.9s10m1M Red metal
    framework tower 3m
North harbour (Puerto Pescaro de Carboneras)
0109.6 **Dique Este** Fl(3)G.12s10m5M Green hexagonal
    tower 4m
0109.7 **Contradique** Fl(3)R.12s8m3M Red hexagonal
    tower 6m

Port communications

Puerto de Hornos Ibéricos VHF Ch 9, 12.

Commercial and fishing harbours

Three harbours, two commercial, large and forbidding,
the Puerto de Hornos Ibéricos SA and the Puerto
Generar del Electricidad and the third a working fishing
harbour. However the first two offer good refuge from
winds from all directions except SE though they should
only be used in an emergency. Local facilities are about
zero but provisions can be found in Carboneras village.
The immediate area is dominated by the huge cement
plant and electric generating station but the hinterland
is wild and attractive. The fishing harbour is busy and
has no special facilities for yachts. In poor weather it is
likely to be crowded and a yacht would have to take its
chance alongside a fishing boat.

Approach

From the south After Cabo de Gata the coast is broken
by headlands enclosing sandy bays. Puerto Genovés is a
wide sandy bay and the Ensenada de San José, which has
a small harbour and village, can be identified. Further N,
El Fraile (489m) is conspicuous as are the Isleta del
Moro and Punta de la Polacra (263m) which has a
tower. Cala de San Pedro which has a few houses and
Agua Amarga may also be seen. The white lighthouse of
Mesa de Roldán (221m) can be seen from afar. Once
the points of Le Media Naranja and Los Muertos have
been rounded the large breakwaters and the industrial
buildings belching smoke will be seen.

From the north From Puerto de Garrucha, backed by
the town of the same name, the coast is flat, sandy and
unbroken, with high ranges of hills inland and some low
cliffs. The town of Mojacar may be seen on its hill ¼M
then the buildings stop and the mountains begin, which

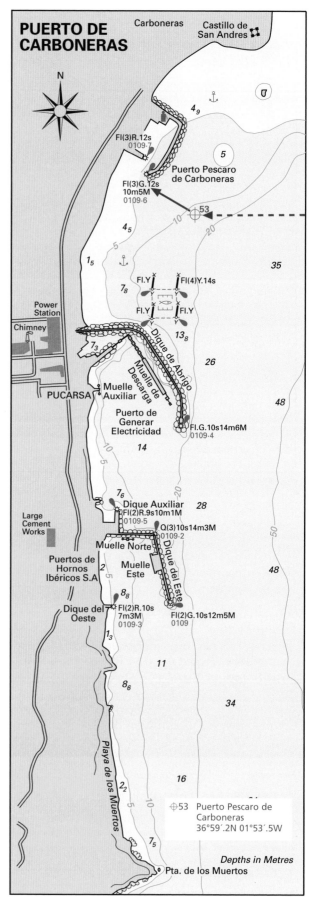

Plan 24

The two commercial harbours at Carboneras with Puerto Pescaro at top right

last until shortly before Carboneras. The village of Carboneras stands behind a rather inconspicuous point with El Islote and Isla de San Andreas (14m) extending 600m off the point. Foul ground stretches nearly ½ M from this point in a SE direction, otherwise the coast is free of dangers and can be followed at 400m. Once the Isla de San Andreas has been passed, the harbour walls and buildings may be seen. A 3.5m deep passage, running NE-SW, 150m wide, exists between this island and El Islote.

GPS approach

For the Puerto Pescaro steer to ⊕53 from an easterly quadrant and steer for breakwater end (approx. 0.3M).

Entrances

Both big harbours may be entered on a NW course leaving the head of either Dique Este 50m to starboard. Pay attention to and keep out of the way of any

commercial vessel manoeuvring. The entrance to the Puerto Pescaro is straightforward but shoals and may be alive with traffic.

Berths

A temporary berth may be available in the S harbour alongside the quay if not in use. It has been rumoured that the fishing harbour is to be extended and become a fishing and yacht harbour. However during a visit in September 2004 only one small pontoon for local small craft was seen in the NE corner and no plans for further pontoons were forthcoming.

Anchorages

A temporary anchorage may be available in 5m sand and stone on the E side of the south and middle harbours, close inshore and clear of commercial works.

Outside, there are two possibilities: between Puerto de Carboneras and Puerto Pescaro and between Puerto Pescaro and El Islote. Both are open to the SE but the latter has better shelter from the NE. Sand, stone and weed.

Formalities

In the commercial harbours, contact the shore by radio for permission to stay. In the fishing harbour, inquire ashore.

⚓ MARINA DE LAS TORRES   37°09´.7N 01°49´W

An open coastal anchorage off the mouth of Río de Aguas in 5m sand, stone and weed. Exposed between NE and SE. The towns of Mojacar and Garrucha lie 2M and 1M away. There is a small landing jetty nearby. A road runs behind the beach and there is a conspicuous old factory chimney.

Puerto Pescaro de Carboneras

25. Puerto de Garrucha

37°11′N 01°49′.1W

Charts

British Admiralty *1515, 77*. Imray *M12*
French *4718*. Spanish *462*

⊕55 37°10′.5N 01°48′.8W

Lights

0110 **Garrucha LtHo** Oc(4)13s19m13M White tower house 10m Reserve light 8M
0110.5 **Espigón head** Q(3)10s4m3M ♦ card BYB 3m
0111·5 **Dique (unattached)** Q(3)10s4m3M ♦ card BYB 3m
0111 **Dique de Levante head** head Fl(3)G.9s13m5M Green tower 11m
0112 **Dique de Poniente head** Fl(3)R.9s6m3M Red tower 3m

Port communications

VHF Ch 9. Club Maritimo ☎ 950 46 00 48
Fax 950 13 24 10 *Email* pdgarrucha@distrito.com
url www.eppa.es.

Busy fishing harbour

A small fishing harbour, which is usually crowded, with a commercial quay. The harbour is easy to approach and enter but is open towards the SE. The little village has simple facilities, shops and a market where everyday requirements can be obtained. The harbour is clean and there is a slipway and small shipyard. The W side of the harbour has been converted into a promenade. A short walk to the disused factory by the prominent chimney gives a good idea of the coast and surrounding area. The hill top town of Mojacar is worth a visit by bus or taxi.

Good sandy beaches on each side of the harbour.

Approach

From the south The Sierra Cabrera, whose foothills are easily identified, lead to Garrucha; one of these hills is covered with tourist housing development. An isolated obelisk-like chimney on a small hill behind the town is conspicuous. The lighthouse shows at close range.

From the north The low plain and dry river mouths SSW of Sierra Almagrera lead to Garrucha which has an isolated chimney and cranes on the Dique de Levante.

GPS approach

Steer to ⊕55 from an easterly quadrant and steer for breakwater end (approx. 2.5M).

Anchorage in the approach

Anchor 200m S of elbow of Dique de Poniente in 5m sand.

Entrance

Straightforward but commercial vessels have right of way.

Berths

There is a small marina in the NW corner of the harbour. Secure near the fuel point at head of the 'T'-shaped pontoon near the centre of the harbour projecting from the NW side. Alternatively, berth alongside the broad commercial quay in NE corner of the harbour on the inside of the Dique de Levante. In the SW corner a possible berth is stern-to between fishing craft on N facing side of Dique de Poniente near the landward end; anchor with trip-line from the bow. Confirm berthing arrangements with the office near slipway.

Garrucha

Anchoring in the N end of the harbour is very reluctantly accepted but not with any imminent big ship movements. In strong southerlies a big surge enters the harbour.

Facilities

Maximum length overall: 12m
Simple wood hull repairs by yard on slipway or in workshop in terrace to W of port.
12-tonne crane on Dique de Levante.
Slipways.
Water on quays.

Showers in the office block (key from harbourmaster).
125v and 220v AC supply point on Dique de Poniente and on pontoons.
Gasoleo A and petrol.
Ice from factory on front near *capitán de puerto*'s office.
Club Cultural y Marítimo de Garrucha.
A number of shops and a small market in the village SW of the harbour.
Litter bins around the harbour.

Communications

Bus service to Vera. ☎ Area code 950.

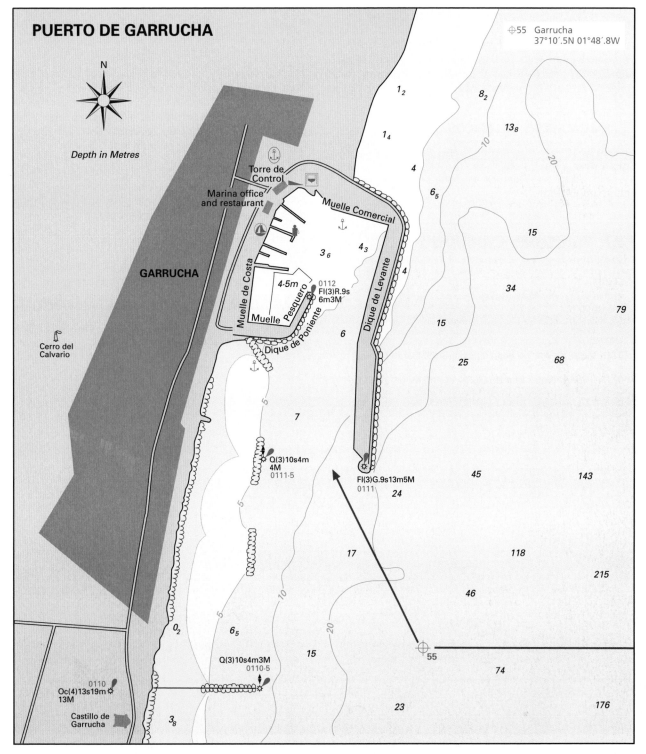

PUERTO DE GARRUCHA

Plan 25

26. Puerto de Villaricos

37°14′.8N 01°46′W

Charts

British Admiralty *774*. Imray *M12*
French *4718*. Spanish *46A, 462*

Lights

0112.5 **Villaricos. Balsa breakwater head** 37°14′.8N
  01°46′.1W Fl(4)G.12s8m5M Green truncated tower 3m
0112.51 **Outer breakwater head** Fl(4)R.15s4m3M Red
  truncated tower 3m

No room for visitors

A pleasant but very small artificial harbour built for the
town's pleasure craft (at last sighting there were only
small motor boats). There is little or no room for
visitors, no harbour facilities. Max length 5.6m.

⚓ PALOMARES Y VILLARICOS

Open anchorages either side of the mouth of the Río
Almanzora. Note the shoals of the delta.

The village of Villaricos is right of centre in the
photograph below.

27. Puerto de Esperanza

37°15′N 01°46′W

Charts

British Admiralty *774*. Imray *M12*
French *4718*
Spanish *46A, 462*

Lights

0113 **Dique de Abrigo head** Q(2)G.6s8m5M Green tower
  3m
0113·1 **Contradique (centre)** Fl(2)R.10s3m3M Red post 1m
0113·2 **Espigón** Fl(3)G.10s3m3M Green square column 2m
0113·4 **Contradique head** Fl(3)R.10s8m3M Red tower 3m

Tiny fishing harbour

Villaricos' tiny fishing harbour is only suitable for small
(<8m) craft for a short stay. It is an attractive setting but
even one visiting craft may be too many. Depths are
reported to be 2m in the approach and port but caution
and careful sounding is advised during any approach.

Approach

From the south The coast north of Garrucha is flat and
sandy with few features and can be followed at about
200 metres offshore except off the delta of the River
Almanzora when 400m should be maintained. The
village of Palomares may be seen south of the river
mouth with the village of Villaricos north of the river.

From the north From the easily identified Ensenada de
Terreros with its off-lying island (24m) and small village,
the coast is cliffed with small sand and stone beaches in
breaks of the cliffs. Inland the hills rise to 350m. The
coast is steep-to, 2 off-lying shallows (6m) – Piedra del
Celor and Losa del Payo – break in heavy seas.

Entrance

Approach the head of the Dique de Abrigo on a W to
NW course, round it at 10m and pass fairly close to the
quay extension with its small green tower.

Facilities

Slipway in SW corner
Shops in village 200m to SW.

⚓ ANCHORAGES 2M TO N OF RÍO ALMANZORA

At least 10 small anchorages in *calas*, some with piers
and quays – use with care.

Delta of Río Almanzora

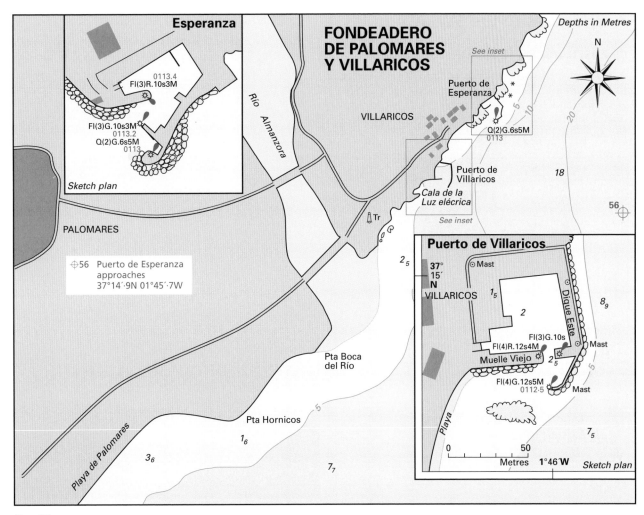

Esperanza

FONDEADERO DE PALOMARES Y VILLARICOS

Depths in Metres

N

See inset

Puerto de Esperanza

VILLARICOS

0113.4
FI(3)R.10s3M

FI(3)G.10s3M
0113.2
Q(2)G.6s5M
0113

Sketch plan

Río Almanzora

Q(2)G.6s5M
0113

18

PALOMARES

Puerto de Villaricos

Cala de la Luz elécrica

See inset

⊕56 Puerto de Esperanza approaches
37°14´·9N 01°45´·7W

56⊕

Tr

2₅

Puerto de Villaricos

37°
15´
N
VILLARICOS

⊙ Mast

1₅

2

Dique Este

8₉

FI(3)G.10s
FI(4)R.12s4M
Muelle Viejo
2₅

Mast

Pta Boca del Río

FI(4)G.12s5M
0112·5

Mast

Playa

Pta Hornicos

1₆

3₆

7₅

Playa de Palomares

7₇

0   50
Metres   1°46´W   *Sketch plan*

Plan 26

Esperanza

Anchorages to the SW of Aguilas

⚓ ENSENADA DE TERREROS 37°21′N 01°39′.7W

A well-protected anchorage but open to SE and subject to swell from E. The 600m passage between the Punta el Cañon and Isla de los Terreros (34m) is 6m deep. Anchor off San Juan de los Terreros in N part of bay. A few shops and the main road.

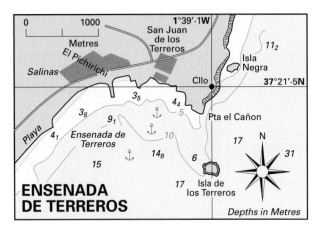

Plan IVd

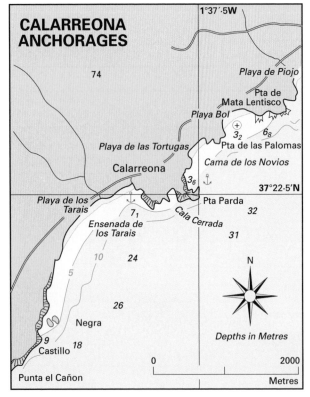

Plan IVe

⚓ PUNTA PARDA 37°22′.5N 01°37′.5W

At the N end of Ensenada de los Tarais, which is open between E and S, there are two anchorages on the west side of Punta Parda, off Cala Reona and Cala Cerrada, and one on the east, Cama de los Novios (beware of the small island in the entrance to this bay). Anchor according to draught, sand and weed. Whether the name, Cama de los Novios, the bed of the newly-married, reflects turbulent or peaceful nights is anyone's guess.

Punta Parda looking into Cala Cerrada; Cama de los Novios is behind the point looking NW

28. Puertos de Aguilas y del Hornillo

37°24′.4N 01°34′.4W

Currents

Currents inside these two bays tend to set in the direction of recent winds.

Charts

British Admiralty *1515, 774.* Imray *M12*
French *6341, 4718.* Spanish *463*

⊕57 37°24′N 01°34′.2W

Lights

Approach
0114 **Punta Negra** Fl(2)5s30m13M Black and white bands 23m
0117.5 **Islote de la Aguilica** Fl.G.3s19m3M Square white building

Commercial Harbour
0116 **Mole** head Fl(2)R.6s9m3M Red post 5m
0116·1 **Contradique head** Fl(3)G.9s5m2M Grey Post 3m

Yacht Harbour (Darsena Deportiva)
0116.2 **Dique Sur head** Fl(2)G.5s6m2M White truncated tower, green top 5m
0116·4 **Dique Oeste** Oc.R.5s5m2M White truncated tower, red top 4m

Port communications

Port VHF Ch 9 ☎/*Fax* 968 41 02 28
Club Náutico de Aguilas VHF Ch 9 ☎/*Fax* 968 41 19 51
Marina mobile 670445725 *Email* admon@cnaguilas.com
url www.cnaguilas.com

Useful anchorage harbour

Two bays, separated by a headland with a tourist development. The western bay, Aguilas, has a small fishing port on its west shore and a small crowded yacht harbour on its north shore. To the east, the other side of the headland, is El Hornillo, an old anchorage with a project for a marina close to the north east. Both bays are open to the ESE and uncomfortable in a wind from this direction but have attractive surroundings.

Aguilas was an important Roman port which fell into disuse after repeated invasions by the Berbers. In 1765 the village and harbour were rebuilt and the castle restored by Count Aranda, a minister of Charles III. A climb to the castle of San Juan (18th century) on Montaña de Aguilas above the harbour is worthwhile for the view. Good beaches on either side of the harbour.

Note that there are two headlands with lights named Punta Negra in this area: Punta Negra de Aguilas, normally listed under Punta Negra and Punta Negra de Mazarrón, normally listed under Mazarrón.

Approach

From the SW Follow the coast, passing the conspicuous Isla de los Terreros. In the distance four high, steep-sided headlands will be seen (Mt de Aguilas, Mt de la Aguilica, Isla el Fraile and Mt Cope). Aguilas lies behind the first headland, which has a small castle on its summit. A tall lone chimney stands in the bay to the W of the first headland.

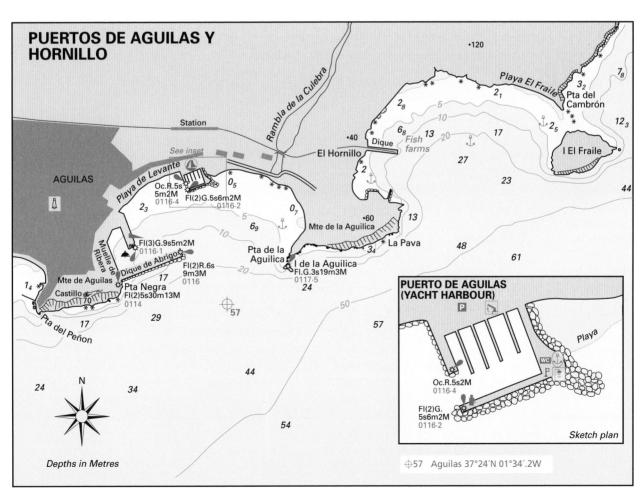

Plan 28

The fishing harbour at Puerto Aguilas and the yacht haven at upper right

From the NE Having rounded the large promontory of Mt Cope, a group of tree high, steep-sided rocky headlands will be seen, the first actually on an island. The harbour lies between the second and third headland.

GPS approach

Steer to ⊕57 from a southeasterly quadrant and steer for breakwater end (approx. 0.2M).

Entrance

In Aguilas, give the head of mole a 50m berth; a buoyed channel leads to the yacht harbour. Fishing nets are sometimes laid near the entrance to both bays. In heavy weather the entrance to both harbours might be dangerous.

Berths

In Aguilas yacht harbour secure to any vacant berth or as directed by harbour staff. In the fishing harbour a possibility is to go alongside at the root of the mole, clear of commercial craft; alternatively secure stern-to a fishing quay with a bow anchor using an anchor trip-line. Before arriving, check that there is room with the harbourmaster by radio.

Anchorages

It is possible to anchor almost anywhere in the bay clear of the quays. Suggested anchorages are shown on the plan.

Facilities

Aguilas Fishing Harbour
50-tonne travel-lift and hardstanding.
12-tonne crane.
Slipway at the SW corner.
Engine repair mechanics in the town.
Small repairs to woodwork and hulls can be carried out at workshop by slipway.
Chandlers shop near the fish quay, another near the yacht harbour.
Water on the commercial mole. Supply also available at lonja de pescadores.
Ice from a factory to W of the town or at the harbourmaster's office.
Darsena Deportiva
Maximum length overall: 12m.
Water and electricity on the quays.
Gasoleo A and petrol.
Club Náutico de Aguilas at yacht harbour.
A good selection of shops in the town and a small market.

Communications

Bus and rail services. ☎ Area code 968.

Anchorages between Aguilas and Mazarron

⚓ CALA BARDINA 37°25´.6N 01°30´.5W

The first 50m offshore is cordoned off for swimmers and small boats. A channel for these boats is marked with a red and a green buoy – watch out for a submerged rock some 20m south of the green buoy! There is still plenty of room to anchor in 6 to 8 metres outside the buoys. Well protected from the N and E by Mt Cope (244m) but open between SE and SW and with swell from E winds.

⚓ ENSENADA DE LA FUENTE 37°26´.1N 01°28´.7W

An anchorage open to NE but well protected by Mt Cope from other directions. Anchor in SW corner of the bay in 3m sand.

⚓ OTHER ANCHORAGES BETWEEN MONTAÑA COPE AND PUERTO DE MAZARRÓN

A large number of small coastal anchorages exist on this stretch of coast, see plan. Use with care. Most are off small, sandy beaches and any obstructions can be seen in the clear water. Some anchorages have a stony bottom but most are sand or shingle.

Plan IVf

29. Puerto Deportivo de Mazarrón

37°33´.4N 01°16´.3W

Charts

British Admiralty *774*. Imray *M12*
French *6341, 4718*. Spanish *4632, 463*

⊕59 37°33´.3N 01°16´.3W

Lights

0122 **Yacht club jetty head** Fl.R.2s10m3M Red metal
tower, white band 9m
To the east
0120 **Mazarrón LtHo** Oc(1+2)13·5s65m15M White tower
11m

Port communications

VHF Ch 9. Yacht club ☎ 968 59 40 11 *Fax* 968 59 52 53

Pleasant harbour good shelter

Situated round the corner and about a mile west of the
old fishing harbour of Mazarrón, it has better facilities
for visiting yachts and is more pleasant to visit than the
old harbour. It offers very good shelter from all
directions. There are beaches beside the harbour.

Note that there are two headlands with lights named
Punta Negra in this area: Punta Negra de Mazarrón,
normally listed under Mazarrón, and Punta Negra de
Aguilas, normally listed under Punta Negra.

Approach

Tunny nets are sometimes laid off this section of coast
and there are presently fish farms 1M SE of Pta del
Calnegre and 1M S of Isla de Adentro. Submarines
exercise in the south of this area.

From the SW The Sierra de las Moreras, with two peaks
(458 and 429m), and the Isla de Adentro (56m) are
recognisable. Punta Negra de Mazarrón with its
lighthouse and large statue of Jesus is unmistakable. The
harbour lies to W of Isla de Adentro.

From the NE The 4M-wide Ensenada de Mazarrón is
easy to identify as is Punta Negra, described above,
which has the appearance of an island from this
direction. When Punta Negra has been closed Isla de
Adentro will be seen; the harbour lies to W of this
island.

GPS approach

Steer to ⊕59 from a southerly quadrant and steer for
breakwater end (approx 0.15M), leaving the Isla de
Adentro well to starboard.

Anchorage in the approach

Depths to the NE of the harbour are shallow and the
bottom is rocky so anchoring is not recommended but
there is a very attractive sandy cove just west of the
harbour with 3m in its centre.

Entrance

From the SW Approach Isla de Adentro on a NE course
and, when 200m from it, turn onto a N course towards
the harbour breakwater. Leave it 10m to port. Beware
the rocky islet, Los Esculles, lying just to the north of the
line between the north side of Isla de Adentro and the
marina entrance.

From the NE Having identified the statue and Isla de
Adentro round the Isla leaving it 200m to starboard (do
not attempt to pass to the north of the Isla as the water
is shallow with rocky outcrops) and proceed on a NNW
course to close the breakwater end. Note warning about
Los Esculles in previous paragraph.

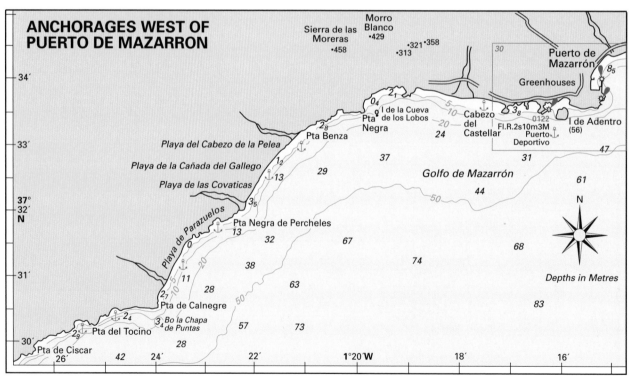

Plan IVg

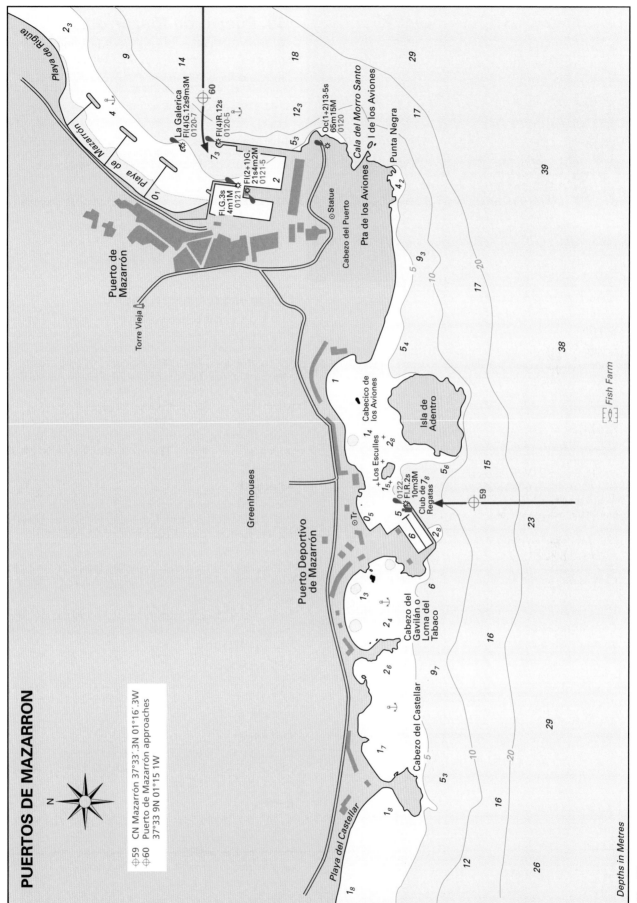

PUERTOS DE MAZARRON

N

⊕59 CN Mazarrón 37°33´.3N 01°16´.3W
⊕60 Puerto de Mazarrón approaches
      37°33´9N 01°15´1W

Playa de Rígüite

2₃

9

14

La Galerica
Fl(4)G.12s9m3M
0120·7

Fl(4)R.12s
0120·5

60

18

12₃

Oc(1+2)13·5s
65m15M
0120

7₃

5₃

Cala del Morro Santo

Fl(2+1)G.
2·1s4m2M
0121·5

2

Fl.G.3s
4m1M
0121

Statue

Puerto de
Mazarrón

Torre Vieja

Cabezo del Puerto

Pta de los Aviones

Cabecico de
los Aviones

Punta Negra

I de los Aviones

29

17

4₂

9₃

5

10

17

20

Playa de Mazarrón

0₁

4

39

38

Greenhouses

1

Los Esculles
1₄
2₈
1₅
0122·
Fl.R.2s
10m3M
Club de
Regatas
7₈

2₈

59

23

Isla de
Adentro

5₆

15

Puerto Deportivo
de Mazarrón

Tr

0₅

5

6

1₃

2₄

Cabezo del
Gavilán o
Loma del
Tabaco

6

16

2₆

9₇

Cabezo del Castellar

1₇

5

10

20

29

Playa del Castellar

5₃

16

1₈

12

26

1₈

Fish Farm

Depths in Metres

Plan 30

Puerto Deportivo de Mazarrón

30. Puerto de Mazarrón

37°33′.9N 01°15′.W

Charts

British Admiralty *774*. Imray *M12*
French *6341, 4718*. Spanish *4632, 463*

⊕60 37°33′.9N 01°15′.1W

Lights

0120 **Mazarrón LtHo** Oc(1+2)13.5s65m15M White tower
    11m Reserve light range 8M
0120.7 **Islote de la Galerica** Fl(4)G.12s9m3M Metal
    framework tower, green top 7m
Harbour
0120.5 **Dique de Abrigo head** Fl(4)R.12s9m5M Grey post
0121 **Contradique head** Fl.G.3s4m1M Grey post 3m
0121·5 **Mole NE** Fl(2+1)G.21s4m2M Grey post 3m

Port communications

VHF Ch 9. ☎ 968 59 40 11 *Fax* 968 59 52 53.

Berths

Secure to quay on port-hand side of entrance near fuel
pumps and ask at the Club de Regatas office for a
berth. Visitors berths are limited to three at the end of
the 'T' pontoon. Visitors may be put elsewhere if there
is room.

Facilities

Maximum length overall: 25m (four yachts only; more at lesser
    length).
Marine Engineer (Volvo agency).
Slipway at N side of harbour and for dinghies at E side.
8-tonne crane.
Hardstandings.
Water taps on pontoons and quays.
220v AC points on pontoons and quays.
Gasoleo A and petrol.
Ice at entrance.
Club de Regatas de Mazarrón has a bar, restaurant, showers
    etc.
Provisions from village of Mazarrón.

Communications

☎ Area code 968. Taxi ☎ 59 51 22.

Fishing and commercial harbour

This fishing and commercial harbour at the W end of
the Ensenada de Mazarrón is easy to enter and offers
good protection from all directions except NE. There
are reasonable facilities ashore but the town of
Mazarrón about 3M inland has good shops and may be
reached by taxi or bus. A climb to the lighthouse is
worthwhile for the view. Good beaches in the bay.

Note that there are two headlands with lights named
Punta Negra in this area: Punta Negra de Mazarrón,
normally listed under Mazarrón, and Punta Negra de
Aguilas, normally listed under Punta Negra.

Approach

Tunny nets are sometimes laid off this section of coast
and there is a fish farm 1M south of Isla de Adentro.
Submarines exercise in the south of the area.

From the SW The Sierra de las Moreras and a few
islands close to the coast are recognisable. Punta Negra
with its lighthouse and a large statue of Jesus is
especially conspicuous.

From the NE Punta Negra resembles an island and, with
its lighthouse and statue, is conspicuous across the wide
Rada de Mazarrón.

GPS approach

Steer to ⊕60 from an easterly quadrant and steer for
breakwater end (approx. 0.14M) leaving La Galerica well
to starboard.

Entrance

Approach the head of the breakwater on a westerly
course, keeping well clear of Isla de la Galerica and
round the head at 25m.

Berths

As this is mainly a commercial harbour, the facilities for
yachts are almost non-existent. The inner harbour is
shallow and crowded with local moorings and berthing
on the quays is frowned upon. The advice is to call the
capitanía on Ch 9 and request a berth (stating one's
draught).

Puerto de Mazarrón

Moorings

The heavy permanent moorings laid over a large area in the best-sheltered areas outside the harbour are for fishing craft as are the moorings inside the harbour. Some of these moorings have only a bundle of corks on a rope riser leading to their chains.

Anchorages

Anchor to E or N of the harbour entrance. Keep clear of La Galerica rock. In the E end of the bay anchor off village of La Subida (see plan below) and N of Punta de la Azohía outside small-craft moorings.

Miscellaneous

The beacons on Punta de la Azohía mark a measured distance of 1857.47m on the N side of the bay, near the centre, on an axis of 104°.

Facilities

Two hards ashore with large travel-lift on centre quay.
Water from fish quay.
Ice from a small factory.
Shops and a supermarket and market in the village. Many more in the town itself some 3M inland.

Communications

Bus to Mazarrón town. ☎ Area code 968.

⚓ ENSENADA DE MAZARRÓN 37°33′.4N 01°10′.6W

It is possible to anchor almost anywhere around this bay in 5M sand and weed. The recommended places are to the sides of the three *ramblas* (dry river beds) or just NE of Punta de la Azohía off the small hamlet of La Subida, both open to S. Watch out for fishing boat moorings. A pair of beacons are situated NE and SW of the hamlet. A small supermarket is located in a housing estate ½M along the road to Mazarrón. In the centre of the bay a small private harbour has been developed alongside and behind the Isla Plana.

There is a fish farm off Punta de la Azohía, but one can go between the farm and the point.

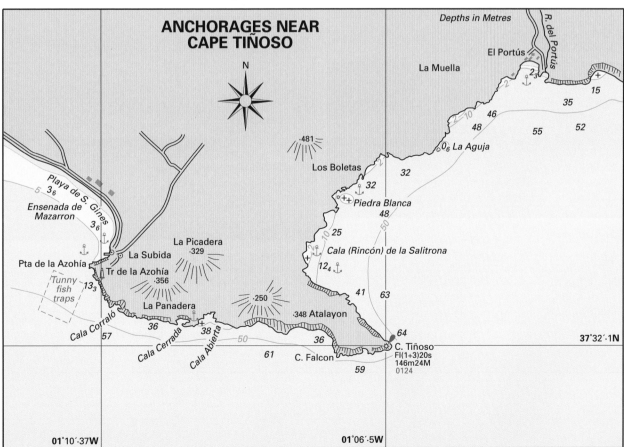

Plan IVh

Punta de Azohía

Rincón de la Salitrona

⚓ **RINCÓN DE LA SALITRONA** 37°37´.2N 01°07´.5W

Anchor off the north beach, in 5m sand and weed, or the south beach which is more sheltered but deeper at 8 to 10m. An alternative is off Los Boletas but pay attention to the rocks, Piedra Blanca.

⚓ **CALA CERRADA** 37°32´.4N 01°09´.25W

Use with caution. Open to S. Anchor in the NE corner, in 8 to 10 metres. The whole *cala* is very deep and is 8m even 20m from the beach.

⚓ **EL PORTÚS** 37°34´.8N 01°04´.4W

Anchor off the sandy beach. Open between SE and SW. Small shops.

Cala Cerrada

El Portús

31. Puerto de Cartagena

37°35′.98N 00°59′.1W

Charts

British Admiralty *774, 1700, 1189, 1194*. Imray *M12*
French *4718, 4719*. Spanish *4642, 464A, 464*

⊕61 37°33′·5N 01°00′W

⊕62 37°35′N 00°58′·9W

Lights

To the west

0124 **Cabo Tiñoso** Fl(1+3)20s146m24M White tower and
building 10m. A magnetic anomaly 3M to S of Cabo
Tiñoso has been reported.

Approaches

Plan below

Western Approach

0125 **Dique, Algameca Grande** Fl(4)R.12s10m7M White and
yellow tower 5m

0125·3 **The Point, Algameca Grande** Fl(3)G.12s8m3M White
and yellow tower 3m

Entrance

0128 **Dique de Navidad** Fl(2)R.10s15m10M White tower red
top 11m

23430(S) **Bajo de Santa Ana** Fl(2)G.7s5M Green conical 5m

Eastern Approach

0127 **Bajo Las Losas** Q(6)+LFl.15s5m5M ⚓ card 5m

Escombreras

0126.2 **Dique Muelle Bastarreche head** Fl.G.3s10m5M White
tower 7m

23200(S) **Bajo de Escombreras** Q(6)+LFl.10s3M ⚓ card buoy
6m

0126 **Islote Escombreras** Fl.5s65m17M Tower with
aluminium cupola on white building 8m

Harbour Plan page 91

0128 **Dique de Navidad** Fl(2)R.10s15m10M White tower red
top 11m

0130 **Dique de la Curra** Fl(3)G.14s14m5M Cylindrical white
tower green cupola 11m

0130.3 **Espalmador floating breakwater** Q.R.1M Red post

0130.5 **Muelle del Carbón head** Fl(2+1)R.14.5s8m3M Red
post, green band 5m

0131.2 **Marina outer breakwater** Q.G.5m1M Green tower
4m

0131.5 **Muelle de Sta Lucia** Fl(4)G.12s5m1M Green post 3m

0132 **Muelle Santiago head** Fl(4)R.11s5m1M Red post 3m

0132.5 **Dique de Alba** Fl(2+1)G.16s5m1M Green column, red
band 3m

Yacht basin

0131.3 **Darsena de Yates breakwater head** 37°35′.7N
00°58′.8W Fl(3)R.9s3m1M Red support 1m

0131.35 **Outer harbour elbow SW** Fl(2+1)G.12s3m1M Green
column, red band

23546(S) **Contradique** Fl(2+1)G.12s3m1M Green column, red
band

Port communications

Port VHF Ch 11, 12, 14. Marina VHF Ch 9.
Puerto Deportivo ☎ 968 32 58 00 *Fax* 968 32 58 15
Email cartagena@apc.es
Real Club de Regatas de Cartagena ☎ 968 50 69 05
Fax 968 50 15 07

Storm signals

Flown from the signal station in Castillo de Galeras.

968 501 509 - marina

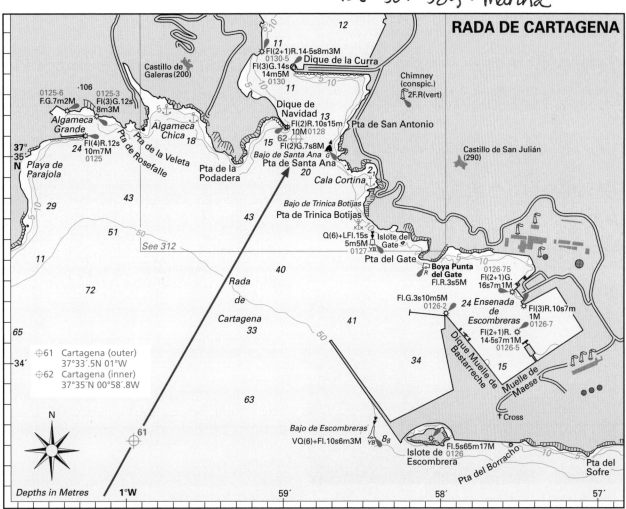

Plan 31

Major harbour with good facilities

A large naval, commercial and fishing port of great antiquity which is easy to approach and enter under almost any conditions. It is an attractive city with good shops. The yacht club is pleasant but is for members – an introduction is needed. Visiting yachts go to the marina. The harbour and quays are sometimes oily and with a SE wind, smoke and fumes from the refinery at Escombrera can be unpleasant.

As of 2004 the yacht club has been moved to a very modern building on the cruise liner landing in the centre of the Muelle de Alfonso XII. New piers have been constructed for berths for large (+25 metres) pleasure craft to the east of the old marina. It is hoped to have everything in place for the 2005 season. It is interesting to note that even though the marina is being extended it was one of the few places to admit to having spare spaces for visitors.

Developed by Hasdrubal about 243 BC it became the centre of Carthaginian influence in Europe, helped by slaves working the gold and silver mines of the region. Hasdrubal's brother, Hannibal, used it a base for his expedition across the Alps and it became the primary target of Scipio the elder ('Africanus' - *Cathargo delenda est*). The Romans duly destroyed Carthaginian influence. St James the Great is said to have landed here in AD 36 bringing Christianity to Spain from Palestine (a sea passage which according to legend took four days). It subsequently passed into the hands of the Barbarians and then Moors. Philip II fortified the surrounding hills in the 16th century, Drake stole its guns in 1585 and took them to Jamaica, Charles III established the arsenal and naval base in the 18th century and the Republicans held out for months against Madrid during the Civil War in 1936. But the chief remnants of its troubled history lie in the minds of its inhabitants, not its artefacts. There is a good view of the harbour from the Castillo de la Concepción and the old churches are worth visiting. A ten-day local holiday starts the Sunday before Trinity Sunday.

Approach

From all directions the entrance to Rada de Cartagena is made obvious by the high steep reddish cliffs of Cabo

New works at Esperanza – from SE

Cartagena

Tiñoso to the W and Islote de Escombrera to the E. The large oil refinery near this island is visible from afar. A large chimney, with black top and white band is conspicuous between Castillo de San Juan and Punta de San Antonio. There is vast construction work going on to enlarge the port of Escombrera. The passage between the Islote and Punta del Borracho has been closed while an 800 metre breakwater now runs NW from the west point of the Islote.

From the west The course goes past Puerto de Algameca Grande, a naval port on the W side of the Rada de Cartagena which is prohibited to yachts. Large unlit mooring buoys are located opposite Algameca Grande and Chico. A firing range exists to the S of this port and submarines exercise in the area.

From the east From Cabo de Palos follow the land keeping a good watch out for fish farms, which proliferate in this area especially off Portman and Cala de Gorguel. Pass south of Cabo del Agua and Islote de Escombreras and steer parallel to the new breakwater until the entrance to Cartagena proper opens up. It is recommended to keep well clear of all the ongoing construction work Although the port may be still used in dire emergency one will normally be sent away to the marina.

GPS approach

Steer to ⊕61 from the southerly sector and make towards ⊕62. Leave Bajo de Sta. Anna to starboard and make for the end of the Dique de la Curra.

Anchorages

Anchoring is forbidden in the harbour or its immediate approaches. Anchoring is possible in Rincón de la Salitrona behind and to N of Cabo Tiñoso, El Portús 4M to W of the harbour, Algameca Chica and Cala Cortina (pay attention to rock on N side). Algameca Chica is smelly and may have fishing nets. Cala Cortina has a rocky bottom. Expect to be moved if you finish up in a defence or commercial area.

Entrance

Straightforward but check that there are no large vessels entering or leaving port.

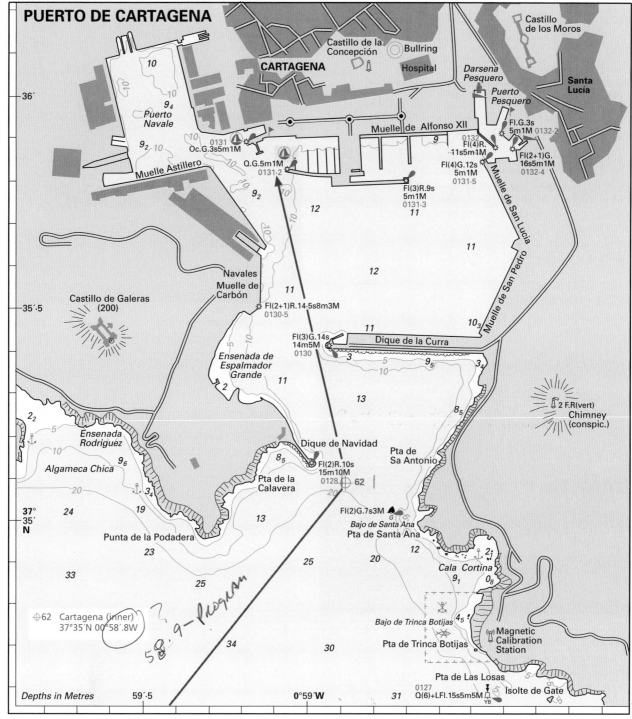

Plan 31a

Berths

Go to the Marina, some surge from ships.

Charges

Low.

Facilities

Maximum length overall: 25m.

All types of repairs, mostly by the naval workshops; contact the marina for advice.

Cranes up to 20 tonnes; contact *capitán de puerto*.

Marine radio shop next to the Scandinavian Consul's office in the Muralla del Mar.

Several chandlers, two near Dársena Pesquera.

Charts from Esqui Náuticas, Campos.

Water and 230/380v AC on marina pontoons.

Gasoleo A and petrol at the marina.

Hypermarket 'Continente' about a kilometre away – ask for directions or take a taxi. Many varied provision shops and two markets in the town, none near.

Launderette in Plaza de San Francisco.

Communications

Murcia airport 30 minutes by taxi, international flights.

Railway to Murcia from FEVE and Los Nietos from RENFE station and bus services. An occasional service by sea to the Canary Isles.

☎ Area code 968. Taxi rank at marina.

32. Puerto de Portmán

Lights

0134 **Punta de la Chapa** Oc.3.5s49m13M tower on white
   building 8m
0134.5 **Breakwater head** Fl(2)R.6s6m3M Red post 4m
0134.3 **Bajo de la Bola** Q(6)+LFl.10s5M ⚓ card buoy 4m

Silted up port with fish farms

Called Portus Magnus by the Romans, Portmán has
been completely silted up by effluent from the lead and
zinc mines inland. The scars in the hillside and the new
wind farm on the top of the hill inland make
recognition of Portmán relatively easy. There is a huge
fish farm to the west of the bay which leaves little space
to anchor. The small dinghy harbour, on the east side,
has a breakwater running out from the beach with a red
column at its end. The harbour is totally sheltered but
only has about 0.5m depth at the entrance and is only
for dinghies and RIBS. There is a *club náutico* on the
west side of the beach but there are no facilities at all in

Puerto de Portmán

the small village. Anchor between the two buoys in the
bay in about 4m and land on the beach by dinghy –
open between SE and SW.

⚓ CALA DEL GORGUEL

An unlit fish farm virtually blocks the entrance to this
cala, approach with care from the east. The *cala* is full
of floating gear and boats for the farm. Anchor (if there
is room) in small rocky cove in 5m mud off the beach.
There are off-lying rocks on W side of beach. Open
between SE and S. There are also fish farms, mostly
unlit, off-shore between La Manceba and Cabo Negrete.

Cala de Gorguel

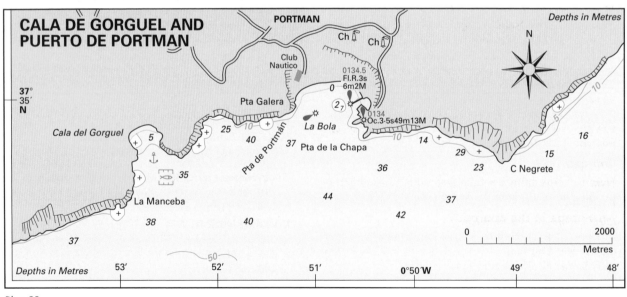

CALA DE GORGUEL AND PUERTO DE PORTMAN

Plan 32

33. Puerto de Cabo de Palos (Cala Avellán)

37°37′.8N 00°42′.8W

Charts

British Admiralty *774, 1700*. Imray *M12*
French *4718, 4719*. Spanish *464, 471*

⊕64 37°37′.5N 00°41′.8W

Lights

0137 **Espigón de la Sal** Fl(2)G.10s6m5M Green post 3m
0137·3 **Beacon** Fl(2)R.12s5m3M White post (4m), on red concrete base 1m
0136.9 **Escollo Las Melvas** Q(6)+LFl.15s5m5M ⍗ card post YB 3m
To the northeast
0136 **Cabo de Palos** Fl(2)10s81m23M Siren Mo(P)40s Grey round tower 51m
To the southwest
0136.5 **Los Punchosos** Q(3)10s8m5M Grey pole 5m

Port communications

VHF Ch 9. ☎ 968 56 35 15

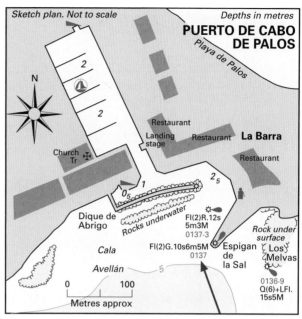

Plan 33   ⊕ 64 37°37′.65N 00°41′.95W

Small yacht and fishing harbour

A small yacht and fishing harbour located at the western edge of a prodigious tourist development running along the edge of the Mar Menor. It and its surroundings are crowded. A pleasant short walk out to the lighthouse. Excellent sandy beaches to N.

The zig-zag entrance requires care and is not really suitable for yachts over 12m.

Approach

From the south From Cartagena to Cabo de Palos the coast has steep rocky cliffs with a few sandy bays lying between points. The hinterland is rugged and hilly. There are no dangers more than 200m off-shore and the coast is steep-to. Portmán may be recognised by the vast hillside of open-cast mining behind it with a wind farm with 8 turbines on top of the hill. The large lighthouse at Cabo de Palos (81m) is easily identified. The harbour lies ½M to the W of it. Pay attention to off-lying rocks in the approach to the harbour.

From the north Isla Grosa (95m) is unmistakable. The coast as far as the prominent Cabo de Palos, is low, flat, sandy and lined with high-rise buildings. No dangers lie more than 600m off-shore. Round Cabo de Palos at 200m paying attention to isolated rocks and islets in the western part of the bay inside this distance, in particular, the rock just under water southeast of Espigón de la Sal, which is now marked by a S cardinal beacon, Las Melvas.

GPS approach

Steer to ⊕64 from a southeasterly quadrant and steer for the end of Espigón de Sal (approx. 0.33M).

Anchorage in the approach

The bottom to the S of Cabo de Palos peninsula is rocky out to the 20m contour. It is better to anchor in 5m sand to the N of this peninsula.

Entrance

Approach the harbour keeping the church, which has an unusual open-work, tripod tower with a bell on a cross bar and a cross on top, approximately NNW (between 325° and 345°), keeping the awash rock, Las Melvas, with its S cardinal pole, well to starboard. Turn to starboard around the end of the Espigón de la Sal (with its green post) keeping close to the quay, leaving the white pole on the 2m diameter red beacon well to port. Then turn to port round the end of the Dique de Abrigo and go alongside the quay parallel to the *dique*.

Berths

Although there are pontoons inside the harbour these are for locals only and visitor berths are alongside the quay in the outer harbour.

Facilities

Maximum length overall: 10m.
A slipway at N end of the harbour and a small slipway in outer harbour to W of entrance to inner harbour.
Chandlery and diesel in the village.
Water taps and electricity on quays.
A few local shops.
See also the entry on facilities under Mar Menor, page 98.

Communications

Bus services to Cartagena, Murcia and La Manga where there is a large supermarket. ☎ Area code 968.

⚓ CABO DE PALOS

Anchorage in bay to NW of Cabo de Palos open to NE in 5m sand and stones. Shops in nearby Playa Honda and at La Barra. Note there is now a traffic separation scheme (TSS) some 9 miles ESE of the lighthouse which should not seriously affect pleasure craft as they are generally closer to the point but one should be aware of its position.

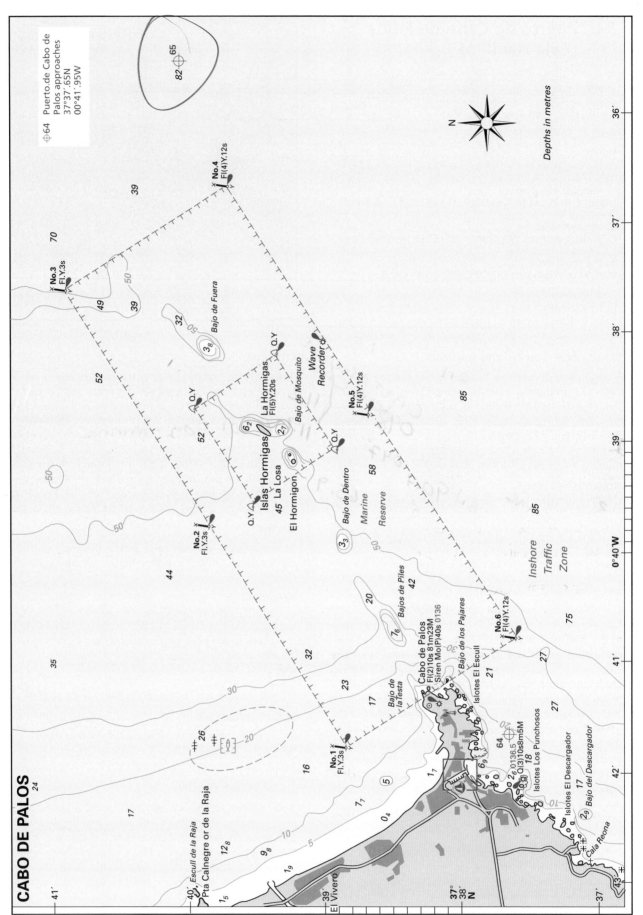

CABO DE PALOS

Puerto de Cabo de
Palos approaches
37°37´·65N
00°41´·95W

Depths in metres

No.3
Fl.Y.3s

No.4
Fl(4)Y.12s

Bajo de Fuera

Q.Y

La Hormigas
Fl(5)Y.20s

Islas Hormigas
La Losa

El Hormigon

Bajo de Mosquito

Wave
Recorder

No.5
Fl(4)Y.12s

Bajo de Dentro

Marine
Reserve

Q.Y

No.2
Fl.Y.3s

Bajos de Piles

Inshore
Traffic
Zone

Bajo de
la Testa

Cabo de Palos
Fl(2)10s 81m23M
Siren Mo(P)40s 0136

Bajo de los Pajares

No.6
Fl(4)Y.12s

Islotes El Escull

No.1
Fl.Y.3s

Islotes Los Punchosos

Q(3)10s8m5M

Islotes El Descargador

Bajo del Descargador

Cala Reona

Pta Calnegre or de la Raja
Escull de la Raja

El Vivero

N

Puerto Cabo de Palos – note underwater rock in the lower right-hand corner (now marked by beacon) looking N to Mar Menor on left and Isla Grosa on right

MARINE RESERVE CABO DE PALOS

This low sandy point with its 51m-high grey lighthouse has a large marine reserve some 2M by 4M extending to the ENE. It is marked by 6 buoys, the 3 northern ones are Fl.Y.3s while the 3 southern ones are Fl(4)Y.12s. There is an inner reserve, around Islas Hormigas, marked with 4 buoys Q.Y some of which may be missing at times. There is also a yellow, spherical wave recorder buoy at 37°39´.3N 00°38´.2W with a light Q(5)Y.20s.

⚓ PLAYA DE PALOS

Coastal anchorage along a 6M stretch of sandy beach in 5m sand and weed. Wide open E and facing wall to wall high-rise buildings – access to the coast road is through private properties. A shallow patch, Banco El Tabal (1.7m), is near the centre of the beach.

⚓ ISLA GROSA

Anchorage in the W quarter of the island to suit draught in clay with weed. The island, 95m high, offers some protection from sea and wind. There are houses on the W side and a landing place. This area is occupied by the military and approach within 300 metres is discouraged.

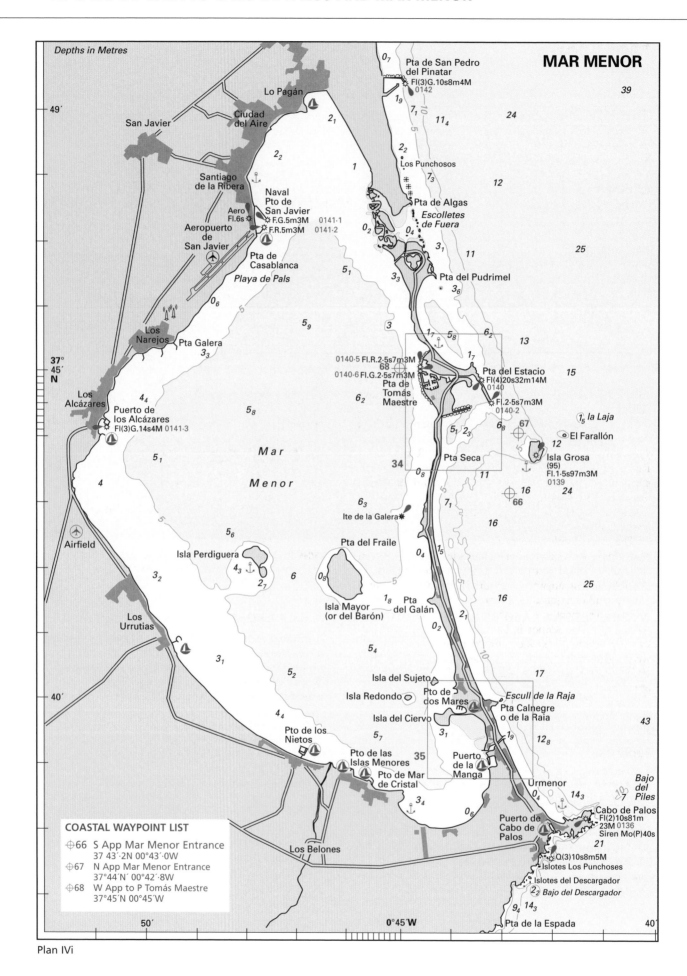

Depths in Metres

MAR MENOR

39

Pta de San Pedro
del Pinatar
Fl(3)G.10s8m4M
0142

Lo Pagán

San Javier

Ciudad
del Aire

2₁

24

7₁ 10

11₄

Santiago
de la Ribera

2₂

2₂

Los Punchosos

12

1

Naval
Pto de
San Javier
F.G.5m3M
F.R.5m3M

0141·1
0141·2

0₂

Pta de Algas
Escolletes
de Fuera

0₄

Aero
Fl.6s

Aeropuerto
de
San Javier

Pta de
Casablanca
Playa de Pals

0₆

5₁

3₃

3₁

11

25

Pta del Pudrimel

3₆

3

5₉

5₈

1₇

6₂

13

Los
Narejos

Pta Galera

3₃

0140·5 Fl.R.2·5s7m3M

0140·6 Fl.G.2·5s7m3M

68

Pta del Estacio
Fl(4)20s32m14M
0140

15

Los
Alcázares

4₄

5₈

Pta de
Tomás
Maestre

6₂

Fl.2·5s7m3M
0140·2

1₅ la Laja

Puerto de
los Alcázares
Fl(3)G.14s4M 0141·3

5₁

2₃

6₈

67

El Farallón

12

34

Mar

Menor

0₈

5₁

Pta Seca

11

Isla Grosa
(95)
Fl.1·5s97m3M
0139

16

66

24

4

5₁

6₃

7₁

16

5₆

Ite de la Galera

Airfield

Isla Perdiguera

4₃

Pta del Fraile

0₄

1₅

25

3₂

6

0₈

5

16

Isla Mayor
(or del Barón)

1₈

Pta
del Galán

2₁

Los
Urrutias

3₁

0₂

5₂

Isla del Sujeto

17

4₄

Isla Redondo

Pto de
dos Mares

Escull de la Raja

Pta Calnegre
o de la Raia

43

Pto de los
Nietos

5₇

Isla del Ciervo

3₁

1₉

12₈

35

Pto de las
Islas Menores

Pto de Mar
de Cristal

Puerto
de la
Manga

Urmenor

0₄

14₃

7 Bajo
del
Piles

3₇

0₆

Puerto de
Cabo de
Palos

Cabo de Palos
Fl(2)10s81m
23M 0136
Siren Mo(P)40s

Los Belones

Q(3)10s8m5M
Islotes Los Punchoses

Islotes del Descargador

2₂ Bajo del Descargador

9₄ 14₃

Pta de la Espada

50′

0°45′W

40

COASTAL WAYPOINT LIST

⊕66 S App Mar Menor Entrance
     37 43′·2N 00°43′·0W
⊕67 N App Mar Menor Entrance
     37°44′N 00°42′·8W
⊕68 W App to P Tomás Maestre
     37°45′N 00°45′W

Plan IVi

Mar Menor

An inland sea

An extraordinary inland sea some 12M long and 6M wide separated from the Mediterranean by a narrow band of sand, La Manga, from which a line of mini sky-scrapers rise. In addition to the intensive encouragement of tourists on land, yacht harbours are being built around the shores of the inland sea. The towns themselves are generally dull and the ports small and shallow but in terms of pottering around, anchoring off, small boating and so forth the Mar has its attractions.

Of the three entrances, one is deep and two very shallow. The major entrance is through Puerto de Tomás Maestre, which is the largest harbour of the Mar Menor and is supposedly dredged to 4m though 3m may be nearer the mark. Details of the approach and entrance are given later; the other two entrances are not described. The second largest harbour, San Javier in the NW, is a naval air force harbour and part of the air academy. It is not open to visitors. Seven small harbours are built around the Mar. A number of moorings have been laid but they are generally private.

The five islands are Isla Mayor or del Barón (102m), Perdiguera (45m), del Ciervo (46m) which is actually joined to La Manga by a causeway, Rondella or Redonda and del Sujeto. The first two are large and steep-to. The passage between Isla Mayor and La Manga has uncertain depths, generally less than 1m, and the passage between Isla del Sujeto and La Manga has even less water.

There are depths of 5 to 6m over the greater part of Mar Menor with gently shallowing sides and the bottom is sand or mud with weed. This makes anchoring possible almost anywhere, according to draught, but a strong wind can quickly kick up a nasty sea with marked currents. The north part is shallower than the south and though the Mar Menor is not tidal, the water level can vary by as much as 50cm or more over a period of weeks, driven by winds or changed by rain. In general terms, do not get on the shoreward side of any harbour entrance.

Beware floating nets; They may be set in a circle about 100m in diameter around a central buoy and supported by small floats which are difficult to see.

Facilities

The better shops of the area are along La Manga and at Los Belones. Shopping elsewhere is basic. There are banks on La Manga (see Puerto de la Manga) Los Nietos and at La Union.

Communications

San Javier airfield, besides holding the Air Force Academy, handles charter flights during the summer. A light railway runs between Los Nietos, La Union and Cartagena (where the station is fairly close to the Continente hypermarket).

34. Puerto de Tomás Maestre

Entrance from the Mediterranean 37°44′.3N 00°43′.4W (between beacons of Los Escolletes).
Entrance from the Mar Menor 37°44′.5N 00°43′.8W

Charts

British Admiralty *1700.* Imray *M12*
French *4719, 7295.* Spanish *4710, 471*

⊕66 32°43′.2N 00°43′0W
⊕67 37°44′N 00°42′.8W
⊕68 37°45′N 00°45′W

Lights

Entrance from seawards
To the south
0136.8 **Cabo de Palos** Fl(2)10s81m23M Siren Mo(P)40s Grey round tower 51m
0139 **Isla Grosa** 3Fl.1.5s97m3M Red round tower 2m
0138 **Islote La Hormiga** Fl(3)14s24m8M White tower 12m
Entrance from seaward
0140 **Punta del Estacio** Fl(4)20s32m14M White tower, black bands 29m
0140.2 **Los Escolletes** Fl.2.5s7m3M Concrete tower 5m
23954(S) **Buoy** Fl(2)G.5s3M Lateral Starboard
23956(S) **Buoy** Fl(2)R.5s3M Lateral Port
Note that the entrance channel may be marked by small buoys in high season
Canal del Estacio
0140.1 **Starboard Baliza** 3 F.GR.5m2M Green post 5m
0140.15 **Port Baliza** F.RG.2m Red post
Note that 0140.1 has a green sector to seaward and a red sector to the interior of the canal; 0140.15 has a red sector to seaward and a green sector to the interior of the canal.
Mar Menor entrance
0140.5 **Dique N** Fl.R.2s7m3M Concrete tower 4m
0140.6 **Dique S** Fl.G.2s7m3M Concrete tower 4m.
Note that the entrance channel may be marked with small buoys in high season

Port communications

VHF Ch 9. *Capitanía* ☎ 968 14 08 16 *Fax* 968 33 70 89
Email puertomaestre@puertomaestre.com
url www.puertomaestre.com

Tomas Maestre – canal, harbour, marinas

A modern marina has been built into the 1½ M long canal which connects the sea with the Mar Menor. In normal conditions approach and entrance are easy but because the area is shallow, entry should not be attempted in strong E or SE winds which kick up heavy seas. Facilities are good except that provision shops are limited. It forms a useful base for the exploration of the Mar Menor and as a staging point between the port of Cartagena and the harbours further N. Golf course and swimming pool nearby.

From June through September the entrance channel from the Mediterranean through the outer harbour may be marked with small buoys. The channel into and out of the Mar Menor itself may be marked with two green and two red lightbuoys joined by floating ropes with small white floats and yellow buoys. These were not in evidence in October 2004.

Approach from seaward

From the south Round the prominent and conspicuous Cabo de Palos at 200m off and follow the low-lying coast in a NNW direction at 1¼M. The narrow sand spit has wall-to-wall high-rise buildings along it with a small gap just before the approach to Tomas Maestre. The canal approach is 1M to NW of the off-shore Isla Grosa (95m).

From the north Cabo Roig is prominent and reddish in colour. It has a tower and some buildings above a small yacht harbour which lies on the S side of the cape. Two other small yacht harbours, which may be recognised, lie 1½M and 3M further S. Puerto de San Pedro del Pinatar is easily recognised by its high breakwater.

Follow the coast, which sprouts high rise buildings as Punta de Estacio is approached, in a SSE direction and at least ¼M offshore. Isla Grosa (95m) which is peaked should be easily recognised. Pass about half way between the island and Los Escolletes and then head N/NW for the entrance beacons. NE of Isla Grosa is the rock El Farallón and further out, a shoal of 1.3m – see charts. A shallow rocky spit sticks out a short distance south of Los Escolletes.

GPS approach

From the south steer to ⊕66 and from the north steer to ⊕67 and then steer to pass between the port and starboard buoys marking the canal entrance.

Anchorages in the approach

From the south Anchor to the west of Isla Grosa (see page 95).
From the north Anchor off Playa del Pudrimel (see page 109).
Outer harbour Anchorage (see note plan 34).

Canal Entrance

From seawards Having passed about halfway between Los Escolletes and Isla Grosa (coming from the north) or keeping Isla Grosa well to starboard (coming from the south) identify the 2 port and starboard buoys marking the entrance to the canal. Proceed on a west of north course to pass between the buoys and on through the outer harbour passing between the 2 posts marking the narrow canal entrance. In summer there may be a number of small buoys marking the channel through the outer harbour. Passing the posts the channel bends round to a WNW'ly course towards the swing bridge. Note that a falling barometer or an E sector winds can cause a 2 knot or more inflowing current; a rising barometer with W sector winds an outflowing current. The new lift bridge opens Monday to Friday at 1100 and 1700 and at 1100, 1400 and 1700 at weekends. The headroom is 7.5metres when closed. Clients of the marina may call VHF Ch 9 or call 968 14 07 25 at any time to have it opened. The canal continues for a further ½ mile past Tomás Maestre marina into the Mar Menor itself. In high season the channel into and out of the Mar Menor itself may be marked with 2 green and 2 red lightbuoys joined by floating ropes with small white floats attached.

From Mar Menor Straightforward between the pier heads but beware traffic.

Marina Entrance

The yacht harbour is on the south side of the canal, opposite the workshop area which has conspicuous working hangars.

Berths

Normal stern-to berths are available. Usually someone is around to tell you where to go. Otherwise, make up where you can and if nobody moves you, go to the *capitanía* under the entrance archway (a long way from most of the marina) to confirm your location.

Charges

High in Summer, medium in winter.

Facilities

Maximum length overall: 22m.
Facilities for most types of repairs (the boatyard is expensive).
100-tonnes slipway.
50 and 15-tonne travel-hoists.
5-tonnes crane.
Chandlers (also provide gas and one which repairs sails).
Water on quays and pontoons.
Shower block on pontoon.
220 and 380v AC on pontoons and quays.
Ice on fuel quay or from office.
Gasoleo A and petrol (the fuelling jetty is at the entrance and may be an awkward lie if there is a current running in the canal).

Communications

☎ Area code 968. Taxis ☎ 56 30 39. There may be an hourly bus to La Manga for shopping.

Tomás Maestre marina from south

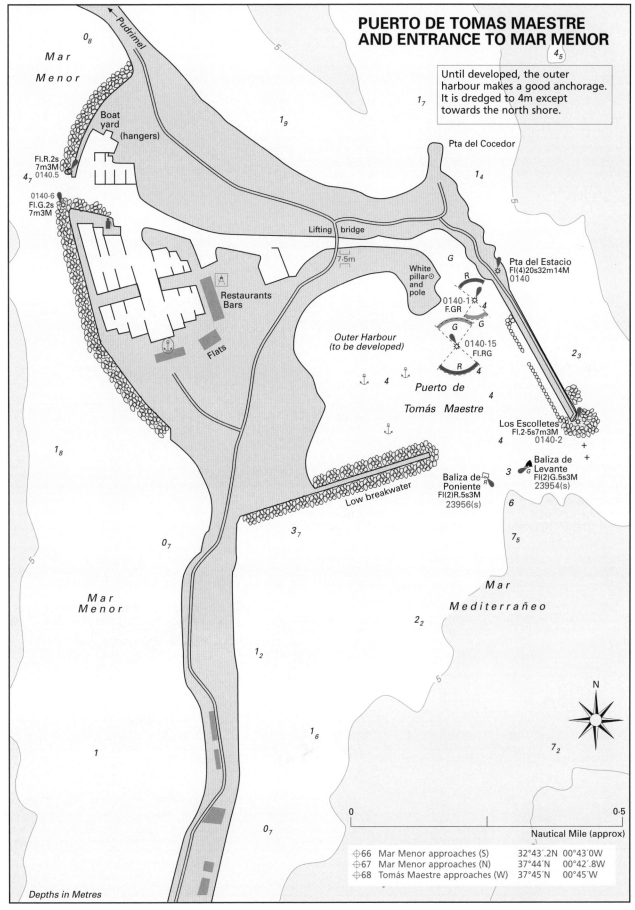

**PUERTO DE TOMAS MAESTRE
AND ENTRANCE TO MAR MENOR**

Until developed, the outer harbour makes a good anchorage. It is dredged to 4m except towards the north shore.

Mar Menor

Pudrimel

0₈

Boat yard
(hangers)

Fl.R.2s
7m3M
4₇ 0140.5

0140·6
Fl.G.2s
7m3M

1₉

1₇

4₅

Pta del Cocedor

1₄

Lifting bridge

7.5m

White pillar⊙ and pole

G

R

0140·1☀
F.GR

G   G

Pta del Estacio
Fl(4)20s32m14M
0140

4

Outer Harbour
(to be developed)

R

0140·15
Fl.RG

4

Puerto de

Tomás Maestre

2₃

4

Los Escolletes
Fl.2·5s7m3M
0140·2

+

+

R

4

Baliza de Levante
Fl(2)G.5s3M
23954(s)

3

Baliza de Poniente
Fl(2)R.5s3M
23956(s)

6

Restaurants Bars

Flats

Low breakwater

3₇

1₈

0₇

7₅

Mar

Mediterrañeo

2₂

1₂

1₆

1

0₇

0₇

N

7₂

Depths in Metres

0

0.5

Nautical Mile (approx)

⊕66	Mar Menor approaches (S)	32°43′.2N	00°43′0W
⊕67	Mar Menor approaches (N)	37°44′N	00°42′.8W
⊕68	Tomás Maestre approaches (W)	37°45′N	00°45′W

Plan 34

Tomás Maestre from the southeast

Tomás Maestre from the east

35. Puerto de Dos Mares

37°40´N 00°44´.5W

Shopping stop off

May be useful for shopping along La Manga. Limiting factors are a depth of about 1·9m and maximum length overall length of about 12m. It may pay to investigate by dinghy before entering.

Approach

There is no channel between Isla Sujeto and La Manga. Enter between the red and green buoys on the north side of the entrance, with 1.9m in the channel.

Berth

Bows to floating pontoons.

36. Puerto de la Manga

37°38´.8N 00°43´.6W

Lights

0140.7 **Breakwater head** Iso.R.40s Grey post 5m.
0140.72 **Right bank** Iso.G.40s Grey post 5m

Port communications

Club Náutico la Isleta ☎/*Fax* 968 14 53 39

A private club

A private club where visitors are made welcome though not particularly encouraged. If in doubt about depths, a visit by dinghy would pay off.

The south and east sides of the harbour are beaches used for bathing.

Approach

The passage east of Isla Mayor should only be taken with local knowledge and there is no passage east of Isla

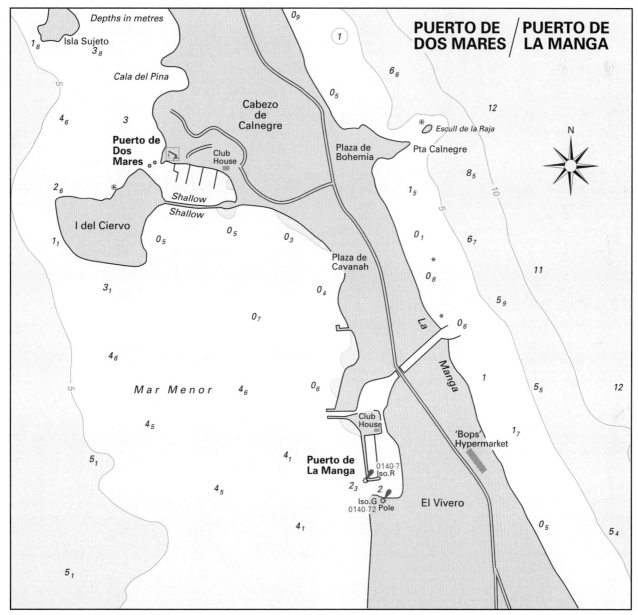

Plan 35

Puerto de la Manga

Plan 37

del Sujeto. It is best to keep west of those two and of Redonda as well.

Entrance

Said to be 1·8m. Come in from the west. The harbour wall is marked 'Club Náutico La Isleta' and the entrance is at the southern end. Keep between the line of buoys, if placed (they are all likely to be small, red and spherical).

Berth

Bows-to piers.

Facilities

Maximum length overall: 12m.
Water and electricity at the berths.
The shops of La Manga: Bop's hypermarket, shops, banks at Plazas Cavanah and Bohemia.
Club Náutico La Isleta has a bar, showers and a part-time restaurant.
Do not pump ship in harbour.

37. Puerto de Mar de Cristal

37°38'.7N 00°45'.7W

Lights

0140.8 **Breakwater head** F.R.5m Red and white round tower 5m
0140.75 **Contradique** F.G.5m White tower, green bands

Port communications

VHF Ch 9. ☎ 968 58 33 00.

Small and shallow harbour

A small artificial harbour built as a part of a housing development and located on the SE corner of the Mar Menor. Easy to approach and enter. The facilities are limited.

Approach

In the NW, from the hill El Carmole (112m) and the tower of Los Urrutias the coast is almost straight, low and flat, and most is under cultivation. The village of Los Nietos, the harbours of Los Nietos and Islas Menores may be seen. In the SE, Punta de Plomo is low

and has a lone house on it.

Entrance

When entering keep as far off-shore as is consistant with entering as the water shoals sharply near the shore.

Berths

The arrivals berth is alongside the North Wall, immediately to port on entering. If no room there, go alongside another boat and ask ashore.

Facilities

Maximum length overall: 10m.
Slipway in SW corner of the harbour.
Water on quays and pontoons.
220v AC points on quays and pontoons.
Club Náutico de Mar de Cristal.
Some shops in housing development.

Puerto de Mar de Cristal

38. Puerto de las Islas Menores

37°38´.9N 00°46´.1W

Lights

0140.85 **Outer breakwater** F.G White tower, green bands
0140.851 **Breakwater head** F.R White tower, red bands

Port communications

Puerto ☎ 968 13 33 44

Small, shallow, private harbour

A small shallow private harbour suitable for dinghies, runabouts and small yachts. Easy to approach and enter. It has a palatial yacht club with associated facilities, but other facilities are limited. It is not a place for cruising yachts.

Approach

From the SE Punta de Plomo with a single large house can be identified as can the Puerto de Mar de Cristal ¾M further E. The harbour projects into the Mar Menor and its large clubhouse is conspicuous.

From the NW The low, flat and almost straight coast is relatively featureless with the exception of El Carmoli (112m) and the town of Los Urrutias, until the large yacht harbour Puerto de Los Nietos, which is conspicuous, is reached. ¾M beyond it lies the low Punta Lengua de Vaca and ½M beyond lies the Punta de Los Barrancones with the harbour on the point.

Anchorage in the approach

Anchor to suit draught to N of this harbour in sand and weed.

Puerto de las Islas Menores

Entrance

Straightforward but harbour shoals to 1m.

Berths

Secure to the inside of Dique del Norte and ask at yacht club for allocation of a berth.

Facilities

Maximum length overall: 8m.
Slipway at yacht club.
Small davit-type crane at head of Dique del Norte.
Water from yacht club.
Small shops near harbour.
The Club Náutico des Islas Menores has bar, restaurant and
   showers.

39. Puerto de los Nietos

37°39´.2N 00°47´W

Lights

0140.9 **Muelle Norte NW head** LFl.R.5s5m White tower,
   red bands 3m
0140.92 **Muelle Norte E corner** F.R.4m Grey post 4m
0140.95 **Contradique head** Oc.G.3.5s5m White tower,
   green bands 3m

Port communications

VHF Ch 4 or 9. *Capitanía* ☎ and *Fax* 968 56 07 37
Club Náutico de Los Nietos ☎ 968 13 33 00

Large yacht harbour

A large artificial yacht harbour. Yachts can winter ashore or afloat.

Approach

Pass between Islas Perdiguera and Mayor and head south. El Carmoli hill to the west will identify Los

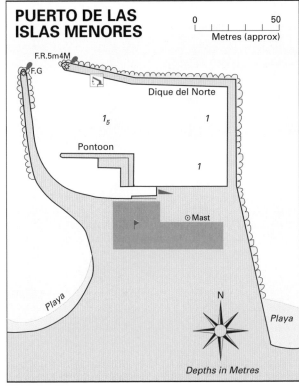

PUERTO DE LAS ISLAS MENORES

0   50
Metres (approx)

F.R.5m4M
F.G

Dique del Norte

1₅   1

Pontoon

1

⊙ Mast

Playa

N

Playa

Depths in Metres

Plan 38

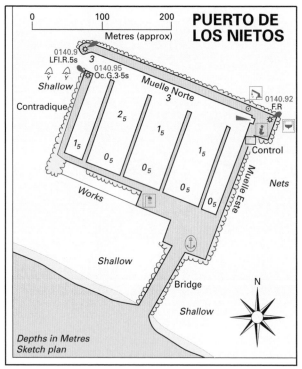

Plan 39

Puerto de los Nietos

Urrutias. To the south, there is a small, dark wood, just east of the Rambla del Beal. Los Nietos is just east of the wood. The breakwater and masts will be seen as the coast is approached.

Anchorage in the approach

Anchorage is possible in sand and weed anywhere to N of this harbour to suit draught.

Entrance

Approach the head of the Muelle Norte on a S heading. There may be a line of multi-coloured buoys to leave to starboard. Do not go inshore of the harbour entrance as the water shoals quickly.

Berths

Secure alongside the Muelle de Espera, immediately to port on entry (go alongside another if necessary) and ask at the office. Alternatively, call on Ch 9 or 4 before entering.
Charges
Low.

Facilities

Maximum length overall: 15m.
Slipway at the NE side of yacht club.
An 8-tonne crane at NE corner of the harbour.
A 28-tonne mobile crane.
Hardstanding for winter lay-ups.
Water taps on quays and pontoons (but tastes funny).
220v AC points on quays and pontoons.
Club Náutico de Los Nietos, ☎ 968 13 33 00, has a restaurant open at weekends, bar, showers and washing machine.
Supermarkets, ferreterías with gas, Post Office, butcher, baker, bank etc. at Los Belones, 2½km SE.
Bank without a cash point.

Communications

Light railway to Cartagena (where the station is close to the hypermarket Continente). ☎ Area code 968.

40. Puerto de los Urrutias

37°40′.6N 00°49′.3W

Lights
0140.97 **Dique de Levante head** F.R
0140.972 **Breakwater head** F.R

Port communications
VHF Ch 9. Club de Regatas Mar Menor ☎ 968 13 44 38.
Email informacion@clubregatasmarmenor.com
url www.clubregatasmarmenor.com

Easy approach but shallow

The harbour lies at the SE end of the village of Urrutias which is underneath the odd-shaped El Carmoli hill. Easy to approach and enter. Spanish holiday village with a good beach to the N of the harbour.

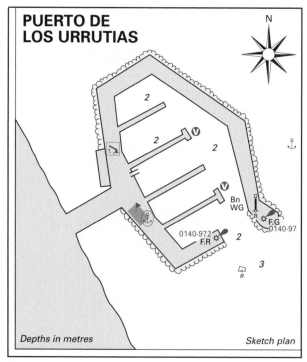

Plan 40

Puerto de los Urrutias

Approach

From the north Past the airport and Los Alcázares. There is a conspicuous hangar-type building before the village and the yacht club is the last major building.

From the south Urrutias lies 2.5M NW of Puerto de los Nietos.

Anchorage

N or S of entrance to suit draught in sand and weed.

Berths

Secure to east wall and ask at the club secretary's office.

Charges

High.

Facilities

Maximum length overall: 15m.
Slipway by crane.
10-tonne crane.
Water taps on pontoons and quays.
220v AC on pontoons and quays.
A few shops in the village, street-market every Thursday.
Club de Regatas Mar Menor has a restaurant, bar, showers and washroom.
Dinghy sailing school.

Communications

☎ Area code 968.

⚓ ISLA PERDIGUERA

Anchor to the SW in 4m sand and mud. Beach bars ashore at weekends.

41. Puerto de los Alcázares

37°44′N 00°50′.9W

Lights

0141.3 **Dique Este head** Fl(2)G.12s4M White tower, green top
0141.4 **Dique Oeste** Fl(2)R.14s4M White tower, red top

Port communications

Club Náutico los Alcazares VHF Ch 9 ☎/Fax 968 57 51 29

Shallow harbour

A shoal (2m or less), artificial yacht harbour alongside an attractive old Victorian-type seaside resort, least touched by mass tourism. Easy to approach and enter. The coast is lined with many piers and shelters of various sizes to enable the inhabitants to fish and bathe. The nearby Aeropuerto de San Javier, its associated harbour and a large amount of land around are part of the Spanish Naval Air Academy and should not be entered.

Approach

From the SE Follow the low flat coast in a NE–N direction. The town of Los Urrutias and El Carmoli (112m), a conical hill, will be recognised. Further E a light aircraft field and a camp site may be seen. Just S of this harbour is a long pier and some large old hangars. The houses of the town of Los Alcázares will be seen from afar.

From the NE The large town of Santiago de la Ribera and the Aeropuerto de San Javier, which has a large

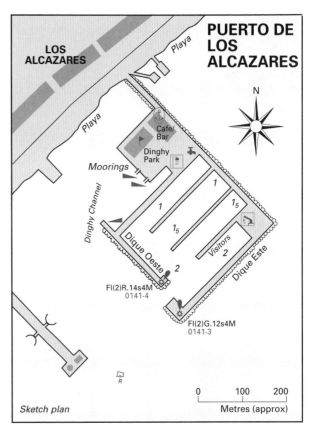

Plan 41

Puerto de los Alcázares

shallow harbour alongside (entrance forbidden), will be easily recognised. Punta Galera and Punta de las Olas are not easily identified. The town of Los Alcázares can be seen from afar.

Anchorage in the approach

Anchor off the harbour in suitable depth to suit draught in sand and weed.

Entrance

Approach the head of Dique Este on a course between W and NNW. A line of white buoys parallel to the military espigón marks the boundary of the no-go area; leave them to port.

Berths

Go alongside the pier immediately opposite the entrance and ask at the office.

Facilities

Maximum length overall: 15m.
Simple repairs possible.
Two slipways and a crane at E corner of the harbour.
Water taps on quays and pontoons.
220v AC points on quays and pontoons.
Many shops in the town including supermarket and a large market.
The Club Náutico de Mar Menor at N corner of harbour has limited facilities but they include open-air showers and a bar.

Communications

Excellent and regular buses to Alicante, Cartagena. Coaches to Bilbao, Madrid, Barcelona. ☎ Area code 968.

⚓ PUERTO SANTIAGO DE RIBERA

An open anchorage off a large town serving the air base and the air port and with tourist interests. The *club náutico* has a pier for small boats.

42. Puerto de Lo Pagan

37°49′N 00°47′W

Lights

24016.4(S) **Entrance buoy** Fl(2)G.7s Lateral starboard
24016.5(S) **Entrance buoy** Fl(2)R.7s Lateral port
0141.55 **Dique head** F.G. Green post
0141.455 **Contradique head** F.R. Red post

Port Communications

Club náutico ☎ 968 18 69 69 *Fax* 968 18 69 58
Email info@clubnauticolopagan.com
url www.clubnauticolopagan.com

New marina but shallow

A new marina has been developed over the last few years off Lo Pagan at the north end of the Mar Menor. It has berths for about 350 craft and has reasonable shore side facilities of fuel, cranage and a slip. The water is very shallow at the north end of the Mar Menor and there are buoys to indicate the 'deep' entrance channel which is understood to be 1.8 metres, but great care should be exercised in the approach with constant attention paid to the echo-sounder.

Berths

It is essential to call ahead to enquire whether there is a berth available for your vessel, as there are only 20 berths allocated for visitors and these are mostly taken in the high season.

Facilities

All facilities are available for the yachtsman and there is reasonable shopping in the nearby town of Lo Pagan. Close by is the 'Parque Regional de las Salinas' which is an important wetlands area which is of great interest to birdwatchers. Note however, that if one does not wish to enter the Mar Menor, Puerto de San Pedro del Pinatar (see below) is but 3 kilometres to the east and is also close to this park.

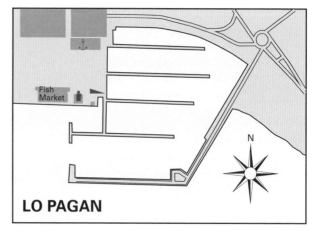

LO PAGAN

Plan 42

Planning guide and distances

⚓ Anchorage

Miles	Harbours & Anchorages	Headlands
21M	⚓ Puerto Genovés	Cabo de Gata
	⚓ Ensenada de San José/Cala Higuera	
	23. Puerto de San José page 71	
	⚓ Ensenada de los Escullos	
	⚓ Ensenada de Rodalquilar	
18M	⚓ Las Negras	
		Punta de la Polacra
	⚓ Cala de San Pedro	
	⚓ Ensenada de Agua Amarga	
	24. Puerto de Carboneras page 74	
	⚓ 2 commercial harbours – emergency only and Puerto Pescaro	
14M	⚓ Marina de las Torres	
	⚓ Punta de la Media Naranja	
	25. Puerto de Garrucha page 75	
5M	⚓ Palomares y Villaricos	Río de Aguas
	26. Puerto de Villaricos page 78	Río Almanzora
0.3M	**27. Puerto de Esperanza** page 78	
	⚓ Anchorages 2M to N of Río Almanzora	
14M	⚓ Ensenada de Terreros	
	⚓ Punta Parda	
	28. Puertos de Aguilas y del Hornillo page 81	
		Punta Parda
19M	⚓ Cala Bardina	
	⚓ Ensenada de la Fuente	
	29. Puerto Deportivo de Mazarrón page 84	
3M		Punta Negra
	30. Puerto de Mazarrón page 86	
	⚓ Ensenada de Mazarrón	
	⚓ Cala Cerrada	
15M	⚓ Rincón de la Salitrona	
	⚓ El Portús	Cabo Tinoso
	31. Puerto de Cartagena page 89	
8M	⚓ Cala del Gorguel	
	32. Puerto de Portmán page 92	
9M		Cabo del Agua
	33 Puerto de Cabo de Palos page 93	
	⚓ Cabo de Palos	
8M	⚓ Playa de Palos	
	⚓ Isla Grosa	
	34. Puerto de Tomás Maestre page 97	
	35. Puerto de Dos Mares page 101	
	36. Puerto de la Manga page 101	
	37. Puerto de Mar de Cristal page 102	
	38. Puerto de las Islas Menores page 103	
	39. Puerto de los Nietos page 103	
5M	**40. Puerto de los Urrutias** page 104	
	41. Puerto de los Alcázares page 105	
	⚓ Puerto Santiago de Ribera	
	42. Puerto de Lo Pagan page 106	
	⚓ Ensenada del Esparto	

Miles	Harbours & Anchorages	Headlands
3M	**43. Puerto de San Pedro del Pinatar** page 109	
3M	**44. Puerto de la Horadada** page 111	
2M	**45. Puerto de Campoamor** page 112	
5M	**46. Puerto de Cabo Roig** page 113	
9M	**47. Puerto de Torrevieja** page 114	
	48. Marina de la Dunas (Puerto de Guardamar)	
6M	page 116	Cabo Cervera
	⚓ Bahía de Santa Pola	
	49. Puerto de Santa Pola page 118	
2M	**50. Puerto de Espato** page 120	
4M	**51. Puerto de Isla de Tabarca** page 120	
11M	**52. Puerto de Alicante** page 122	
3M	⚓ Ensenada de la Albufereta	
	53 Puerto de San Juan page 126	
7M	⚓ Playa de la Huerta	
	54. Puerto de Campello page 127	
9M		Cabo de las Huertas
	55. Puerto de Villajoyosa (Alcoco) page 128	
6M	**56. Puerto de Benidorm** page 130	
	⚓ Ensenada de Benidorm	
	⚓ Cabezo del Tosal	
7M	⚓ Anchorage E of Punta de Canfali	
	⚓ Anchorage W of Punta de la Cueva del Barbero	Punta de la Esalata
	⚓ Anchorages NW of Punta del Albir	
		Punta del Albir
2M	**57. Puerto de Altea** page 132	
1M	**58. Puerto de la Olla de Altea** page 134	
1M	**59. Puerto de Mary Montaña** page 135	
2M	**60. Marina Greenwich (Mascarat)** page 136	
	⚓ Punta Mascarat	
2M	**61. Puerto Blanco** page 138	Cabo Toix
	⚓ Ensenada de Calpe	
	62. Puerto de Calpe page 140	
3M	⚓ Cala la Fosa	Punta Ifach
	63. Puerto de las Basetas page 142	
	⚓ Cala Canaret	
3M	⚓ Cala Blanco	
	⚓ Cabo Blanco	
	⚓ Cala del Dragon	Cabo Blanco
	64. Puerto de Moraira page 145	
	⚓ El Rinconet	
	⚓ Anchorages between Cabo Moraira and Jávea	
	⚓ La Grandadilla	
11M	⚓ Isla del Descubridor	
	⚓ Punta Negra	
	⚓ Isla del Portichol	Cabo de la Nao
	⚓ Cabo de San Martin	
	⚓ Cala Calce	
	⚓ Cala de la Fontana	
5M	**65. Puerto de Jávea** page 148	
	66. Puerto de Dénia page 152 Cabo de San Antonio	

V. COSTA BLANCA
Puerto de San Pedro del Pinatar to Dénia

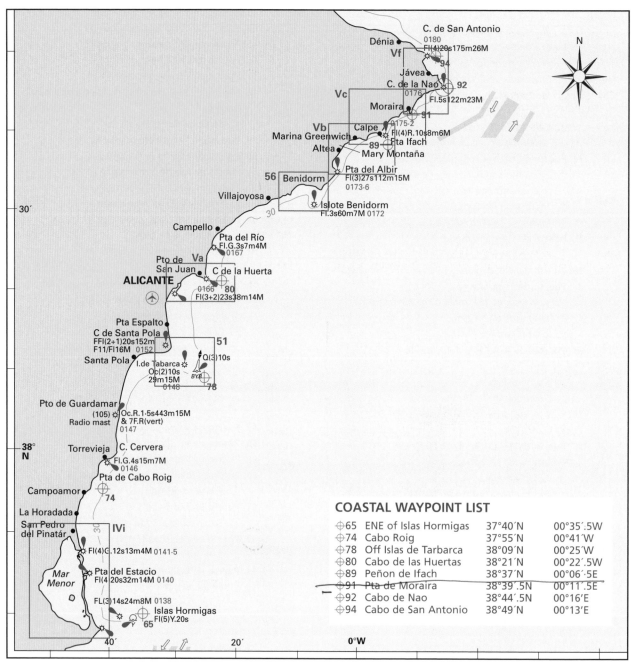

Plan V

PORTS

43. Puerto de San Pedro del Pinatar	52. Puerto de Alicante	60. Marina Greenwich (Mascaret)
44. Puerto de la Horadada	53. Puerto de San Juan	61. Puerto Blanco
45. Puerto de Campoamor	54. Puerto de Campello	62. Puerto de Calpe
46. Puerto de Cabo Roig	55. Puerto de Villajoyosa (Alcocó)	63. Puerto de las Basetas
47. Puerto de Torrevieja		64. Puerto de Moirara
48. Puerto de Guardamar	56. Puerto de Benidorm	65. Puerto de Jávea
49. Puerto de Santa Pola	57. Puerto de Altea	66. Puerto de Dénia
50. Puerto de Espato	58. Puerto de la Olla de Altea	
51. Puerto de Isla de Tabarca	59. Puerto de Mary Montaña	

43. Puerto de San Pedro del Pinatar

37°49´.2N 00°45´.3W

Charts

British Admiralty *1700*. Imray *M12*
French *7295, 4719*. Spanish *471, 4710*

⊕70 37°49´.2N 00°44´.9W

Lights

0141.5 **Dique Norte** Fl(4)G.12s13m4M Green post 3m
0141.6 **Dique Sur** Fl(4)R.12s6m3M Grey mast 3m

Port communications

☎/Fax 968 18 26 78
Email puertosanpedro@puertosanpedro.com
url www.puertosanpedro.com

Modern marina

A 400-berth marina at San Pedro del Pinatar, which was built in the inner part of the harbour in 2001/2, has now been fully completed. There are 4 pontoons extending from the Dique Norte and a new quay has been built to virtually enclose the inner harbour. At the entrance to the new marina there is a 2.5m green post F.G to

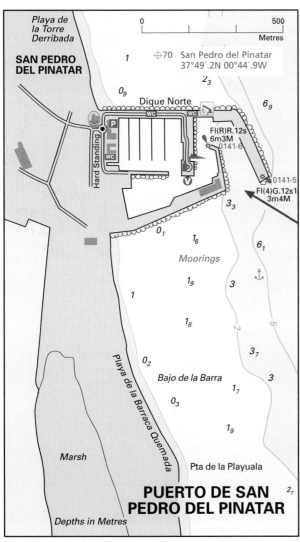

Plan 43

starboard and a 2·5m red post F.R to port. The visitors berth is alongside the end of the starboard-hand jetty and is reported to have a depth of at least 1.5 metres. The 2004 visit saw all shoreside facilities completed and San Pedro is now a fully working marina with all the usual facilities. There is a nice club, a small restaurant, a subaqua school, tennis and small shops all on site. However, out of season stores would probably have to be obtained in either the village or Lo Pagan which is some way away from the marina.

Approach

The high breakwater of Puerto de San Pedro del Pinatar can be seen from afar (and is a useful coastal mark).

From the south Follow the coast up from Punta del Estacio. Development along the sand strip bordering the Mar Menor dies away before the harbour is reached.

From the north Pass Punta de la Torre de la Horadada which has a tower on the point with buildings at its base and yacht harbour on its S side. There is a rocky reef off this head; keep at least 200m off. From there on, keep half a mile off-shore to avoid small rocky islets.

GPS approach

Steer to ⊕70 from the eastern sector and steer for the end of the breakwater (approx. 0.13M).

Entrance

Approach the end of the Dique Norte on a westerly heading rounding the head at 30 metres, keeping a close watch for fishing vessels leaving the harbour. Steer west of north and round the head of the Dique Sur keeping reasonably close to the Dique Norte. Steer south through the outer harbour, turning to starboard at the end of the internal quay.

Berths

Having entered the harbour moor to the end of the internal quay and enquire at the fuel berth or at the *capitanía* in the NW corner of the marina for berth availability.

Facilities

Maximum length 15 metres.
30-ton travel-hoist and crane.
Electricity and water at all berths.
Fuel.
Showers, WC and rubbish bins.
Club náutico
Bar and small shops for essentials.

ENSENADA DEL ESPARTO

This anchorage lies 4M south of San Pedro del Pinatar.
    Anchor in sand and weed off the Playa del Pudrimel, open to NE. Road along coast with housing development.

San Pedro del Pinatar

Puerto de la Horadada

44. Puerto de la Horadada

37°52′N 00°45′.5W

Charts

British Admiralty *1700.* Imray *M12*
French *7295, 4719.* Spanish *471*

⊕71 37°51′·8N 00°45′·3W

Lights

0142 **Dique de Levante head** Fl(3)G.10s8m4M Green and
     white column 6m
0143 **Inner spur head** Fl(3)G.10s9m4M Green and white
     column 6m
0143.5 **Contradique head** Fl(2)R.7s9m4M Red and white
     column 6m

Port communications

VHF Ch 9. *Capitanía* ☎ 965 35 16 87 *Fax* 968 19 02 40
Email torrehoradada@jazzfree.com

Shallow approaches to yacht harbour

A yacht harbour established in an old fishing anchorage
to S of Punta de la Horadada. It is well-protected from
all directions except S. Swell between W and S can make
the approach dangerous as the water is shallow but
otherwise it is easy to approach and enter. Facilities are
limited.

Approach

The approach to this harbour is shallow and strangers
should sound their way in.

From the south The long, low 10M-long sand strip that
separates the Mar Menor from the sea is unmistakable
as is Isla Grosa (95m) and the breakwater of the harbour
of San Pedro del Pinatar. Between Pinatar and
Horadada, 3M north, give the coast a ½ M berth to
avoid rocky islets. The Torre de la Horadada on a low
promontory has buildings at its foot and is conspicuous.
It has a rocky reef with exposed heads extending 150m
off it. In the approach, the harbour walls will be seen.

From the north Between the large harbour of Torrevieja
and Punta de la Horadada the coast is only moderately
high with rocky cliffs in places. The small promontory
of Punta Primo (or Delgada) lies between Torrevieja
and Cabo Roig. Cabo Roig is of reddish sandstone and
is prominent with a white tower and buildings on its
summit. A small yacht harbour lies on the S side of
Cabo Roig and another lies to the S of Punta El Cuervo
which is to S of Cabo Roig. There are a number of small
rocks and islets offshore along this section of coast and
a berth of ½ M is advised. The Torre de la Horadada is
conspicuous from the north and has a reef extending
some 150m to the NNE.

GPS approach

Steer to ⊕71 from the eastern sector and steer for the
end of the breakwater (approx. 0.15M).

Entrance

From a position 200m to S of the harbour entrance,
approach sounding continuously. About 50m from the
entrance change to a NW course. Give the inner spur
head at least 25m berth as rocks extend 10m west of it.

Plan 44

⊕71 Puerto de la Horadada
     37°51′.85N 00°45′.3W

Note the entrance frequently silts up, especially after SW
winds and the depth is often less than the 2.5m shown
on the plan. Great care must be exercised with constant
sounding on entry.

Berths

Secure to the first pontoon and ask at the *capitanía*.

Charges

Low.

Facilities

Maximum length overall: 12m.
Small slipway in the NW corner of the harbour with 1m off it.
5-tonne crane to starboard side of the entrance and a large
    mobile crane.
Engine mechanics – Volvo agency.
Water taps on quays and pontoons.
Showers and WC.
220v AC points on quays and pontoons.
Some shops in the village.
Gasoleo A and petrol.

Communications

Coastal bus service on main road. ☎ Area code 96.

45. Puerto de Campoamor (Dehesa de Campoamor)

37°53´.9N 00°45´.9W

Charts

British Admiralty *1700*. Imray *M12*
French *4719*. Spanish *471*
⊕72 37°53´·8N 00°44´·7W

Lights

0144 **Espigón Este** Iso.G.4s8m4M Green metal mast,
    white bands 6m
0144.2 **Contradique head** Fl(2)R.7s8m3M Red metal mast,
    white bands 6m

Buoys

Two small green conical buoys mark submerged rocks
    200m off the root of the contradique.

Port communications

VHF Ch 9. Club Náutico de Campoamor ☎ 965 32 03 86
Fax 965 32 03 88
Email cncampoamor@cncampoamor.com
url www.cncampoamor.com

Plan 45

⊕72 Puerto de Campoamor
      37°53´.8N 00°44´.7W

Harbour mainly for motor boats

A yacht harbour built primarily for motor boaters on the
site of an old anchorage. It is organised as a residential
club; there are a few berths for transit yachts but visitors
who stay for any length of time may be expected to join
the club, if found acceptable. Approach and entrance are
not difficult but care must be taken as it is shallow.
Facilities in the harbour and village cater for normal
requests. Swell from S–SW tends to enter the harbour.
Fine sandy beaches.

Approach

From the south The high breakwater of Puerto de San
Pedro del Pinatar is conspicuous. The low coast, which
should be given a berth of ½M or more to avoid isolated
patches of rocks and rocky islets, stretches as far as the
Punta de la Horadada which has a *torre* with a building
at its foot. The coast further N has low cliffs. Punta El
Cuervo, which has a shoal 50m off its eastern edge, is
inconspicuous unlike the high-rise apartment blocks
behind Puerto de Campoamor.

From the north The large Puerto de Torrevieja is easily
recognised. The coast to the S should be given a ½M
berth due to off-lying dangers; this coastline has low
rocky sandstone cliffs. Cabo Roig which is of a reddish
colour has a tower on its summit and a small yacht
harbour lies on its S side. Puerto de Campoamor lies just
under 2M to S. There is a shallow river valley just to N
of the harbour.

GPS approach

Steer to ⊕72 from the southeastern quadrant and steer
for the end of the breakwater (approx. 0.15M).

Entrance

Keep well away from the harbour walls until the heads
of the two *diques* are in line on approximately 320° and
then approach, sounding. There is a shoal patch (0.3m)
500m SSE of the harbour, on a line with the entrance of
approximately 157°–337°. When 50m away, divert to

port and then round the head of Dique de Levante.

Berths

Secure to the outer pontoon and ask at the control
office in a hut on the centre pontoon or at the yacht
club if no one is in the office.

Facilities

Maximum length overall: 20m.
Small hardstanding.
Slipway in the W corner of the harbour.
3-tonne crane also in the W corner of the harbour.
Water taps on the quays and pontoons.
220v AC points on quays and pontoons.
Gasoleo A and petrol.
Supermarket in the village.
Club Náutico de Campoamor on the W side of the harbour
    has a bar, showers etc.

Communications

Bus service on the main road. ☎ Area code 96.

Campoamor

46. Puerto de Cabo Roig

37°54′N 00°43′W

Charts

British Admiralty *1700*. Imray *M12*
French *4719*. Spanish *471*

⊕73 37°54′·6N 00°43′·7W

Lights

0145 **Dique de Levante head** Fl.G.3s9m4M Green and
white pole 6m

0145.5 **Contradique head** Fl(2)R.7s8m4M Red and white
pole

Inland to the North

0147 **Guardamar del Segura** 38°04′.4N 00°39′.7W, Aero,
Oc.R.1.5s443m15M and 7F.R(vert).

Port communications

VHF Ch 9. *Capitanía* ☎ 966 76 01 67 *Fax* 966 76 05 74.

Major reconstruction due completion 2005

A small, attractive yacht harbour at a well-established
anchorage, only open to the SW. It is tucked away on the
W side of Cabo Roig which is entirely given over to low-
rise, detached buildings and gardens. The beach to the
N is buoyed-off for swimmers. Inshore there is a small
village at some distance which has everyday supplies.
There is a castle nearby, sand and pebble beaches either
side of the harbour and a golf course at Villamartin, 5M.

Approach

From the south From Puerto de San Pedro del Pinatar
the coast northwards should be given a ½M berth as
there are islets and submerged rocks. Puerto de Torre de
la Horadada can be recognised by the tower and
buildings on the top of the point of the same name.
From here low rocky cliffs stretch 2M to Punta El
Cuervo where there is another yacht harbour, Puerto de
Campoamor, backed by a group of high-rise apartment
buildings. 1½M further along the coast to N is the
reddish sandstone Cabo Roig with a large white tower
surrounded by trees and villas. The harbour is to SW of
the point below the tower.

From the north The Bahía de Santa Pola is 14M wide.
The coast is low in the N half and has low rocky cliffs
in the S. Sierra de Callosa (547m), 11½M to WNW of
Guardamar, a town on the coast 5M to N of Cabo
Cervera, is a good landmark as is the radio mast at
Guardamar del Segura. The breakwaters of Puerto de
Torrevieja and the town of the same name are
conspicuous. 2M to S of this harbour is Punta Prima (or
Delgada) which has rocky cliffs and 2M further on is
the prominent Cabo Roig which has a white tower on
its summit. The harbour lies SW of the tower.

GPS approach

Steer to ⊕73 from the southern sector and steer for the
end of the breakwater, sounding carefully (approx.
0.1M).

Entrance

Sand often builds up off the head of the Dique de
Levante and it is wise to give it a good 30 metre berth.
There may be a small green buoy near the end of the

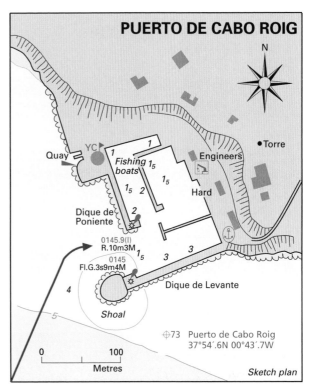

PUERTO DE CABO ROIG

⊕73 Puerto de Cabo Roig
37°54′.6N 00°43′.7W

Sketch plan

Plan 46

dique, which signals the extent of the accumulated sand.
Care must be exercised on entry with constant sounding
recommended.

Berths

Secure to a pontoon T-piece and ask at the *capitanía* or
the *club náutico*.

Facilities

Maximum length overall: 12m.
Slipway on NE side of the harbour – 1.5m of water off it.
1-tonne crane beside the slipway.
Water taps on quays and pontoons.
220v AC points on quays and pontoons.
Supermarket in village.
Club Náutico de Cabo Roig has all normal facilities.

Communications

Bus service on main road 1M inland to Torrevieja.
☎ Area code 96.

Puerto de Cabo Roig

47. Puerto de Torrevieja

37°58´.3N 00°41´.2W

Charts

British Admiralty *1544, 1700.* Imray *M12*
French *4719, 6515.* Spanish *4710*

⊕75 37°57´·5N 00°41´·1W

Lights

0146 **Dique de Levante head** Fl.G.4s15m7M Octagonal
   tower 10m
0146.2 **Muelle de la Sal** Fl(3)R.11.5s11m2M Metal
   framework tower 6m
0146.3 **Pontoon head** F.R
0146.4 **Dársena Pesquera breakwater NW head**
   Fl(2)G.7s4m2M Green structure 3m
0146.6 **Club Náutico jetty E head** Fl(4)R.11s4m2M Red
   column 3m
To the north
0148 **Isla de Tabarca** Oc(2)10s29m15M White tower 14m
Inland to the north
0147 **Guardamar del Segura**, Aero Oc.R.1.5s 443m15M
   and 7F.R(vert).

Port communications

VHF Ch 06, 11, 14. Marina Internacional de Torrevieja SA,
☎ 965 71 36 50 *Fax* 965 71 42 66 *Email* marina.int@ctv.es.
Real Club Nautico de Torrevieja ☎ 965 71 01 12
Fax 965 71 08 82 *Email* info@rcnt.com *url* www.rcnt.com

Useful major harbour

A nice clean harbour with some good yacht berths on
pontoons, a good yacht club and an excellent anchorage
west of the marina (rare along the coast), but where
yachts have sometimes been banned by the
harbourmaster. This has been challenged by the local
yachtsmen but it seems to be a general feature all along
this stretch of coast which comes under the jurisdiction
of Valencia. The yacht harbour, Marina Internacional de
Torrevieja SA is on the northwest side of the harbour.
The commercial quay, Muelle de la Sal, handles large
quantities of salt. The approach and entrance are simple
and there is good shelter from winds except those from
S to SW which make parts of the harbour
uncomfortable. It is understood that plans are made for
an 890-berth marina off the Dique de Levante in the
eastern part of the harbour. It was stated that it was to
be ready in 2005 but as no work had commenced in
2004 it is difficult to believe that statement. However,
although all the berths are presently privately owned
and occupied in the marina there is a policy to allow
visiting craft to use berths that are unoccupied (unlike
many other harbours on this coast).

The town is of no great interest but it has several
restaurants and there are shops quite close to the
harbour. A visit to the saltworks, the 'Salt Cellar of the
World', is of interest. Good beaches on either side of the
harbour.

Torrevieja

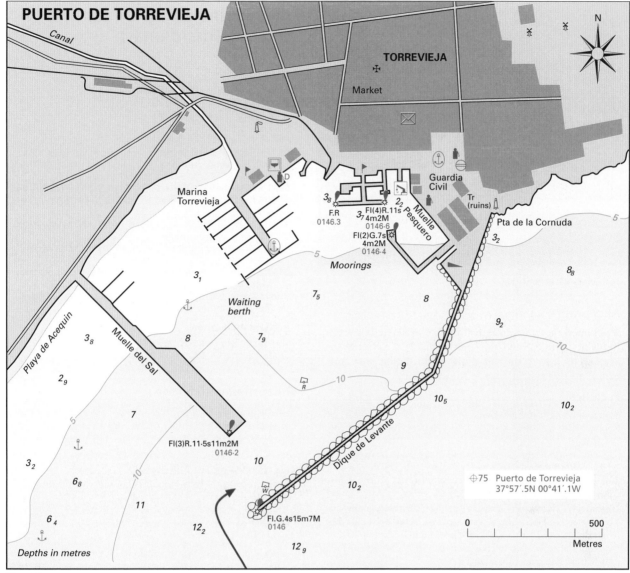

PUERTO DE TORREVIEJA

TORREVIEJA

Market

Guardia
Civil

Marina
Torrevieja

Tr
(ruins)

Pta de la Cornuda

3₈
F.R
0146.3

Fl(4)R.11s
4m2M
0146·6

2₂

Muelle Pesquero

3₇

Fl(2)G.7s
4m2M
0146·4

3₂

8₈

Moorings

5

7₅

8

9₂

9

Waiting
berth

8

7₉

Muelle del Sal

3₁

10

Playa de Acequin

3₈

2₉

7

10₅

10₂

R

Dique de Levante

9

⊕75 Puerto de Torrevieja
37°57´.5N 00°41´.1W

3₂

6₈

Fl(3)R.11·5s11m2M
0146·2

10

0   500

Metres

6₄

11

10₂

12₂

Fl.G.4s15m7M
0146

Depths in metres

12₉

Plan 47

Approach

From the south Isla Grosa (95m), off the breakwater of
Puerto de Tomás Maestre and near the centre of the
10M building strip separating Mar Menor from the sea,
is unmistakable as is the high breakwater of Puerto San
Pedro del Pinatar. The following three promontories all
have yacht harbours on their S sides: Punta de la Torre
de la Horadada with a tower on the point and buildings
around its base; Punta El Cuervo which has a group of
high-rise buildings; and the reddish-coloured Cabo Roig
which has a white tower. Keep at least ½M off the coast.
From Punta Prima (or Delgada) the rocky cliffs fall away
to a low, flat coast near Torrevieja. The breakwaters and
town of Torrevieja are visible from afar though quite
well inset from Cabo Cervera.

From the north Cross the wide Bahía de Santa Pola
which has cliffs in its S part. The Sierra de Callosa
(547m) 11½M to WNW of the town of Guardamar and
the radio mast at Guardamar del Segura are useful
marks. Cabo Cervera is prominent but low; to S of it are
several smaller rocky points with coves between. The

harbour breakwaters appear when these points have
been rounded.

GPS approach

Steer to ⊕75 from the southeastern quadrant and steer
for the end of the breakwater (approx. 0.4M).

Anchorage in the approach

Anchor just west of the Muelle Sal to suit draught but
keeping out of the way of the harbour entrance.

Entrance

Straightforward but fishing boats move at speed and, at
night, often without lights. Their wash can make the
outer berths at the marina uncomfortable.

Berths

Go the Marina Torrevieja or The Réal Club Náutico de
Torrevieja on the north side of the fishing harbour. The
pontoons at the root of the Muelle de Sal are for small
craft only as they are in very shallow water.

Torrevieja yacht harbour

Anchoring

It is hoped that anchoring will remain available between the Muelle de Sal and the marina but it is essential to keep well clear of the salt ships' manoeuvring area and expect to pay a small charge for anchoring.

Facilities

Maximum length overall: 40m.
Repairs and technical service area, contact yacht club for advice.
Slipway alongside the yacht club and a large one near root of Dique de Levante.
80-tonne travel-lift.
Cranes up to 12 tonnes.
Chandlery – Network Yacht & Rigging Services (run by an English couple) have a well stocked shop between the International Marina and the Club Nautico Marina. There is another chandler in the town and also one outside of town on the road to Cartagena.
Water taps on the pontoon and on the quay.
220v AC points on pontoons.
Gasoleo A and petrol.
Ice from factory near customs office or from club.
The Réal Club Náutico de Torrevieja has good facilities including bar, restaurants, lounges, terraces and showers. Visitors are made welcome.
Good shops and small market in the town.
Supermarket in street behind the garage on the N side of the main road in town.
Launderette in the marina or two streets back from the *club náutico*.

Communications

Rail and bus services. ☎ Area code 96. Taxi ☎ 571 22 77.

48. Marina de las Dunas (Puerto Guardamar)

38°06′.5N 00°38′.6W

Charts

British Admiralty *1700*. Imray *M12*
French *4719*. Spanish *472, 4721*

⊕76 38°06′.7N 00°38′.0E

Lights

0147 **Guardamar del Segura** , Aero, Oc.R.1.5s443m15M and 7F.R(vert). Antenna white and red bands 440m (light is 2.5M S and 0.5M inland of marina)
0147.5 **S Breakwater head** Fl(3)R.9s8m5M Red tower 5m
0147.51 **N Breakwater head** Fl(3)G.9s8m3M Green tower 5m
0147.52 **Middle breakwater head** Fl(4)G.11s8m1M Green tower on white base 5m
0147.7 **Starboard hand entrance** Fl.G.4s4m1M Green tower, red band, white base 4m
0147.72 **Port hand entrance** Fl.R.4s4m1M Red tower on white base 4m
Buoys A number of small yellow and white buoys mark the 3m channel into the marina.

Port communications

VHF Ch 9. *Capitanía* ☎ 965 97 19 38
Email marinadunas@terra.es

Quiet sheltered marina

The mouth of the Río Segura has been widened and a channel dug to the south of the old river mouth to give access to a 500-berth marina. The land approach is to the NW corner where a new road leads to the town of Guardamar – about 1km away.

The marina is fully operational with a café and some small shops.

Approach

From the south The large harbour and town of Torrevieja is easily recognised. To N of this harbour are a series of points with small *calas* between, the coast being rocky cliffs. The coast from Cabo Cervera to N is low and sandy. The town of Guardamar, which has a ruined castle, lies 1M to S of the mouth of the Río Segura which has rocky breakwaters. The radio mast Guardamar del Segura is 4½M to NNW of Cabo Cervera.

From the north Cross the Bahía de Santa Pola from Cabo de Santa Pola on a SW course leaving Isla de Tabarca to port and Puerto de Santa Pola to starboard, both of which are easily identified. 2½M to N of Río Segura is the Torre del Pinet off which at 2M ESE lies a fish farm. The coast is low and sandy.

GPS approach

Steer to ⊕76 from the eastern sector and steer for between the breakwaters (approx. 0.21M).

Entrance

Although the entrance has been dredged to 6m between the breakwaters it is liable to silting. Approach the mouth of the river, half way between the green and red towers at the ends of the breakwaters on a SW course, sounding carefully. Once inside the mouth keep

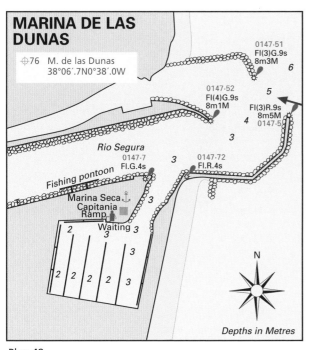

MARINA DE LAS DUNAS

⊕76 M. de las Dunas
38°06'.7N 0°38'.0W

0147·51
Fl(3)G.9s
8m3M
6

0147·52
Fl(4)G.9s
8m1M
5

Fl(3)R.9s
8m5M
4
0147·5

3

Río Segura
0147·7
Fl.G.4s
3
0147·72
Fl.R.4s

Fishing pontoon

Marina Seca ⚓
Capitania
Ramp
2
Waiting 3
3
3
3
3

2 2 2 2 3

N

Depths in Metres

Plan 48

between the lines of yellow buoys until abeam of the marina entrance, turn to port and enter the marina itself. The waiting berth is immediately to starboard on entering, in front of the *capitanía*.

Charges

Medium.

Facilities

Maximum length 15m.
Café and small shops in high season.
Electricity and water on pontoons.
Repair yard with crane and travel-hoist.
Hardstanding with covered hangers.
Fuel berth.
Showers and toilets.
Parking.
24-hour security.

⚓ BAHÍA DE SANTA POLA

Anchor to suit draught along the coast from Cabo Cervera to Santa Pola in sand, mud and stones with weed. Sandy beach with low cliffs, road inland and some development. Flamingos use the meres.

Río Segura and Marina de las Dunas

49. Puerto de Santa Pola

38°11'.2N 00°33'.8W

Charts

British Admiralty *473, 1700*. Imray *M12*
French *7304, 4719*. Spanish *4721, 472*

⊕77 38°10'.7N 00°33'.9W

Lights

To the south
0147 **Guardamar del Segura** , Aero, Oc.R.1.5s 443m15M
 and 7F.R(vert)
Harbour
0154 **Dique de Levante head** Fl.G.5s9m4M Green and
 white tower 5m
0155 **Contradique head** Fl(2)R.7s6m3M Red and white
 octagonal tower 5m
0154.3 **Espigón head** 38°11'.3N 00°33'.6W Fl(2)G.7s5m2M
 Green and white post 3m
To the east
24420(S) **Wave buoy** 38°15'.1N 00°24'.9W Q(5)Y.20s
 Yellow spherical
To the northeast
0152 **Cabo Santa Pola** FFl(2+1)20s152mF11M/Fl16M
 Square white tower with metal superstructure 15m vis
 over 270° arc

Port communications

Club náutico VHF Ch 9. ☎ 965 41 24 03 *Fax* 966 69 02 61
Email admin@cnauticosantapola.com
url www.cnauticosantapola.com

Busy fishing port with friendly club

An old Roman port and settlement, now a busy, small
fishing port with a good harbour for visiting yachts and
an unattractive tourist town. There are repair yards,
adequate shops and a good market. In high season, the
disco may be very noisy.

There is a 16th-century castle and for the energetic,
excellent views of the coast from Cabo de Santa Pola.
The *salinas* west of the town has flamingos, stilts,
avocets and other birds in winter and spring. Beaches on
both sides of the harbour.

Approach

From the south The town of Guardamar and nearby
Guardamar del Segura are easily identified, as is Cabo
de Santa Pola which lies to NE of this harbour. There is
a large yellow crane and building at the end of the
Dique de Levante and a large blue boat shed at the end
of the *contradique*.

From the north Cabo de Santa Pola and the Isla de
Tabarca are easily recognised. There is a large yellow
crane and building at the end of the Dique de Levante
and a large blue boat shed at the end of the
contradique.

Puerto de Santa Pola

GPS approach

Steer to ⊕77 from the southern quadrant and steer for the breakwater head (approx. 0.34M).

Anchorage in the approach

Anchor 200m to E of the Dique de Levante in 4 to 5 metres on mud and weed.

Entrance

Approach on a NE course and round head of Dique de Levante at 20m to starboard. Keep a watch for fishing boats leaving at speed.

Berths

There are 2 areas to berth, to the north are the public pontoons and to the west are the yacht club pontoons. The public pontoons are limited to craft of less than 8m maximum length and are administered by the *capitanía*. Normal 10m+ craft on approach should call the YC on VHF Ch 9 (or phone) for berth availability - there are no actual visitor berths but the club will do their best to find a berth for you but they are very limited, non-existent in high season.

Facilities

Maximum length overall: 15m.
Two major fishing boat repair and building yards located to the E of the harbour will undertake yacht repairs.
Hard at the shipyard and at N of harbour.
Two large slipways on the coast to E of the harbour.
Cranes at the shipyards and two on Dique de Levante. A special crane for yachts to S of pontoons.
Two small chandlers in the town near quays.
Water from taps on the quays and pontoons.
220v/380v AC in shipyard.
Gasoleo A.
Ice available in the town and on fuel quay.
Club Náutico de Santa Pola with bar, restaurant and swimming pool.
A number of fairly good shops in town and a good market.

Communications

Bus service on the main road. ☎ Area code 96.
Taxi ☎ 541 35 36.

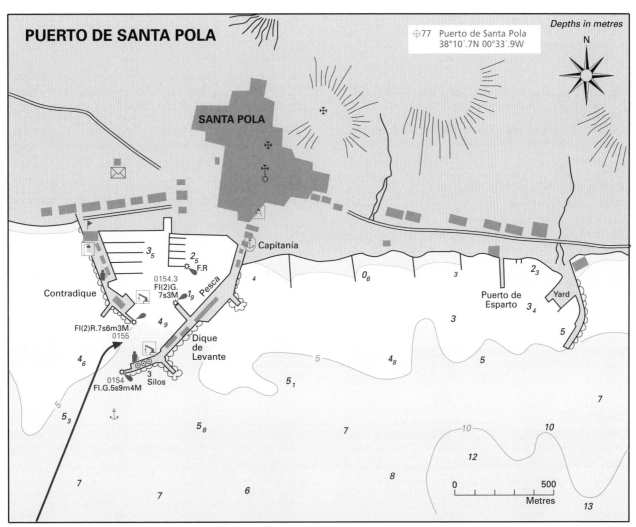

Plan 49

50. Puerto de Espato

38°11′.2N 00°38′W

Service station

This is more of a service station than a port, immediately to the north of Punta Espato. It has large slipways, hardstandings and a travel-lift.

Anchorage in the approach

A good anchorage in 7m sand and weed lies 500m to S of Punta de Espato.

Facilities

Some heavy engineering.
50-tonne travel-lift.
Hardstanding.

Puerto de Espato

51. Puerto de Isla de Tabarca (Isla Plana)

38°10′N 00°28′W

Charts

British Admiralty *473, 1700.* Imray *M12*
French *7304, 4719.* Spanish *472A, 472*

Lights

0148 **Isla Tabarca** Oc(2)10s29m15M White round tower 14m
Harbour
0149 **Dique-escolera** Fl(2)R.6s10m3M Metallic tower 4m
24290(S) **Bajo de la Nao** Q(3)10s5M ♦ card buoy 4m

Island and marine reserve

The island was once an old pirate base. They were eventually driven out and a small fortified village built to hold the island against further occupation and garrisoned by Spaniards who were exchanged prisoners of war. The inhabitants have, for generations, lived a very frugal, isolated life based on a small fishing fleet. There is an old fort from the reign of Charles III which is falling into disrepair and small beaches on the S and E side of the island.

A large area around this island is a reserve where fishing, diving and anchoring is forbidden (see chart page 121). The reserve is marked by 6 buoys, the northern three are Fl(4)Y.12s, while the southern three are Fl(5)15s, all with cross topmarks.

Approach

From the SW Make for the prominent Cabo de Santa Pola, passing about halfway between the extreme W of the island and the mainland. When the N coast of the island has opened up and the lighthouse bears 300°, approach with the lighthouse lined up with the head of the *dique*.

From the NE Aim at the centre of the island. In the closer approach the *dique* will be seen. Head for it on a SE-ly course.

Entrance

Go for the *dique* head between 300° and 315° and leave it 30m to port.

Berths

Secure to quay. In any swell, use an anchor to hold off. Leave space for ferries to the mainland and fishing boats near the head of the *dique*.

Anchorage

There are restricted anchoring zones, north and south of the harbour, over about 400m.

Facilities

Water from the village if you must – it is in short supply, stored in a cistern and issued each evening.
A few small shops in the village.

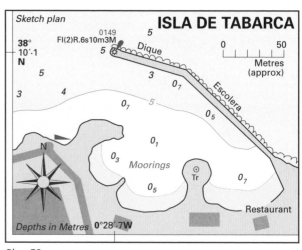

Plan 50

Isla Tabarca

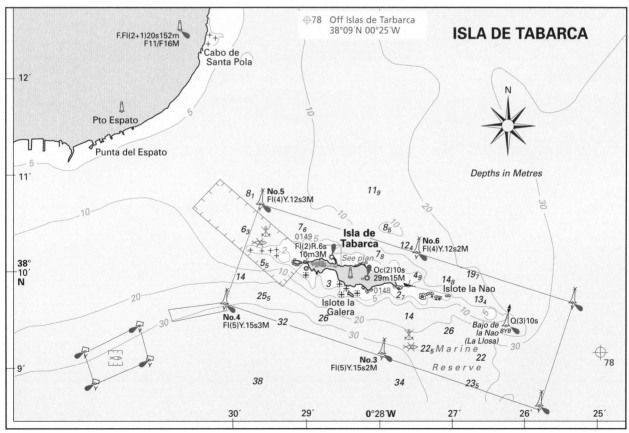

Plan 51

52. Puerto de Alicante

38°20´.3N 00°28´.9W

Charts

British Admiralty *469, 473, 1700.* Imray *M12*
French *6515, 7304, 4719.* Spanish *4722, 472A, 472*

⊕79 38°19´.35N 00°29´.1W

Lights

To the south
0152 **Cabo Santa Pola** FFl(2+1)20s152mF11M/Fl16M Square
  white tower with metal superstructure 15m vis over
  270° arc
0148 **Isla Tabarca** Oc(2)10s29m15M White round tower
  14m
Harbour
0158 **Dique de Abrigo de Levante head** Fl.G.5s14m11M
  Green truncated tower 9m
0158.4 **Terminal granelles sólidos SW end** Fl.R.5s9m6M Red
  cylindrical tower on white support 6m
0158.6 **Terminal granelles sólidos NE end** Fl(2)R.7s9m3M
  Red cylindrical tower on white base 3m
0159 **Muelle 11 S corner** Fl(2+1)R.22s8m5M Red tower,
  green band 6m
0159.3 **Muelle 11 N corner** Fl(3)R.8s8m3M Red tower on
  white base 6m
0160 **Muelle A SW corner** Fl(2+1)R.8s8m3M Red metal
  column, green band 6m
0162 **Muelle de Poniente head** Fl(4)R.11s7m3M Red and
  white post 4m

0161 **Muelles 8 and 10 head** Fl(3)G.8.5s8m3M Green tower
  on white base 6m
0160.5 **Real Club pontoon S head** Fl(2+1)R.21s3m2M Red
  post green band 2m
0160.6 **Real Club pontoon N head** Fl.R.5s3m3M Red post 2m
New Fishing Harbour
0157.5 **East breakwater head** Fl(3)G.9s10m
0157.7 **Outer breakwater head** Fl(3)R.9s6M
24510a(S) **Buoy W** Q(9) 15s3M ⌶ card buoy
24510b(S) **Buoy** Fl(2+1)R.21s3M
24510c(S) **Buoy** E Q(3)10s3M ♦ card buoy
To the east
0166 **Cabo de las Huertas** 38°21´.2N 00°24´.3W
  Fl(5)19s38m14M White tower 9m

Buoys
There are some large mooring buoys to SW of port and two
smaller black and yellow outfall buoys to E of the entrance.

Port communications

Port VHF Ch 14, 20 ☎ 965 20 22 55
Marina VHF Ch 9 ☎ 965 21 36 00 *Fax* 965 21 36 65
Email recepcion@marinaalicante.com
url www.marinaalicante.com
Real Club de Regatas ☎ 965 92 12 50 *Fax* 965 22 85 42
Email oficina@rcra.es *url* www.rcra.es

Alicante

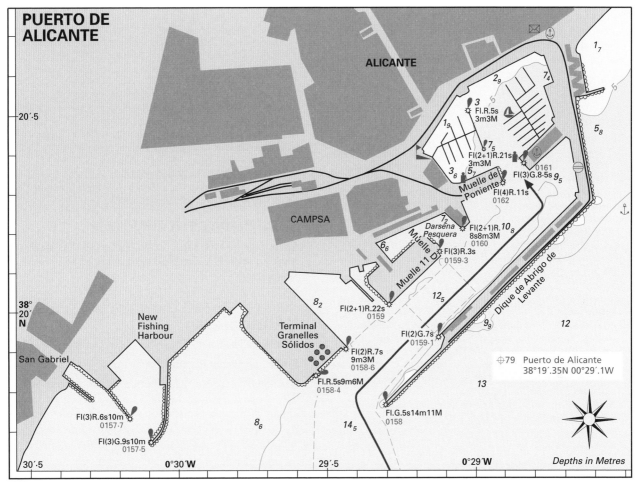

PUERTO DE ALICANTE

Plan 52

Large city, marina centrally located

A large commercial and fishing port, good facilities for yachtsmen which have encroached into the former anchorage. Easy to enter and obtain shelter in almost any conditions.

The new fishing harbour has now been completed to the SW of the port with a conspicuous new breakwater with sheds behind it. This is not a harbour for yachts so do not approach it at present. However infilling is still going on between the new breakwater and the Terminal Granelles Sólidos. Keep clear of any buoys that may be laid in the area.

The city, founded by the Carthaginians and named Akraheuta was the centre of the Punic empire. The Romans renamed it Lucentum from which the Moors derived Lekant and their successors, Alicante. It was obscured to British eyes until the early 18th century when it was assaulted by Sir John Leake and defended by General O'Mahoney; it became the seat of a British mercantile colony and was occupied by the British during the Peninsular War. More recently it was a Republican centre during the civil war; Primo de Rivera, founder of the Falange, was somewhat hurriedly executed in Alicante in 1936.

The festival, Foqueres de San Juan (St John's bonfires), on 24 June is worth attending. Good sandy beaches either side of the port. The beach to NE is the nearest.

Approach

From the south Round Cabo de Santa Pola, pass inside Isla de Tabarca and the hills behind the port topped by a castle will appear and be easily identified.

From the north Cabo de las Huertas is prominent with a whitish hill behind. Beyond it, three steep hills of a light yellow colour are noticeable.

GPS approach

Steer to ⊕79 from the southeastern quadrant and steer for the northern breakwater head (approx. 0.4M). Do not be tempted to steer for the new southern breakwater head which is now the main fishing harbour.

Entrance

Infilling work is going on to extend the Terminal Granelles Sólidos to the SW and to construct a new fishing harbour. A new *dique* has been constructed and there may be several buoys indicating the extent of the work. Keep well clear of this construction work. After rounding the Abrigo de Levante, follow it at 100m ignoring the first two entrances to port. The entrance to the inner harbour is the third gap. Keep clear of ships entering and leaving.

Berths

Call the marina on VHF Ch 9 (or phone) and moor at the waiting berth just to the NE of the fuel berth, immediately to starboard on entering the marina. Go to the office with your documents to arrange a berth, spaces are very limited but the marina does its best to accommodate visitors. All berths have finger pontoons.

Charges

High.

Facilities

Maximum length overall: 24m.

Repairs of a limited nature can be undertaken. Contact Alicante Marine Services. The shipyard is prepared to slip, clean and paint yachts.

Two slipways in W corner of the inner harbour with capacity of up to 500 tonnes.

A number of cranes in the port with capacity of up to 30 tonnes.

Several chandlery shops in the town.

Water from taps on quays and pontoons.

220v AC supply points.

Gasoleo A and petrol.

Ice from door no. 2 of the ice factory in Dársena Pesquera or from club.

The Real Club de Regatas de Alicante has good facilities. It is both a social and a yacht club and an introduction may be required. Contact the secretary before using the club.

Many shops of all kinds and qualities but inconveniently placed for the marina. There is a good market about 1M into the city; use a no. 6, 7 or 8 bus.

Several launderettes some distance into the city.

TV satellite connections available for larger craft.

The Real Club de Regatas has moved to a new building over the slipway in the west corner of the inner harbour. Tripper boats now ply from the old position of the YC at the centre of the NW side of the inner harbour.

Communications

Major international airport – good for crew change. Rail service to Madrid. One terminal of the narrow gauge coast railway which runs a tourist excursion train as far as Dénia. Bus service along the coast. International airport (with connections to British provincial airports). Ferries to the Islas Baleares, Marseille and other ports.
☎ Area code 96. Taxi ☎ 525 25 11.
British Consulate Plaza Calvo Sotelo 1/2 Post: Apartado 564
☎ 521 61 90, 521 60 22 *Fax* 514 05 28.

⚓ ENSENADA DE LA ALBUFERETA

Anchorage in 3m sand in N corner of the Bahía de Alicante open E. Coast road with many houses and flats. Shops nearby.

L'Albufereta

38°21′N 00°28′W

Small, shallow dinghy harbour

A small artificial dinghy harbour with depths of less than a metre, little shelter and no facilities apart from a dinghy ramp and hardstanding. Real Club des Regates and some sailing schools use this harbour extensively.

Alicante's new fishing harbour SW of port

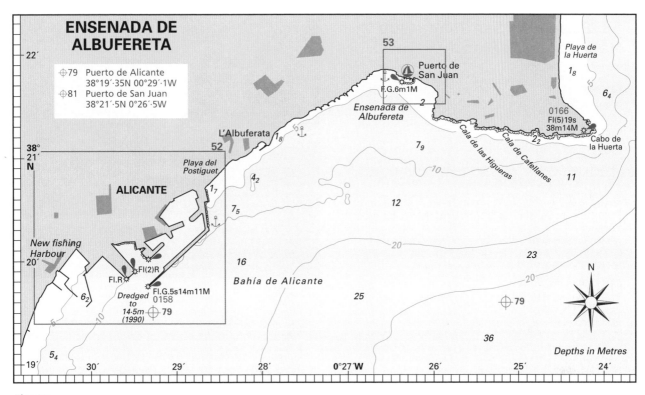

ENSENADA DE ALBUFERETA

⊕79   Puerto de Alicante
38°19′·35N 00°29′·1W
⊕81   Puerto de San Juan
38°21′·5N 0°26′·5W

Plan Va

L'Albufereta

53. Puerto de San Juan (Club Náutico Costa Blanca)

38°21′.7N 00°26′.3W

Charts

British Admiralty *469, 1700.* Imray *M12*
French *7304, 4719.* Spanish *472A, 472*

⊕81 38°21′.5N 00°26′.5W

Lights

0164 **Dique head** F.G.6m1M Green and white column 3m
0164.2 **Contradique head** F.R.6m1M Red and white
   column 3m
To the east
0166 **Cabo de las Huertas** Fl(5)19s38m14M White tower
   9m
24685(S) **Buoy** 38°21′·3N 00°26′·2W Q(6)+LFl.15s4M ⟊
   cardinal some 50m W of a submerged quay (under
   construction) off Puertoamor

Port communications

VHF Ch 9 Club Náutico Costa Blanca ☎ 965 15 44 91
Fax 965 26 59 86
Email cncostablanca@cdromsa.es

San Juan

Friendly but limited

A small popular yacht harbour with a very friendly *club
náutico* which can handle up to 12m yachts but as it is
very crowded, especially in summer, one must ring
ahead to ascertain whether a berth is available. Although
well sheltered by Cabo de la Huerta and normally with
an easy approach and entrance, a heavy swell from the
SSW could make the final stage difficult. Facilities for
yachts are limited. Sandy beaches either side of the
harbour.

Approach

From the south – see Alicante. The prominent Cabo de
Santa Pola the off-lying Isla de Tabarca, the hills, town
and port of Alicante are all easily recognised. The
harbour is 3M NE of Puerto de Alicante and 2M to W
of Cabo de las Huertas.

From the north After Villajoyosa the coast is low and
sandy with many small seaside villages. A small range of
coastal hills 8M to SW of Villajoyosa and a small
peninsula, La Illeta, which has a harbour on its S side
may be recognised. The low 'Punta del Río' has a
number of high-rise buildings on it; Cabo de las Huerta
is a low promontory with the Monte de las Matas
(181m) just inland. Give it a ¼M berth as there is a
submerged reef off it, then round Punta de la Cala and
the harbour will open up 1½M to W.

GPS approach

Steer to ⊕81 from the southern quadrant and steer for
the breakwater head (approx. 0.17M).

Anchorage in the approach

Anchor 200m to S of the harbour in 5m sand.

Entrance

Straightforward but look out for small craft.

Berths

Secure to a vacant berth just inside the entrance and ask
at the clubhouse.

Facilities

Maximum length overall: 12m.
Slipway in N, centre and E of the harbour.
2-tonne semi-mobile crane on the central spur.
Water taps around harbour.
220v AC points around the harbour.
Club Náutico de San Juan beside the harbour with all normal
   facilities.
Several supermarkets nearby.

Communications

Bus service along the coast. ☎ Area code 96.

⚓ PLAYA DE LA HUERTA (PLATJA DE SAN JUAN)

Coastal anchorage open to E in 5m sand and weed.
Road and houses along shore, sandy beach.

Plan 53

54. Puerto de Campello

38°25′.8N 00°23′.1W

Charts

British Admiralty *1700*. Imray *M12*
French *4719*. Spanish *473*

⊕82 38°25′.6N 00°23′.0W

Lights

To the south
0166 **Cabo de las Huertas** Fl(5)19s38m14M White tower
    9m
Harbour
0167 **Dique de Levante** Fl.G.3s8m4M Green rhombic
    (with hole) tower 5m
0167.2 **Contradique head** Fl(2)R.8s7m3M Red round
    concrete tower 4m

Port communications

VHF Ch 9. *Capitanía* ☎ 965 63 17 48. *Fax* 965 63 19 64
Email cncampello@alc.es

Puerto de Campello

Small modern marina

Formerly a small fishing village and anchorage now submerged in holiday homes and apartments. The harbour is easy to approach and enter. It has better facilities than several locally. Good shelter inside but swell enters with strong winds between SE and W. The caves, Cuevas de Canalobre, 10M inland, are of interest. Very good sandy beaches either side of the harbour. A pleasant town.

Approach

From the south The low promontory of Cabo de la Huerta, backed by Monte de las Matas (190m), is conspicuous. Give the headland ¼M berth as an underwater reef runs out SE-ly from it. The coast northwards is low, flat and dull with a long, sandy beach and seaside villages backed by high-rise buildings.

The (usually dry) mouth of the Río Montenegre (or de Castellá) is just S of Punta del Río which is low and flat but has a group of high-rise buildings. The harbour

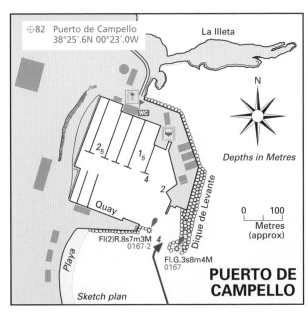

Plan 54

can be recognised by a grey/black tower block with red sun blinds on its SW side and an old tower with 2 creamy coloured high rise buildings to its NW.

From the north The harbour and town of Villajoyosa are easily recognised. The coast to S is of broken cliffs with small coves and small hills inland. La Illeta is quite low and inconspicuous but the harbour can be recognised by the 2 creamy-coloured high-rise buildings to the NW of the old tower and harbour.

GPS approach

Steer to ⊕82 from the eastern quadrant and steer for the breakwater head (approx. 0.13M).

Anchorage in the approach

Anchor in 5m sand 100m to S of the entrance.

Entrance

Approach the harbour entrance on a NW heading and enter leaving the head of Dique de Levante at least 25m to starboard, or even more at night, as the *dique* sticks out a long way past the beacon, especially to the west.

Berths

Call office on Ch 9 or secure to a vacant berth and ask at the yacht club.

Facilities

Maximum length overall: 15m.
Electricians, radio, radar and engine mechanics, shipwright.
Slipway in NE corner of the harbour.
45-tonne travel-lift and covered dry storage (including a 'filing cabinet' for 200 motor boats).
Water taps on quays pontoons.
220v AC points on pontoons.
Gasoleo A and petrol.
The Club Náutico de Campello has showers, a restaurant, and launderette.
A few local shops with a supermarket a few hundred metres to the south.

Communications

Bus service along the coast and rail to Alicante and along the coast to Dénia in the N. ☎ Area code 96. Taxi
☎ 563 02 11.

55. Puerto de Villajoyosa (Alcocó)

38°30´.4N 00°13´.1W

Charts

British Admiralty *1700*. Imray *M12*
French *7295, 4719*. Spanish *473, 4731*

⊕83 38°30´.2N 00°13´.3W

Lights

To the southwest
0166 **Cabo de las Huertas** Fl(5)19s38m14M White tower 9m
Harbour
0168 **Dique de Levante head** Fl.G.3s14m4M Green tower, white base 7m
0169 **Dique de Poniente head** Fl(2)R.6s7m3M Red octagonal tower, white base 6m
0168.5 **Espigón head** Fl(2)R.6s8m5M Red octagonal tower, white base 6m
To the east
0172 **Islote de Benidorm** Fl.3s60m7M White truncated pyramid 4m

Port communications

VHF Ch 9. ☎ 965 89 36 06 *Fax* 966 85 15 04
Email secretaria@cnlavila.org *url* www.cnlavila.org

Useful harbour lacking shelter

A fishing harbour now largely given over to yachts. Approach and entrance are easy but shelter is not very good and with SE and S winds it can be uncomfortable. The harbour is sometimes oily and depths change with silting and dredging.

The old wall, ruined castle and fortified church in the town are interesting as is the Amadorio dam, some miles inland. About 24 to 31 July, there is a Christian feast in honour of the patron saint Sta Marta. Good beaches on either side of the harbour.

Approach

From the SW Cabo de la Huerta which has a conspicuous lighthouse is easily recognised as are the many high-rise buildings at Villajoyosa. A very large white tower block of flats, Cinco Torres (60m), lies just inland of this harbour.

From the NE Having rounded the long high rocky feature of Sierra Helada, the mass of high-rise buildings of Benidorm with its outlying Isla Benidorm are easily identified, together with the large white tower block of flats, Cinco Torres (60m), inland of this harbour.

GPS approach

Steer to ⊕83 from the southeastern quadrant and steer for the breakwater head (approx. 0.13M).

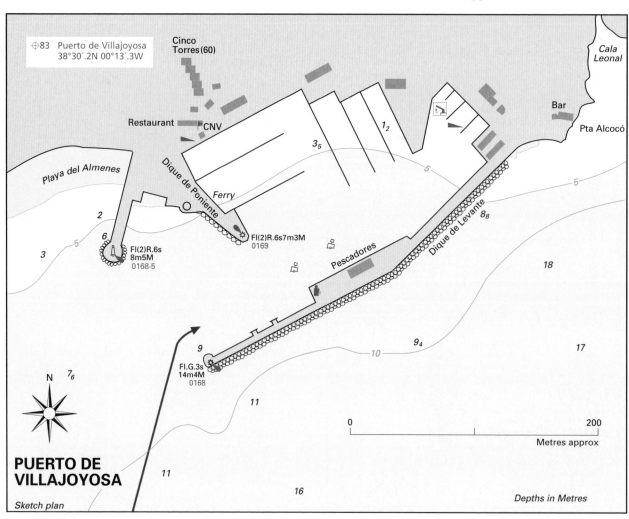

Plan 55

Villajoyosa

Anchorage in the approach

Anchor 200m to W of the head of Dique de Levante in 8m mud and weed.

Entrance

Approach the entrance on a N course and round the head of Dique de Levante at 20m, passing between it and the artificial island with a light at the end of the submerged Espigón Antiarena on the north side of the entrance. The harbour tends to silt up and is periodically dredged and depths shown may not be correct. Keep clear of ferry berth near head of Dique de Poniente.

Berths

Secure to the pontoon just inside the Dique de Poniente and inquire at the yacht club for a more sheltered berth within.

Facilities

Maximum length overall: 20m.
Major repairs and engine work by the shipyard at the NE end of the harbour.
Slipway at the NE corner of the harbour, 100 tonnes and 3m.
35-tonne travel-hoist.
5 and 10-tonne cranes at the slipway.

Water taps on the Dique de Levante and pontoons.
220v AC points on pontoons.
Gasoleo A and petrol.
Club Náutico Alcocó-Villajoyosa.
A few small local shops but there are many in the town about 1M away.
Launderettes in town.

Communications

Buses and railway. ☎ Area code 96 Taxi ☎ 589 00 24.

56. Puerto de Benidorm

38°32'N 00°08'W

Charts

British Admiralty *1700*. Imray *M12*
French *4719*. Spanish *473, 4731*

⊕84 38°31'·9N 00°08'·2W

Lights

0172.5 **Dique de Abrigo head** Fl.G.3s8m4M White hut, green tower 3m
To the south
0172 **Islote de Benidorm** Fl.3s60m7M White truncated pyramid 4m

Port communications

VHF Ch 9. Club Náutico de Benidorm ☎ 96 585 30 67
Fax 965 86 65 63 *Email* cnauticobenidorm@ctv.es

Tiny harbour

The small, old fishing harbour, consisting of one jetty, is now overwhelmed by one of the biggest tourist developments on the coast. It has minimal shelter. Approach and entrance are easy except in winds from S to SW, when it is impossible and the harbour untenable. The needs of yachts per se are not catered for but anchoring off is feasible and if any crew feels neglected, there is plenty of tourist bustle ashore. Long sandy beaches on either side of the harbour.

Approach

From the SW Follow the flat and rather monotonous coast from Villajoyosa towards the high massive rocky feature of Sierra Helada, which is seen from afar and stands beyond Benidorm. Islote Benidorm, a pyramid-shaped island, lies off the harbour. The small, white, rocky-cliffed Punta de Canfáli with houses and a blue-domed church on it lies just beyond the *dique*.

From the NE Round the massive bulk of Sierra Helada and the harbour will be found just beyond it, near the white, rocky-cliffed Punta de Canfáli and among a mass of high-rise buildings. A water-ski area with overhead tow lines on metal posts is laid out in the bay to E of Punta de Canfali.

GPS approach

Steer to ⊕84 from the southern quadrant and steer for the breakwater head (approx. 0.17M).

Anchorage in the approach

Anchor 150m to NW of the head of the *dique* in 6m sand.

Entrance

Approach the head of the *dique* on a N course; round it at 50m. Beware underwater debris closer to the *dique*.

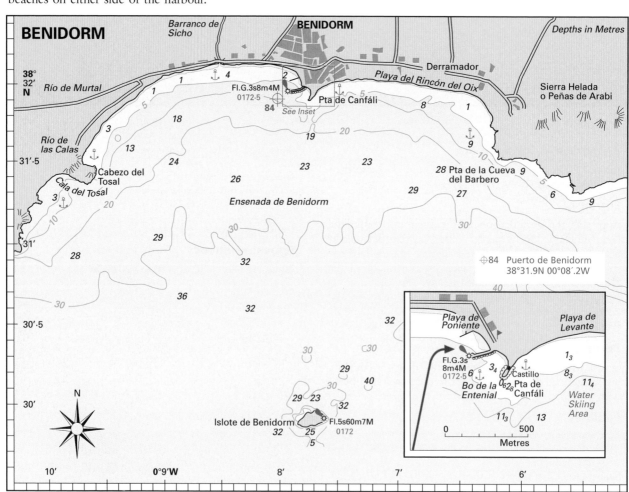

Plan 56

Berths

A temporary berth may be found alongside the NW face of the *dique* but it is frequently used by ferries and fishing boats.

Anchorage

It is possible to anchor on either side of the *dique*, well clear of it, in about 6m sand.

Facilities

Engine mechanics in town, mainly with experience in cars.
Hardstanding by the yacht club.
Chandler's shop in the town.
Water from tap near the root of the *dique*.
Many shops in the town and a market.
Club Náutico de Benidorm has a bar, lounge, restaurant, terrace and showers.
Several launderettes in town.

Communications

Bus, rail, taxis, car hire. ☎ Area code 96.

Benidorm harbour from SE

⚓ ENSENADA DE BENIDORM

Anchorage along the sandy beaches stretching between Cabezo del Tosal and Punta de la Escalata backed by massive high-rise buildings for package holidaymakers and open to S. Anchor in suitable depth offshore; sandy bottom.

⚓ CABEZO DEL TOSAL

There are anchorages N and S of this promontory, both open to the East. Anchor in 3m, sand.

⚓ ANCHORAGE E OF PUNTA DE CANFALI

Anchor in 3m sand open to S. Considerable holiday development ashore with skyscrapers. A water-ski circuit is established in this anchorage. Not recommended in summer for this reason.

⚓ ANCHORAGE W OF PUNTA DE LA CUEVA DEL BARBERO

A small anchorage open to S and swell from W. Road and development ashore, sand and shingle beach, bottom has rocky patches.

⚓ ANCHORAGES TO NW OF PUNTA DEL ALBIR
38°34′N 00°03′.1W

Three anchorages well protected except from N–NE by the Sierra Helada (438m). Sandy bottom with rocky patches. Down draughts from S–SW winds may be experienced.

Cabezo de Tosal, south anchorage from SW

Punta del Albir lighthouse from SE and first anchorage to NW

57. Puerto de Altea

38°35′.3N 00°03′.2W

Charts

British Admiralty *1700*. Imray *M12*
French *7296, 4719*. Spanish *473, 4732*
⊕85 38°35′.1N 00°03′.12W

Lights

To the south
0173.6 **Punta del Albir** Fl(3)27s112m15M White tower on
house 8m
Harbour
0174 **Dique de Levante head** Fl(3)G.8s12m4M Green
octagonal stone tower 6m
0174.2 **Dique de Poniente head** Fl(2)R.6s9m3M Red
octagonal tower 6m

Port communications

VHF Ch 9. Club Náutico de Altea
☎ 965 84 15 91 *Fax* 965 84 15 79
Email cnaltea@cnaltea.com *url* www.cnaltea.com

Excellent yacht harbour

Built near the place where Scipio landed and sacked the
Greek colony of Honosca, Altea is a busy artificial
fishing harbour with an excellent yacht facility and an
easy approach. Shops are some distance away at the foot
of the town which stands on a hill. The area is
surrounded by high mountains which make it attractive.

The old town on the top of the hill and its church are
worth a visit. The village and castle at Guadalest some
9M inland is worth a visit. There are good sandy
beaches on either side of this harbour.

Approach

From the SW Round the high-cliffed feature of Sierra
Helada which has a conspicuous lighthouse on its NE
end, Punta del Albir. From here the harbour walls will
be seen and, beyond them, the church of Altea which
stands on top of a small hill. The church has
conspicuous blue domes.

From the NE The unique high, steep-sided peninsula of
Ifach and the lower Cabo Toix are easily recognised.
When rounded, the blue-domed church on the hilltop at
Altea will be seen. The harbour walls will not be seen
until much closer in.

GPS approach

Steer to ⊕85 from the southern quadrant and steer for
the breakwater head (approx. 0.11M).

Anchorage in the approach

Anchor immediately S of the Dique de Poniente where
a considerable amount of shelter can be gained from the
Dique de Levante. Keep out of the way of speeding
fishing boats using the harbour entrance. Alternatively,
not so good, to NE of the Dique de Levante in 5m sand.

Puerto de Altea

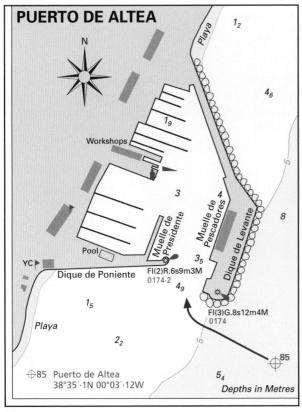

PUERTO DE ALTEA

N

Playa

1₂

4₆

1₉

Workshops

3

4

8

Muelle de Presidente

Muelle de Pescadores

Dique de Levante

Pool

YC ►

Dique de Poniente

3₅

Fl(2)R.6s9m3M
0174·2

4₉

Fl(3)G.8s12m4M
0174

1₅

Playa

2₂

⊕85 Puerto de Altea
38°35′·1N 00°03′·12W

5₄

85

Depths in Metres

Plan 57

frequently dredged which may change the depths. Watch for commercial traffic.

Berths

Secure to Muelle Presidente and ask at the yacht club on the SW corner of Dique Poniente for a berth.

Facilities

Maximum length overall: 23m.
Two shipyards for yacht repairs.
Engine mechanics.
A 100-tonne slipway; other slipways on the NW side of the harbour near head of the spur and root of Muelle Presidente.
30-tonne travel-hoist.
A chandlery on the seafront and others in the town.
Water taps on yacht harbour pontoons and quays.
220v and 380v AC on pontoons and quays.
Gasoleo A and petrol.
Ice is available near the yacht club.
Club Náutico de Altea, located on W side of yacht harbour, has a bar, restaurant, patio, showers and launderette.
Most of the shops and the local market are on or near the main road to the E of the church at the foot of the hill. There are a few small shops near the harbour.
Launderettes in town.
Swimming pool on Dique de Poniente.

Communications

Bus and rail services. ☎ Area code 96. Taxi ☎ 584 02 36.

Entrance

Approach on a NW course and round the head of Dique de Levante at 20m. Enter the yacht harbour behind the Muelle Presidente. The harbour silts up and is

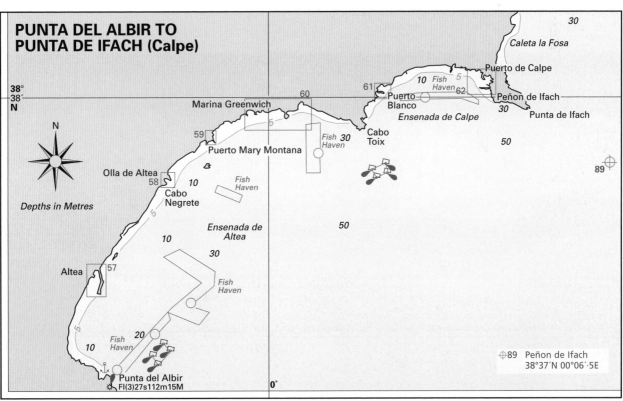

PUNTA DEL ALBIR TO PUNTA DE IFACH (Calpe)

30

Caleta la Fosa

Puerto de Calpe

38°
38′
N

60

61

10 Fish Haven

5

62

Peñon de Ifach

Marina Greenwich

Puerto Blanco

30

Punta de Ifach

N

59

5

Fish 30 Haven

Cabo Toix

Ensenada de Calpe

50

89 ⊕

Puerto Mary Montana

Olla de Altea

58

10

Fish Haven

50

Cabo Negrete

Depths in Metres

Ensenada de Altea

10

30

50

Altea

57

Fish Haven

20

Fish Haven

10

Punta del Albir
Fl(3)27s112m15M

0°

⊕89 Peñon de Ifach
38°37′N 00°06′·5E

Plan Vb

58. Puerto de la Olla de Altea (El Portet)

38°36′8N 00°01′.9W

Charts

British Admiralty *1700*. Imray *M12*
French *4719*. Spanish *473, 4732*

Lights

0174·4 **Dique de Levante** Fl(2)G.9s6m Green round tower white base 4m
0174·6 **Dique de Poniente** Fl(2)R.9s7m Red round tower white base 4m

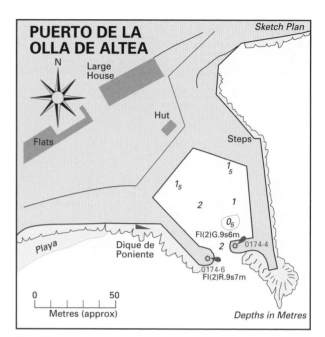

Plan 58

Minute harbour

This minute harbour is only suitable for day boats, dinghies and small yachts which can be hauled ashore in the event of bad weather. Approach and entrance present no problems in good weather but would be dangerous in heavy seas from E. Facilities ashore are limited and in the summer months it is very crowded. Small pebble beaches either side of the harbour. Large beach to S of Cabo Negrete.

Approach

From the south After the large high rocky mass of the Sierra Helada (Peñas de Arabi) (438m) pass outside Isla Mediana (Mitjana). Having cleared Punta del Albir, the town of Altea will be seen. It has a conspicuous church with two blue domes on top of a hill and its harbour lies to the S. Northwards of Altea harbour the coast should be given a 300m berth for ½M when Cabo Negrete will be identified by its rocky point and a large, white house in dark trees. There are rocks off the point. Olla del Altea lies 250m to N of this point and can be identified by a large private house behind the harbour.

From the north Round the prominent and steep-to Cabo Toix. Pass Puerto de Mascarat, which will be identified by its breakwaters and the smaller private harbour of Puerto de Marymontaña. Pass outside Islote and Isleta, two offshore islands, the latter with a shallow patch 0.2m inshore and having passed Isleta, go W towards the harbour. The large private house also shows up from this direction.

Anchorage in the approach

Anchor 250m to E of the harbour in 5m mud and stones.

Olla de Altea

Entrance

Approach the harbour on a W to NW heading and keep a watch on soundings. Enter on a NNW heading at slow speed; note shallow patch to starboard just inside the harbour.

Berths

Secure to quays to starboard, ground on slipways if a bilge keeler or haul out ashore.

Facilities

Slipways on W and N side of the harbour for day boats and dinghies.
Simple everyday requirements from local shops.

Communications

Rail and bus services.

59. Puerto de Mary Montaña

38°37'.5N 00°01'.1W

Charts

British Admiralty *1700*. Imray *M12*
French *4719*. Spanish *473, 4732*

Lights

0174·8 **Dique de Levante head** F. White masonry column 3m
Dique de Poniente head F.R.4m1M White square tower
Note The latter is not official and is occasional.

Private harbour

An attractive private harbour, suitable for small and medium-sized yachts, belonging to a large estate and for use only as a harbour of refuge; it should not be entered without good reason. Facilities are limited to water and electricity. The main coast road lies 500m to NW from the harbour up a hill.

Approach

The approach is shallow. A shallow, rocky area lies to E of the harbour culminating in Islote, a small islet 350m to E–NE of the entrance. A larger rocky island, Isleta, lies 700m to S of the entrance with a reef stretching NW to the coast.

From the south From Altea which can be recognised by its harbour and the town on a hill, which is crowned by a church with two blue domes, the sandy coast runs in a N–NE direction and is backed by a range of hills. Cabo Negrete and the Puerto de la Olla de Altea will only be recognised if close to the shore. In the approach from this direction it is advisable to pass outside Isleta which lies 550m off the shore and then turn on to a N course and approach the harbour, sounding carefully with a lookout posted forward. From Isleta the harbour should be seen, backed by the rocky Montaña Bernia (1129m) which is a pyramid shape. In the closer approach, the triple-arched gateway may be seen behind the harbour wall.

From the north Cabo Toix which is steep-to and the large harbour of Puerto Mascarat are easily recognised. Keep outside the 10m depth contour which lies some 400m from the shore until 100m NE of Isleta. The harbour lies in a N direction and a direct approach can

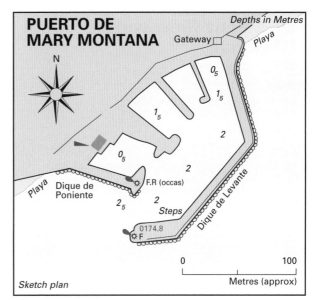

Plan 59

be made from here towards the entrance, sounding carefully and with a lookout forward.

Anchorage in the approach

The area near the harbour is of rock and the nearest suitable anchorage is in 5m sand 300m W of Isleta.

Entrance

Approach the entrance on a N course and enter on a NE heading.

Berths

Secure to the inner side of the Dique de Levante and report to the harbour official at the caseta by the gateway. If no one is to be found there to allocate a berth, proceed some 200/300m up the hill to a large house and report there.

Facilities

Water taps on all quays.
220v AC points on all quays.

Communications

Bus service along the main road and the coastal railway station at Olla de Altea.

Puerto de Mary Montaña

60. Marina Greenwich (Mascarat)

38°37′.7N 00°00′.3W

Charts

British Admiralty *1700*. Imray *M12*
French *4719*. Spanish *473, 4732*

⊕86 38°37′·6N 00°00′·3E

Lights

0174.92 **Dique Sur W head** Fl.G.6s6m4M Green round toweron white base 8m
0174.9 **Dique Sur E head** Fl.3s6m4M White round tower, black base 10m
0174.93 **Contradique head** F.R.6m4M Red round tower, white base 8m

Port communications

VHF Ch 9. Port Office ☎ 965 84 22 00
Fax 965 84 23 07 *Email* marinagreenwich@ctv.es
url www.marinagreenwich.com

Convenient and pleasant marina

The harbour, interestingly lying on the Greenwich meridian, is surrounded by high rocky hills and has an attractive hinterland, worth visiting by car. Building work continues with a very conspicuous blue block of apartments behind the harbour entrance. The eastern end of the marina is being extended to accomodate additional berths. The harbour itself has good facilities. It becomes crowded in summer and it is prudent to book ahead. A small shingle beach to W of the harbour and a golf course nearby.

Approach

From the south Give the coast a 500m berth NE from Altea, which is easily identified by the church on top of the hill with two blue domes, to Puerto de Mascarat. Cabo Negrete and the small Puerto de la Olla de Altea are not conspicuous but the island of Isleta, which should be left to port, will be seen as will the Puerto de Mary Montaña and the small rocky islet of Islote. Approach the harbour entrance on N course.

From the north Round the unmistakable Punta Ifach and cross the Ensenada de Calpe. Puerto de Calpe will be seen NW of the Peñón de Ifach (332m). Cabo Toix, which is steep-to, is prominent and has high cliffs which slope up the higher ground inland. On rounding this point, part of the harbour breakwater will be seen. Punta Mascarat obscures the rest of the harbour when seen from this area. The harbour entrance is at the west end of the breakwater.

GPS approach

Steer to ⊕86 from the southeastern quadrant and steer for the breakwater head (approx. 0.13M).

Anchorage in the approach

Anchor in 5m sand between Punta Mascarat and the E side of the harbour to suit prevalent wind.

Entrance

Approach the Dique Sur western end from the south quadrant, round it to starboard at 20m and steer east for the fuel quay, immediately to port on entering.

Berth

Secure to fuel quay and ask at the port control office.

Facilities

Maximum length overall: 30m.
Engine mechanics and general repairs.
Crane.
50-tonne travel-hoist.
Chandlery behind the harbour.

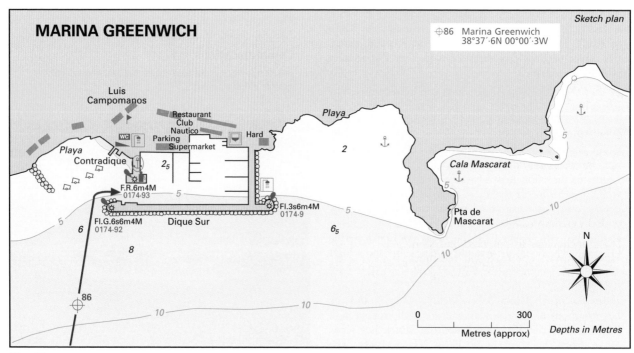

Plan 60

Marina Greenwich (Mascarat)

Water taps on quays and pontoons.
Showers.
220/380v AC points on quays and pontoons.
Gasoleo A and petrol.
Ice on fuel quay.
Shops for everyday requirements and a supermarket behind
the harbour.

Communications

Buses on main road above the harbour. Railway at Olla de
Altea. ☎ Area code 96. Taxi ☎ 584 02 36.

⚓ PUNTA MASCARAT

Three anchorages in 5m sand and stone, one to W of
Punta Mascarat, one to E and the third off the mouth
of Barranco del Collada. By choosing the anchorage, the
high cliffs can give protection except from S winds and
there may be swell from SE or SW. The main road is at
top of the cliffs.

61. Puerto Blanco

38°38′.1N 00°02′.1E

Charts

British Admiralty *1700*. Imray *M12*
French *4719*. Spanish *473, 4732*

⊕87 38°38′·1N 00°02′·24E

Lights

0175 **E breakwater head** F.7m3M Red castellated
      tower 6m

Port communications

Try Ch 9. ☎ 965 83 13 37 *Fax* 965 83 26 32

Small boat harbour

A small-boat harbour lying NNE of Cabo Toix and
800m W of Puerto de Calpe. It may be a useful
alternative when Calpe is full but it may also be full
itself. It has good shelter except in an easterly when
there will be swell in the harbour. Facilities are limited.
Some housing estates in the area.

Approach

From the SW From the conspicuous promontory of
Punta de Albir (112m) the equally conspicuous Cabo
Toix and Punta Ifach will be seen. The harbour lies on
the E side of Cabo Toix which is steep-to.

From the NE From Cabo Moraira set course to round
the conspicuous Punta Ifach, then on to a W course
towards Puerto Blanco which will be seen in the closer
approach just to the N of Cabo Toix.

GPS approach

Steer to ⊕87 from the southeastern quadrant and steer
for the breakwater head (approx. 0.07M).

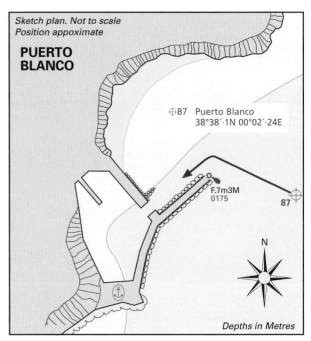

Plan 61

Entrance

Usually straightforward but may not be possible in a
strong easterly.

Berths

Secure to a vacant berth and ask at the *capitanía*.

Charges

Medium.

Facilities

Engineer and workshop available.
Water taps on quay.
Supermarket ½ a mile away.

Puerto Blanco

Peñon de Ifach, looking south

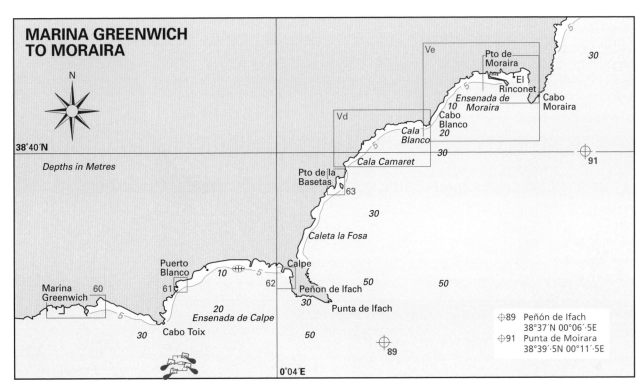

**MARINA GREENWICH
TO MORAIRA**

N

38°40´N

Depths in Metres

Ve
Pto de
Moraira
El
Rinconet
Ensenada de
10 *Moraira*
Cabo
Blanco
20
30

Cabo
Moraira

30

Vd
Cala
Blanco
30
Cala Camaret
91

Pto de la
Basetas
63

30

Caleta la Fosa

Puerto
Blanco
10
5
Calpe
62
50
50
Peñon de Ifach
30
Punta de Ifach

Marina
Greenwich
60
61
5
20
Ensenada de Calpe
30
Cabo Toix

50

⊕89 Peñón de Ifach
38°37´N 00°06´·5E
⊕91 Punta de Moirara
38°39´·5N 00°11´·5E

⊕
89

0°04´E

Plan Vc

⚓ **ENSENADA DE CALPE**

The Ensenada de Calpe lies between Puerto Blanco and Calpe. Anchorage off sandy beach in 3 to 5m sand open E. Pay attention to unmarked wrecks off Playa del Bou and Playa del Almadrat. Road ashore with some apartment buildings.

*1
nice
marina
& town*

62. Puerto de Calpe

38°38'.2N 00°04'.2E

Charts

British Admiralty *1700, 1701.* Imray *M12*
French *7296, 4719.* Spanish *473, 4732*

⊕88 38°38'.12N 00°03'.9E

Lights

0175.2 **Contradique head** Fl(4)R.10s8m6M Truncated
masonry tower, red top 4m
0175.4 **Dique head** Fl.G.4s13m6M Masonry tower, green
top 6m

Port communications

VHF Ch 9. ☎ 965 83 18 09 *Fax* 965 83 49 31
Email cncalpe@ctv.es *url* www.cncalpe.com

Harbour in spectacular location

Located at the base of the spectacular Peñón de Ifach, the old fishing harbour, with a history going back to the Phoenicians, has been transformed by the construction of breakwaters, quays and pontoons for yachts. It is a busy harbour which can be approached and entered with ease. The shelter is good though a SW wind can bring swell into the harbour. It is worth visiting to admire the Peñón de Ifach; a climb from its NW side through a tunnel and along a perilous pathway to the top results in a spectacular view of the coast and a demonstration of the uncontrolled nature of high-rise and other commercial building. Good beaches either side of the harbour. Golf Club de Ifach nearby.

Approach

A dangerous wreck lies ½M to W of the harbour.

From SW having rounded the massive Sierra Helada, the Peñón de Ifach will be seen in the distance appearing as an island. Cabo Toix, another massive cape en route, is easy to identify.

From NE round Cabo de la Nao, high and prominent and has a conspicuous lighthouse on top. Cabo Moraira, another prominent cape with a new yacht harbour to its W is also easy to recognise. The Peñón de Ifach can be seen from afar but appears as an island.

Calpe and the Peñón de Ifach

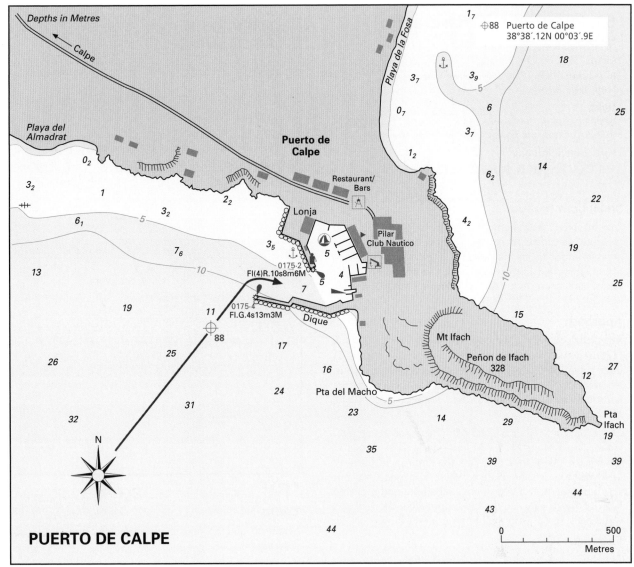

PUERTO DE CALPE

Plan 62

GPS approach

Steer to ⊕88 from the southwestern quadrant and steer for the breakwater head (approx. 0.12M).

Anchorage in the approaches

Anchor 100m to W of the head of the *contradique* in 5m sand or on the other side of Ifach in Cala la Fosa, 5m sand and stone.

Entrance

Straightforward, but it is a bit tight inside and there may be some ship movements. With N winds, there can be strong gusts in the harbour from the Peñón de Ifach.

Berths

Go on to a pontoon and ask at the yacht club office for a berth. The harbour suffers quite a surge in strong SW winds.

Charges

High. — In may 2008 = 22€. Not bad!
wifi at bench infront of office
Nice showers/toilet

Facilities

Maximum length overall: 30m.
The shipyard can carry out most repairs to hull and engines.
Other engine mechanics in the town.
Two slipways at the shipyard.
10-tonne crane.
Chandlery shop in the town and at the shipyard.
Water taps on pontoons but test it before filling tanks.
220v AC on pontoons.
Gasoleo A.
Ice on quay.
Club Náutico de Calpe with the usual facilities.
There are two supermarkets beyond the steps leading over the ridge behind the marina. More shops in Calpe about 1M away.
Launderette at the club house.

Communications

Bus and rail services. ☎ Area code 96.

⚓ CALA DE LA FOSA (N of Peñon de Ifach)

Anchor off middle of Playa de la Fosa in 5m sand. Road and high-rise apartment buildings ashore. Open to E.

63. Puerto de las Basetas

38°39´.6N 00°05´.2E

Charts

British Admiralty *1700, 1701*. Imray *M12*
French *4719*. Spanish *474*

Lights

0175.8 **Dique de Levante head** F.R.6m1M Red tower 3m
0175.9 **Contradique head** F.G.6m1M Green tower 3m

Port communications

VHF Ch 9. Port office ☎ 965 83 12 13.

Small boat harbour

An attractive little harbour but for small yachts and
dinghies only. The entrance is narrow and space inside
is limited, not to say cramped. The sea wall is based on
a line of rocks lying parallel to the shore within which
quays have been built. La Cala 400m to S has a shingle
beach.

Approach

From the south Round the unmistakable Peñón de Ifach
(328m) which is steep-to. The harbour lies 2M N. A
large tower on Cabo Blanco to NE is very conspicuous.
The harbour is difficult to see until close in, when the
harbour wall, with a small white house on it, will be
identified.

From the north Round Cabo Moraira which is steep-to.
Cross the Ensenada de Moraira in a SW direction
closing the coast after 3M. Pass the large yacht harbour
at Moraira and Cabo Blanco, which is steep-to but not
very prominent; it has a sloping silhouette and a cliffed
face on the E side. In the close approach, the harbour
wall and a small white building on it will be seen.

Entrance

Approach the entrance at the N end of the harbour on
a NW-ly course, sounding and with a forward lookout
posted. Go S of the small exposed rock and round the
head of the Dique de Levante taking care of isolated
rocky heads.

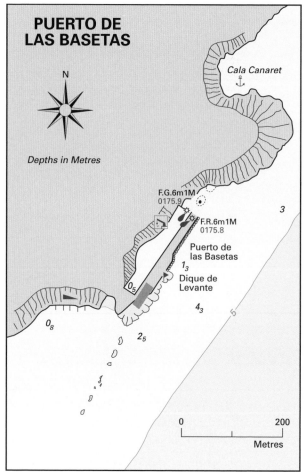

Plan 63

Berths

Secure to quay to port in a suitable gap and consult the
capitanía.

Facilities

Slipways at the S end of the harbour.
Small hardstanding.
3-tonne crane.
Water from a yacht club tap.
220v AC in the Club.
Small yacht club.
Scuba school.

Communications

Bus service to Calpe on coast road behind harbour.
☎ Area code 96.

Puerto de las Basetas

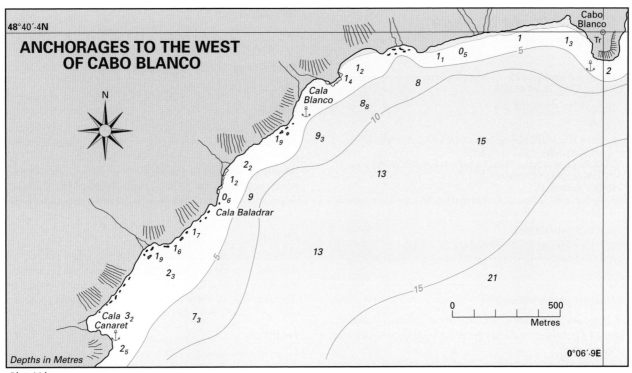

Plan Vd

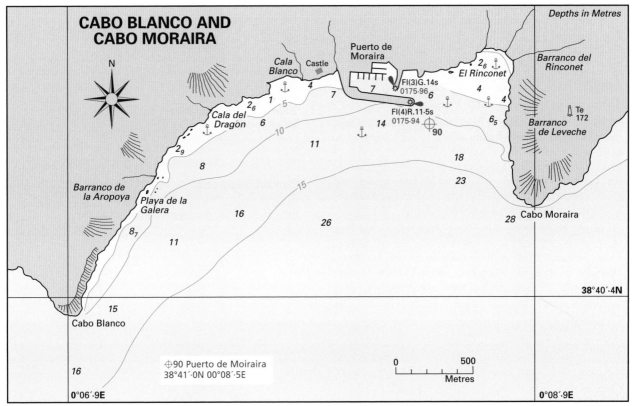

Plan Ve

⚓ CALA CANARET, CALA BLANCO, CABO BLANCO

These anchorages should be used with care. There are submerged rocks which can usually be seen in the clear water. Rocks make poor holding in some areas. All wide open to the SE.

⚓ CALA DEL DRAGON

Anchorage off small sandy bay in 2.5m sand. Wide open to the SE. Road inland.

64. Puerto de Moraira

38°41'.1N 00°08'.3E

Charts

British Admiralty *1700, 1701.* Imray *M12*
French *4719.* Spanish *474*

⊕90 38°41'.0N 00°08'.5E

Lights

0175.94 **Dique de Abrigo head** Fl(4)R.11.5s10m4M White
round tower, red bands 6m
0175.96 **Contradique head** Fl(3)G.14s10m4M White round
tower, green bands 6m
To the northeast
0176 **Cabo de la Nao** Fl.5s122m23M 049°-vis–190° White
octagonal tower and house 20m

Port communications

VHF Ch 9. ☎ 965 74 43 19 *Fax* 965 74 47 50
Email info@cnmoraira.com *url* www.cnmoraira.com

Modern pleasant resort

A large modern yacht harbour in an attractive setting,
one of the easier harbours to enter in bad weather and
well sheltered from wind and waves once inside. The
new harbour takes up some of the old anchorage of the
bay but the most sheltered part which is more suitable
for yachts is still available.

Moraira is a useful point of departure for San
Antonio-Abad in Ibiza, 55M. A climb to the Torre de
Moraira is rewarded with a fantastic view of the coast.
Sandy beach at El Rinconet. Golf Club de Ifach 4M.

Approach

There may be tuna nets in the bay.

From the south After Peñón de Ifach go NE-ly towards
the prominent Cabo Moraira which is high, with steep
cliffs and a tower on its summit (172m). The peak of
Montaña Isabela (La Liorenza) (442m) lies behind. In
the closer approach the houses of Moraira village and
tower blocks will appear. The harbour lies just E of the
semi-circular fort located near the village.

From the north From Cabo de la Nao which has high
steep cliffs, the course is SW towards the prominent
Cabo Moraira, 172m with a tower on its summit. Cabo
Moraira is steep-to. Round it on to a NW course
towards the harbour which is then immediately visible.

GPS approach

Steer to ⊕90 from the southern quadrant and steer for
the breakwater head (approx. 0.13M).

Anchorage in the approach

Anchor in the Ensenada del Rinconet (see below).

Berths

Make up on the fuel quay on the inner side of the
contradique and ask at the *capitanía*. Note that all
berths are privately owned so one should be prepared to
be shifted around if staying for a few days. Some quays
have rocky feet extending some distance. In summer,
when it is very crowded, boats double-up alongside the
Dique de Abrigo.

Charges

High. Note that the *club náutico* only permits a
cumulative total of seven days berthing in the season for
a visiting yacht after which temporary membership of
the club has to be paid at the current weekly rate, in
addition to the berthing charges.

Facilities

Maximum length overall: 30m.
Workshops.
Slipway in NE corner.
50-tonne travel-hoist.
10-tonne crane.
Chandlery shop beside the harbour and another in the village.
230/380v AC on pontoons.
Water taps on quays and pontoons but drinking water only on
the two western pontoons and head of the *contradique*.
Showers.
Gasoleo A.
Butane Gasolinera de Benissa Mon–Fri 1200–1300hrs.
Ice on fuel quay.
Club Náutico de Moraira.
Supermarket close by outside.
Shop at the N side of harbour and several in the village.

Communications

Buses to Jávea and Calpe on coast road. Railway at Benisa.
☎ Area code 96. Taxi ☎ 583 17 16 574 42 81.

Plan 64

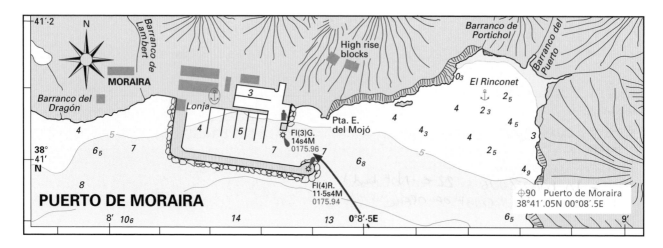

Moraira

⚓ EL RINCONET

Anchor according to depth, sand up to 150m from the shore, sand, rock and weed beyond that. Open between S and SE. See plans on pages 143 and 144.

El Rinconet

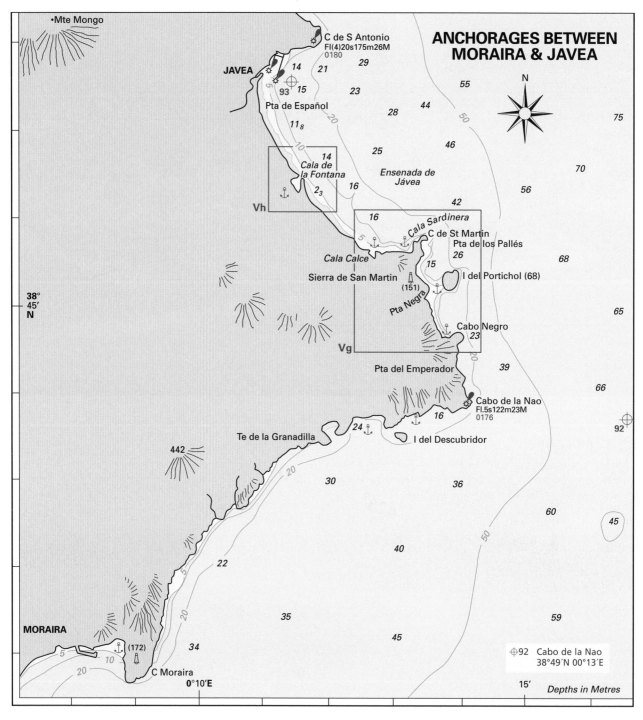

ANCHORAGES BETWEEN MORAIRA & JAVEA

Plan Vf

ANCHORAGES BETWEEN CABO MORAIRA AND JÁVEA

There are several interesting anchorages between Moraira and Jávea. They all need to be treated with caution in terms of wind and swell conditions and because of submerged rocks inshore. Note that there is now a traffic separation scheme (TSS) some 9 miles ESE of Cabo de la Nao which should not seriously affect pleasure craft as they are generally closer to the point but be aware of its presence. In bad weather vessels using the TSS may be directed further inshore - skippers should be aware.

La Granadilla

Isla del Portichol from the SE

Isla del Descubridor

Cabo de San Martin and Cala Sardinera from NE

⚓ LA GRANADILLA

Anchoring may be restricted by yellow buoys marking the swimming area. Beware submerged rocks near both sides of the entrance.

⚓ ISLA DEL DESCUBRIDOR

The island appears as a point. There are many submerged rocks.

⚓ PUNTA NEGRA

The anchorage is on the north side.

Punta Negra

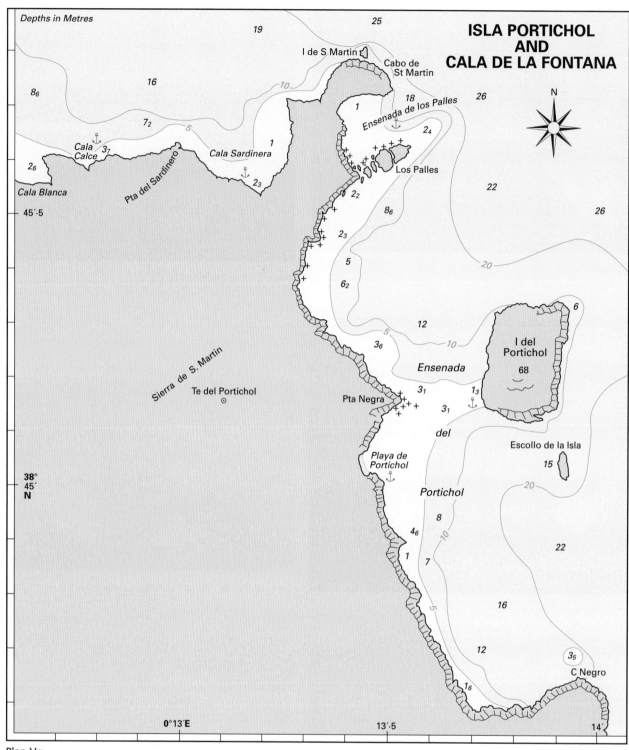

Depths in Metres

ISLA PORTICHOL
AND
CALA DE LA FONTANA

Plan Vg

⚓ **ISLA DEL PORTICHOL**

⚓ **CABO DE SAN MARTIN**

⚓ **CALA SARDINERA**

⚓ **CALA CALCE**

A very small cove offering anchorage for small craft in stone 1.5m. Open between N and NE.

⚓ **CALA DE LA FONTANA** 38°46′.4N 00°11′.5W

A suburb of Jávea. Open between NE and E. The bay is silting up.

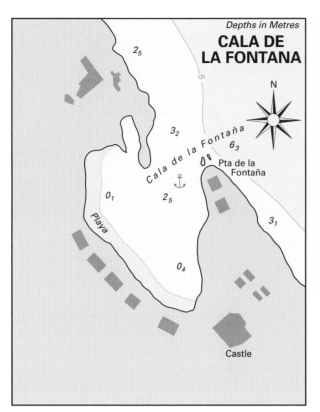

Plan Vh

Depths in Metres
CALA DE LA FONTANA

Cala de la Fontaña

Cabo de San Antonio to the E of Jávea – from the S

65. Puerto de Jávea

38°48'.9N 00°11'2E

Charts

British Admiralty *1700, 1701.* Imray *M12*
French *7296, 4719.* Spanish *474, 4741*

⊕93 38°47'.5N 00°11'.5E

Lights

To the southeast
0176 **Cabo de la Nao** Fl.5s122m23M White octagonal
 tower and house 20m 049°-vis-190°
Harbour
0179 **Dique head** Fl.G.3s11m5M Green octagonal tower
 6m
0179.4 **Contradique head** Fl(2)R.6s9m4M Red tower 6m
On the SW corner of first espigón to starboard on
 entering there is a green post 4m with a light of
 unknown characteristics. Be aware of its existence.
To the northeast
0180 **Cabo de San Antonio** Fl(4)20s175m26M White
 tower and building 17m

Port communications

VHF Ch 9. ☎/*Fax* 965 79 10 25 *Email* cnjavea@teleline.es
url www.cnjavea.com

Pleasant but crowded harbour

A pleasant yachting and fishing harbour, in attractive
surroundings and very full in summer. Approach and
entrance are easy, and there is protection from all winds
except SE to S. Jávea is the nearest harbour to Ibiza.

There are many caves in the area, some of which can
only be visited by boat. The Gothic church at Jávea and
the modern boat-shaped church near the harbour are
both worth visiting. The view from the top of Cabo de
San Antonio is good. There is a fine sandy beach about
a mile south of the marina and a small pebbly one at the
root of the Muelle de Levante.

Approach

From the SE Round Cabo de San Martin which has
several off-lying islets and, sometimes, tunny nets. The
wide Ensenada de Jávea then opens up. The town
stretches south and harbour is in the NW corner under
the steep-sided mountain with abandoned windmills on
the skyline.

From the NW Round Cabo de San Antonio which is a
high, steep-sided, flat-topped promontory with a
conspicuous lighthouse and signal station; follow round
onto a SW course and the harbour wall will be seen in
the closer approach.

From all directions the high pyramid-shaped
Montaña Mongo, which stands to the W of the harbour,
is very conspicuous.

GPS approach

Steer to ⊕93 from the eastern quadrant and steer for
the breakwater head (approx. 0.3M).

Anchorage in the approach

Anchoring is prohibited S of the harbour; see plan.

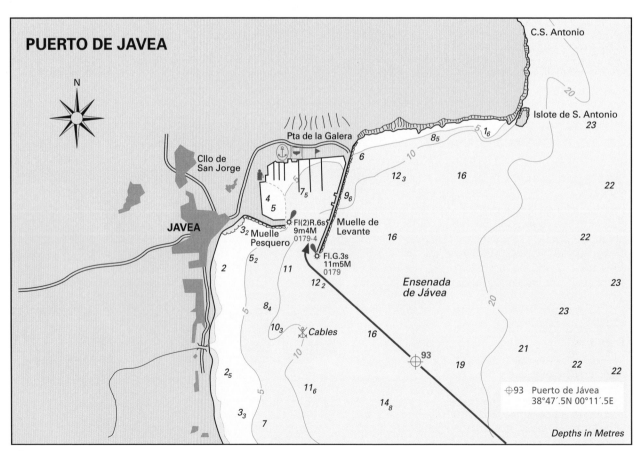

Plan 65

Puerto de Jávea

Entrance

The breakwaters have stone feet and should be given a good 10m berth.

Berths

Berth stern-to the yacht club quay on the N side of harbour with anchor and trip-line from the bow or in a similar manner to a pontoon using the pick-up buoys. An alternative berth is sometimes available on the inner side of the *dique*, secured stern-to. There are underwater projecting rocky foundations to the *dique*: the three short spurs are in constant use.

Charges

High.

Facilities

Maximum length overall: 22m.
Limited hull and engine repairs.
Slipway to the W side of the yacht club.
65-tonne travel-lift and 6-tonne crane.
Water from a hose at the yacht club.
220v AC points at the yacht club.
Ice from the yacht club.

Gasoleo B only.
Club Náutico de Jávea with bar, restaurant, cabins, showers, swimming pool, etc.
Small shops and supermarket near the harbour, large supermarket, most shops, launderette and the market itself are in the town, about a mile away.

Communications

Buses and railway in town. ☎ Area code 96.
Taxis ☎ 579 32 24.

66. Puerto de Dénia

38°50'.5N 00°07'.1E

Charts

British Admiralty *1515, 1700, 1701.* Imray *M12*
French *7296, 4719.* Spanish *474, 4741*

⊕95 38°51'.4N 00°08'.3E

Lights

To the southeast
0180 **Cabo de San Antonio** Fl(4)20s175m26M White
 tower and building 17m

Harbour
0184 **Dique Norte head** Fl(3)G.10.5s13m5M Green tower
 7m
0187 **Dique Norte elbow** Fl(4)G.11s4m4M Green tower
 3m
0187.5 **Espigón Central N head** Fl.G.5s4m3M Green tower
 3m
0187.7 **Espigón Central S head** Fl(2)G.7s3m3M Green post
 2m
0187.9 **Central** Fl(3)G.9s3m2M Green post 2m
0185 **Dique S head** Fl(3)R.10s9m5M Red tower 7m
0188 **Dique S elbow** Fl(4)R.11s5m4M Red tower 3m
0188.5 **Espigón head** Fl.R.5s2m2M Red tower 2m
0188.7 **CN Dique de Abrigo** 38°50'.3N 00°07'.1E
 Fl(2+1)R.20s3m1M Red post, green band 2m
0186 **Ldg Lts 228°** *Front* 38°50'.4N 00°06'.9E
 Fl.R.2.5s10m4M White post, black bands 10m 198°-vis-
 258°
0186.1 *Rear* (150m away) Oc.R.6s14m4M White post,
 black bands 10m 198°-vis-258°

To the northwest
0198 **Cabo Cullera** Fl(3).20s28m25M White tower on
 house 16m
Note that between 0188 and 0188.5 there is a line of
 small red cylindrical buoys which must be left to port
 on entry.

Port communications

VHF Ch 9. Club náutico ☎ 965 78 09 89 *Fax* 965 78 08 50
Email info@cndenia.es *url* www.cndenia.es
VHF Ch 9. Marina de Denia ☎ 966 42 43 07
Fax 966 42 43 87
Email marinadedenia@marinadedenia.com
url www.marinadedenia.com

Commercial harbour with good marina facilities

A fishing, ferry and commercial harbour occupied by all
invaders from the Greeks (600BC) onwards; the latest
are the tourists. Repair and other facilities are good. The
old town, castle and the surrounding area are attractive.
Sandy beaches on either side of the harbour, those to
the N being best.

There is now a new Marina de Dénia just to port on
entering with 400 more berths with depths of 3 to 4m,
but the port is still crowded in high season.

Construction work on the NW part of the harbour
has now been completed and all buoys laid during the
work have been removed. The new marina has also been
completed and is now fully operational with bars,
restaurants, shops etc. which reduces the need to go on
the long walk into the town.

Approach

From the SE Round the high, steep-sided, flat-topped
promontory of Cabo de San Antonio and follow the
coast keeping a mile offshore to avoid shoals. In the
closer approach, Castillo de Dénia will be seen on a
small hill behind the harbour and the Dique del Norte.
Do not cut the corner but make for a position 200m to
NE of the head of this *dique*.

From the NW The low sandy coast is backed by high
ranges of mountains. Montaña Mongo which lies behind
this harbour, and the vertically faced Cabo de San
Antonio which lies beyond it can be seen from afar. In
the closer approach the Castillo de Dénia on its small
hill and the long Dique del Norte will be seen. Keep at
least 1M off the coast owing to shoals and make for a
position 200m to NE of the head of Dique del Norte.

The head of the Dique del Norte has been washed
away and underwater obstructions may still remain up
to 100m to NE of the present visible head.

GPS approach

Steer to ⊕95 from the northeastern quadrant and steer
228° between the breakwater heads (approx. 0.75M), as
one should be on the leading lines.'

Anchorage in the approach

Anchor 300m to the E of the head of Dique del Norte
in 7m sand.

Entrance

From at least 200m to NE, approach the entrance on a
SW course, give the head of Dique del Norte 30m and
follow it in at this distance off.

Berths

There are three marinas in the harbour. The Municipal
Marina, at the NW end, is for small craft (<7m) only
and it is for private berth holders only. The yacht club is
still available for visiting yachts (call *club náutico* on Ch
9) but is expensive. There is a fairly new marina,
immediately to port on entering (call *Marina de Dénia*
on Ch 9 or phone) which has 400 berths and although
further away from the town most stores are now
available on site.

Charges

Medium; at the *club náutico*, high.

Facilities

All ship work bar radar.
Two slipways, maximum 100 tonnes.
Cranes up to 12 tonnes.
Chandler's shop behind the shipyard.
Water from taps around the yacht harbour and on the Muelle
 de Atraque.
Gasoleo A and petrol in the port and, for members only, the
 club náutico.
Ice factory to the E of the Castillo de Dénia. Ice is also
 available from the yacht club.
The Club Náutico de Dénia has a large modern clubhouse
 with bar, lounge, restaurant, showers and so on. It is
 responsible for the S corner of the harbour. An
 introduction may be required.
A good range of shops in the town and an excellent market.
Launderettes in the town.

Communications

Bus service. Dénia is one terminus of the coastal narrow
gauge rail system. Ferries to Islas Baleares.
☎ Area code 96. Taxi ☎ 578 34 98.

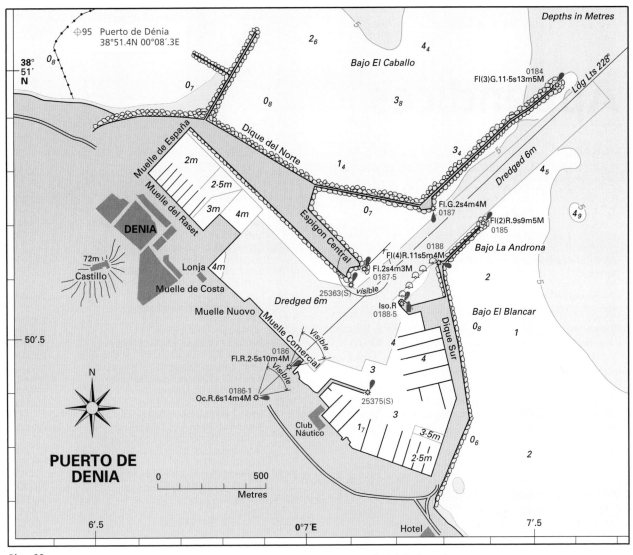

Depths in Metres

⊕95 Puerto de Dénia
38°51.4N 00°08'.3E

38°
51'
N

0₈

Bajo El Caballo

2₆

4₄

FI(3)G.11·5s13m5M

0184

Ldg Lts 228°

0₇

0₈

Muelle de España

Dique del Norte

3₈

3₄

Dredged 6m

4₅

4₉

2m

2·5m

Muelle del Raset

1₄

0₇

FI.G.2s4m4M

0187

Espigón Central

FI(2)R.9s9m5M

0185

DENIA

3m   4m

FI(4)R.11s5m4M

0188

Bajo La Androna

72m

Castillo

Lonja 4m

FI.2s4m3M

0187·5

2

Muelle de Costa

25363(S)   *visible*

Bajo El Blancar

Dredged 6m

Iso.R

0188·5

0₈   1

Muelle Nuovo

Muelle Comercial

Visible

4

Dique Sur

50'.5

N

4

FI.R.2·5s10m4M

0186

Visible

3

0186·1

Oc.R.6s14m4M

25375(S)

3

PUERTO DE
DENIA

0   500

Metres

Club
Náutico

1₇

3·5m

0₆

2·5m

2

6'.5

0°7'E

Hotel

7'.5

Plan 66

Puerto de Dénia from S

Appendices

I. CHARTS

Charts and other publications may be corrected annually by reference to the Admiralty *List of Lights and Fog Signals Volume D* (NP 77) and *E* (NP 78) or weekly via the Admiralty Notices to Mariners.

Note A few charts appear twice in the following list under different island headings. The index diagram only shows large-scale charts where the diagram's scale permits.

Chart agents

Before departure – British Admiralty and Spanish charts from Imray Laurie Norie & Wilson Ltd, Wych House, The Broadway, St Ives, Cambs PE27 5BT ☎ 01480 462114, *Fax* 01480 496109 www.@imray.com. However in the case of Spanish charts, stocks held are limited and it may take some time to fill an order. It may be simpler to order directly from the Instituto Hidrográfico de la Marina, Tolosa Latour 1, DP 11007 Cádiz ☎ (956) 59 94 12, *Fax* (956) 27 53 58 and pay by credit card.

Gibraltar

Gibraltar Chart Agency, 11a Block 5 Watergardens, Gibraltar
☎ +350 76293 *Fax* +350 77293
email gibchartag@gibtelecom.net
www.gibchartagency.com

Spain (Algeciras)

SUISCA SL
Avda. Blas Infante, Centro Blas Local 1, 11201 Agceciras, Cádiz
☎ +34 902 220007 *Fax* +34 902 220 008
email barcelona@suiscasl.com
www.suiscasl.com

BRITISH ADMIRALTY CHARTS

Note Index references refer to sections in *Admiralty World Catalogue NP131* Index E1 Western Mediterranean Sea

Chart	Title	Scale
45	Gibraltar harbour	3,600
142	Strait of Gibraltar	100,000
	Tarifa	25,000
144	Gibraltar	10,000
165	Menorca to Sicilia including Malta	1,100,000
469	Puerto de Alicante	10,000
473	Approaches to Puerto de Alicante	25,000
518	Approaches to Puerto de Valencia	27,500
562	Valencia	10,000
773	Strait of Gibraltar to Isla de Alborán	300,000
774	Motril to Cartagena including Isla de Alborán	300,000
	Isla de Alborán	15,000
1180	Barcelona	10,000
1193	Puerto de Tarragona and approaches	10,000
1196	Approaches to Puerto de Barcelona	30,000
1448	Gibraltar bay	25,000
	Algeciras	12,500
1515	Plans on the east coast of Spain	
	Dénia	15,000

Chart	Title	Scale
	Garrucha	7,500
	Aguilas and El Hornillo	12,500
	Sant Carles de la Rapita and Alcanar	25,000
	Carboneras	15,000
1700	Cartagena to Cabo de San Antonio including Isla Formentera	300,000
1701	Cabo de San Antonio to Villanueva y Geltrú including Islas de Ibiza and Formentera	300,000
1702	Ibiza, Formentera and southern Mallorca	300,000
1703	Mallorca and Menorca	300,000
1704	Punta de la Bana to Islas Medas	300,000
1705	Cabo de San Sebastian to Îles d'Hyères	300,000
1780	Barcelona to Napoli including Islas Baleares, Corse and Sardegna	1,100,000
1850	Approaches to Malaga	25,000
1851	Malaga	10,000
2717	Strait of Gibraltar to Barcelona and Alger including Islas Baleares	1,100,000
2831	Mallorca: Punta Salinas to Cabo de Formentor including Canal de Menorca	120,000
	Puerto de Alcudia	20,000
2832	Mallorca: Punta Salinas to Punta Beca including Isla de Cabrera	120,000
2761	Menorca	60,000
2762	Mahón	7,500
2834	Ibiza and Formentera	120,000
	Ibiza	10,000
	San Antonio Abad	20,000
	Channels between Ibiza and Formentera	50,000
3034	Approaches to Palma	25,000
3035	Palma	10,000
3132	Strait of Gibraltar to Arquipélago da Madeira	1,250,000
3578	Eastern approaches to the Strait of Gibraltar	150,000

SPANISH CHARTS

Chart	Title	Scale
44C	Estrecho de Gibraltar	175,000
45	Estrecho de Gibraltar y Mar de Alborán	350,000
45A	De punta Carnero a cabo Sacratif y de punta Cires a cabo Negro	175,000
45B	De cabo Sacratif a cabo de Gata	175,000
46A	Del cabo de Gata al cabo de Palos	175,000
47A	Del cabo de Palos al cabo de la Nao	175,000
48A	Del puerto de Calpe al puerto de Sagunto y las islas de Ibiza y Formentera	175,000
48B	Del cabo Canet al cabo Tortosa	175,000
48C	De cabo Tortosa a cabo de Tossa	175,000
48E	Islas de Mallorca y Menorca	200,000
49A	Del puerto de Barcelona al Cap Cerbere	75,000
105	Estrecho de Gibraltar. De cabo Roche a punta de la Chullera y de cabo Espartel a cabo Negro	100,000
421	De isla Dragonera a cabo Blanco	50,000
421A	Bahía de Palma Del islote El Toro a cabo Regana	25,000
422	De cabo Regana a punta Salinas	50,000
422A	Freu de Cabrera	25,000

BRITISH ADMIRALTY CHARTS
IMRAY CHARTS

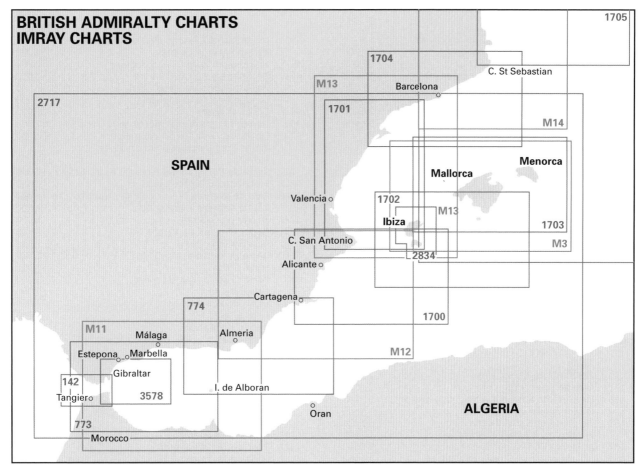

SPANISH CHARTS

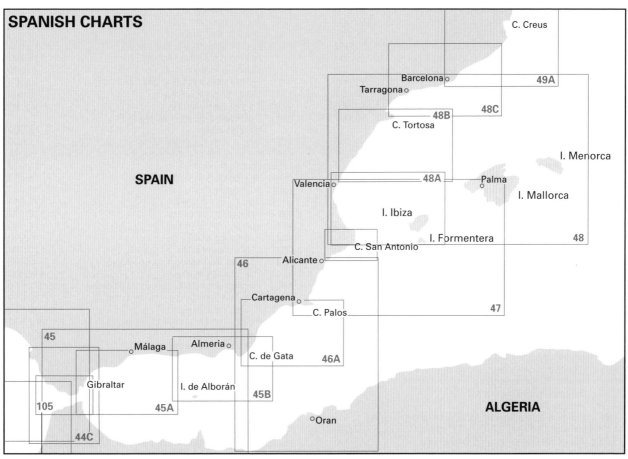

Chart	Title	Scale
423	De punta Plana a Porto Colom con la isla de Cabrera y adyacentes	50,000
424	De Cala Llonga a cabo Farrutx	50,000
425	De cabo Pera a cabo Formentor	50,000
425A	Bahía de Alcudia	25,000
426	De la Bahía de Alcudia al puerto de Sóller	50,000
426A	Aproches del puerto de Mahón	25,000
427	De cala de la Calobra a isla Dragonera	50,000
436	Isla de Menorca 60,000	
445	Estrecho de Gibraltar De punta Camarinal a punta Europa y de cabo Espartel a punta Almina	60,000
445A	Bahía de Algeciras	25,000
445B	Bajo de los Cabezos e isla de Tarifa	25,000
453	De punta Europa a la torre de las Bóvedas	50,000
454	De Estepona a punta de Calaburras	50,000
455	De punta de Calaburras a la ensenada de Vélez-Málaga	50,000
455A	Aproches del puerto de Málaga	25,000
456	De punta de Torrox a cabo Sacratif	50,000
457	De Motril a Adra	50000
458	De Adra a Almería	50,000
459	Golfo de Almería De la punta Sabinar al cabo de Gata	50,000
	Plano: Roquetas de Mar	7,500
461	De cabo de Gata a Mesa de Roldán	50,000
	Planos: Puerto Genovés y ensenada de San José	15,000
	Ensenada de los Escullos	25,000
	Cala de San Pedro	25,000
462	De Mesa de Roldán a isla de los Terreros	50,000
	Plano: Puerto de Garrucha	7,500
463	De punta de Sarriá a cabo Tiñoso	50,000
	Puertos de Aguila y El Hornillo	12,500
463A	De Monte Cope a punta de La Azohía	30,000
464	Del cabo Tiñoso al cabo de Palos	50,000
464A	Del puerto de Mazarrón a cabo del Agua	30,000
471	Del cabo de Palos a cabo Cervera	50,000
472	Bahías de Santa Pola y Alicante	50,000
472A	Aproches del puerto de Alicante	25,000
473	Del cabo de las Huertas a la punta de Ifach	50,000
	Plano: Puerto Deportivo El Campello	7,500
474	De la punta de Ifach al río Bullent	50,000
	Puerto de Morayra	10,000
475	Del río Bullent al cabo Cullera	50,000
476	De cabo Cullera al puerto de Valencia	50,000
478	De cabo Negret a cabo Berbería	60,000
479	Costa sur de la isla de Ibiza e isla de Formentera	60,000
479A	Freus entre Ibiza y Formentera	25,000
481	Del puerto de Valencia al puerto de Sagunto	50,000
481A	Aproches del puerto de Valencia	25,000
482	Del puerto de Sagunto al cabo de Oropesa	60,000
482A	Aproches del puerto de Castellón	25,000
483	Con río Mijares al cabo de Oropesa con las islas Columbretes	60,000
483A	Aproches de las islas Columbretes	25,000
484	De cabo de Oropesa a puerto de Vinaroz	60,000
485	Del puerto de Vinaroz al puerto de La Ampolla	60,000
486	Del puerto del Fangal al puerto de Torredembarra	60,000
487	De cabo Salou al puerto de Villanueva y Geltrú	50,000
487A	Aproches del puerto de Tarragona	25,000
488	Del puerto de Vilanova i la Geltrú al puerto de Barcelona	50,000
488A	Del puerto de Vilanova i la Geltrú al puerto de Barcelona	25,000
	Planos: Puerto de Garraf	5,000
	Puerto de Vallcarca	5,000
489	Del puerto de Barcelona al puerto de Arenys de Mar	50,000
489A	Aproches del puerto de Barcelona	25,000

Chart	Title	Scale
491	Del puerto de Arenys de Mar al puerto de San Feliú de Guixols	50,000
492	De cabo de Tossa a cabo Begur	50,000
493	De cap Negre a cap Cerbere	50,000
	Planos: Puerto de Llaça	10,000
	Fondeadero de Cadaqués	20,000
493A	Golfo de Roses	25,000
965	De punta de Amer al Morro de la Vaca	100,000
970	De Morro de la Vaca a cabo Blanco	100,000
	Plano: Surgidero de la Foradada de Miramar	12,000
4211	Bahía de Palma De las Illetas al islote Galera	10,000
4215	Ensenada de Santa Ponsa	10,000
4216	Freu de Dragonera y puerto de Andratx	15,000
4221	Isla de Cabrera y adyacentes	12,500
4222	Puerto de Cabrera	5,000
4231	Porto Petro y Cala Llonga	7,500
	Cala Figuera	2,500
4240	Bahía de Alcudia	12,500
4241	Porto Colom	5,000
	Porto Cristo o cala Manacor	5,000
	Cala Ratjada	5,000
4242	Bahía de Pollença	7,500
4251	Puerto de Sóller	5,000
4261	Puerto de Mahón	7,500
4262	Puerto de Fornells y bahía de Tirant	10,000
4263	Puerto de Ciutadella	5,000
4450	Puerto de Tarifa	7,500
4451	Bahía de Algeciras - Zona Oeste	10,000
4452	Bahía de Algeciras - Zona Este	10,000
4571	Puertos de Motril y Adra	
	Puerto de Adra	10,000
	Puerto de Motril	7,500
4591	Puerto de Almería	10,000
4621	Puertos de Carboneras	10,000
4632	Rada de Mazarrón	12,500
4642	Puertos de Cartagena y Escombreras	10,000
4710	Puertos de Torrevieja, San Pedro del Pinatar, Tomás Maestre y Cabo de Palos con las islas Hormigas	
	Planos: Puerto de Torrevieja	15,000
	Puerto de Tomás Maestre	15,000
	Cabo de Palos e Islas Hormigas	20,000
	Puerto de San Pedro del Pinatar	10,000
4721	Bahía de Santa Pola	10,000
4722	Puerto de Alicante	10,000
4731	Del Puerto de Villajollosa al Pto De Benidorm	12,500
4732	Del puerto de Altea al puerto de Calpe	12,500
4741	De la ensenada de Javea al Puerto de Denia	15,000
4752	Puerto de Gandía	10,000
4781	Puerto de San Antonio Abad	5,000
4791	Puerto de Ibiza	10,000
4811	Puerto de Valencia	10,000
4812	Puerto de Sagunto	10,000
4821	Puerto de Castellón	10,000
4822	Puerto de Burriana	10,000
4831	Islas Columbretes	10,000
4841	Puertos de Benicarló y Peñíscola	10,000
4842	Puerto de Vinaros	10,000
4851	Puertos de Sant Carles de la Rápita y Alcanar	12,500
4861	Rada de Salou y puerto de Cambrils	10,000
4871	Puerto de Tarragona	10,000
4881	Puerto de Vilanova i la Geltrú	7,500
4882	Puerto de Sitges	10,000
4891	Puerto de Barcelona	12,500
4892	Del puerto de El Masnou al puerto de Premiá de Mar	10,000
4893	Puertos de Mataró y El Balis	10,000
4911	Puertos de El Balis y Arenys de Mar	10,000
4913	Puerto de Blanes	10,000
4922	Ensenada y puerto de Sant Feliú de Guíxols	10,000
4923	Fondeadero y puerto de Palamós	10,000
4924	Cabo San Sebastián e islas Hormigas	10,000

Chart	Title	Scale
4931	Fondeadero de islas Medas y puerto de El Estartit	10,000
4932	Bahía de Roses	10,000
4934	Puerto de la Selva	10,000

FRENCH CHARTS

Service Hydrographique et Oceanographique de la Marine (SHOM)

Chart	Title	Scale
4033	Iles Columbretes	18,000
4717	De Gibraltar à la pointe del Sabinal	250,000
	Cartouche: Port de Motril	10,000
	Mouillages de la Herradura, Los Berengueles, Almunecar, Belilla et Salobrena	80,000
4718	De la Pointe del Sabinal à Carthagène	247,000
	Cartouche: Port Genoves et anse de San Jose	25,000
	Cartouche: Anse de los Escullos	25,000
	Cartouche: Port de San Pedro	25,000
4719	De Carthagène à Valence	242,000

Chart	Title	Scale
4720	De Valence a Tarragone	236,000
4827	De Tarragone au cap de Creux	231,000
5505	Iles Baléares	319,000
6341	Ports de la côte Sud d'Espagne, anse de Mazarron	25,000
	Cartouche: Port de Portman	10,000
	Cartouche: Ports de Aguilas et de el Hornillo	15,000
6515	Ports de la côte Est d'Espagne – Port d'Alicante	10,000
	Cartouche: Port de Torrevieja	15,000
6569	Mer d'Alboran, feuille Nord	202,000
6570	Mer d'Alboran, feuille Sud	203,000
6775	Baie de Palma, de las Illetas a l'ilot Galera	10,000
7008	Du Cabo de San Sébastian à Fos-sur-Mer	25,000
7026	Baie de Algeciras	25,000
7042	Détroit de Gibraltar	100,000
7046	Port de Barcelona	10,000

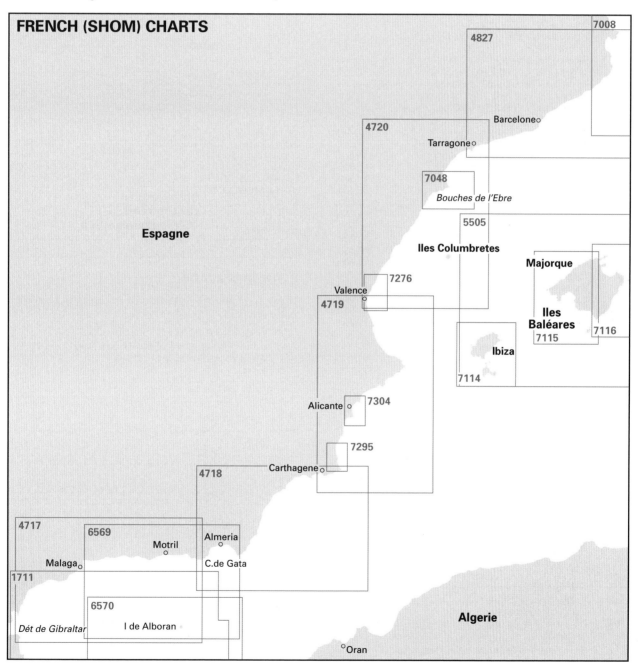

Chart	Title	Scale
7047	Du Cabo de Salou à Tarragona	10,000
7048	Du port de Vinaroz au port de la Ampolla – Delta de l'Ebre (Ebro)	60,000
7115	Mallorca _ Partie Ouest _ De Punta Beca à Punta Salinas	100,000
7116	Mallorca – Partie Est – De Punta Salinas à Cabo Formentor	100,000
7117	Menorca – Ports et Mouillages de Menorca, Ciudadela, Tiranet Cala Fornells, Máhon	100,000
7118	Abords de Palma – De Isla Dragoner à Cabo Blanco, Andraitx, Santa Ponsa	40,000
7119	Ports et Mouillages de Mallorca et Cabrèra Pollensa, Alcudia, Soller, Colom Ratjada, Surgidero de, Foradada, Figuera, Cristó ou Calá Manacor, *Cala* Llonga	12,500
7276	Abords de Valencia	25,000
7294	Puerto de Malaga	10,000
7295	Ports et Mouillages entre Cabo de la Nao et Cabo de Palos Tomás Maestre, Palos, Villajoyosa, Mar Menor	15,000
7296	Ports et mouillages entre Tarragona et Alicante Peñiscola, Castellón de la Plana, Burriana, Jávea, Benicarlo, Sagunto, Denia, San Carlos de la Rápita, Calpe, Gandia	15,000
	Altea	20,000
7298	Ports et mouillages entre la frontière franco-espagnole et Tarragona	
	Puerto de la Selva	10,000
	Puerto de Cadaqués	15,000
	Bahía de Rosas	15,000
	Puerto de El Estartit	15,000
	Puerto de Palamos	15,000
	Puerto de Arenys de Mar	10,000
	Puerto de San Feliú de Guíxols	10,000
	Cala de Llafranc	10,000
	Puerto de Blanes	15,000
	Puerto de Villanueva y Geltrú	15,000
	Sitges et puerto Vallcarca	20,000
	Puerto de Garraf	5,000
7304	Abords de Alicante	10,000
7504	Abords de Almeria	25,000
7505	Du Cabo de Tossa au Cap Cerbère	93,700
7642	Ports de Carthagène et d'Escombreras	10,000

IMRAY CHARTS

M10 Western Mediterranean – Gibraltar to the Ionian Sea 1:2,750,000 WGS 84

M11 Mediterranean Spain – Gibraltar to Cabo de Gata & Morocco de Gata 1:440,000 WGS 84
Plans Strait of Gibraltar, Gibraltar, Ceuta, Almeria, Estepona, Puerto de Almerimar

M12 Mediterranean Spain – Cabo de Gata to Denia & Ibiza 1:500,000 WGS 84
Plans Mar Menor, Alicante, Dénia, Torrevieja, Altea, Villajoyosa

M13 Mediterranean Spain – Dénia to Barcelona 1:440,000 WGS 84
Plans Dénia, Tarragona, Valencia Yacht Harbour, Barcelona Harbour, Barcelona Port Vell, San Antonio (Ibiza)

M14 Mediterranean Spain – Barcelona to Bouches du Rhône 1:440,000 WGS 84
Plans St-Cyprien-Plage, Puerto de l'Escala, Sète, Cap d'Agde, Roses, Palamos, Port Vendres, Barcelona Harbour, Barcelona Port Vell

Chart	Title	Scale

M3 Islas Baleares – Formentera, Ibiza, Mallorca, Menorca 1:350,000 WGS 84
Plans Puerto de Ibiza, Puerto de Colom, Puerto de Palma, Puerto de Máhon, Puerto de San Antonio

M15 Mediterranean France – Marseille to Genoa and La Corse 1:400,000 WGS 84
Plans Baie de Calvi, Iles d'Hyères, Antibes, St-Jean-Cap Ferrat, Golfe de St Tropez, Monaco, Bandol, Genoa, San Remo

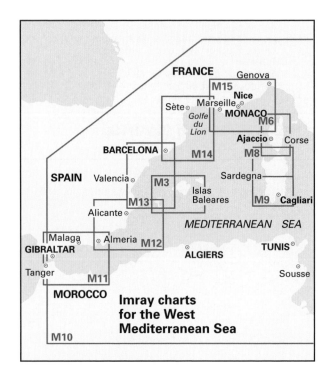

Imray charts for the West Mediterranean Sea

II. FURTHER READING

Many navigational publications are reprinted annually, in which case the latest edition should be carried. Others, including most cruising guides, are updated by means of supplements available from the publishers (web site www.imray.com).

Admiralty publications

NP 289 Leisure Maritime Communications (UK and the Mediterranean)

Mediterranean Pilot Vol I (NP 45) and Supplement covers the south and east coasts of Spain, the Islas Baleares, Sardinia, Sicily and the north coast of Africa

List of Lights and Fog Signals, Vol E (NP 78) (Mediterranean, Black and Red Seas)

List of Radio Signals

Vol 1, Part 1 (NP281/1) Coast Radio Stations (Europe, Africa and Asia)

Vol 2 (NP 282) Radio Navigational Aids, Electronic Position Fixing Systems and Radio Time Signals

Vol 3, Part 1 (NP 283/1) Radio Weather Services and Navigational Warnings (Europe, Africa and Asia)

Vol 4 (NP 284) Meteorological Observation Stations

Vol 5 (NP 285) Global Maritime Distress and Safety

Systems (GMDSS)

Vol 6, Part 2 (NP 286/2) Vessel Traffic Services, Port Operations and Pilot Services (The Mediterranean, Africa and Asia)

Yachtsmen's guides, almanacs etc
English language

Imray Mediterranean Almanac, Rod Heikell & Lu Michell (Imray Laurie Norie & Wilson Ltd). A biennial almanac with second year supplement, packed with information. Particularly good value for yachts on passage when not every cruising guide is likely to be carried.

Mediterranean Cruising Handbook, Rod Heikell (Imray Laurie Norie & Wilson Ltd, 2004). Useful information on techniques such as berthing bow or stern-to, clothing, storing up etc. General information on cruising areas, passages etc.

Islas Baleares RCC Pilotage Foundation - Robin Brandon - Revised by John Marchment (Imray Laurie Norie & Wilson Ltd, 2003).

Mediterranean Spain – Costas del Azahar, Dorada and Brava, Robin Brandon Revised by John Marchment (Imray Laurie Norie & Wilson Ltd, 2002).

North Africa, Graham Hutt (Imray Laurie Norie & Wilson Ltd, 2005). The only yachtsman's guide to the coast between the Strait of Gibraltar and Tunisia. Includes Atlantic Morocco.

Spanish

La Guía del Navegante – La Costa de España y el Algarve (The Yachtsman's Guide). Spanish and English, revised annually. (PubliNáutic Rilnvest SL,). Not a full scale pilot book, but an excellent source of up-to-date information on local services and facilites (partly via the advertisements) with phone numbers etc.

Guia Náutica Turistica y Deportiva de España by the Asamblea de Capitánes de Yate. An expensive and colourful guide book covering all the Spanish coasts and including some useful data on harbours but no pilotage information. The plans are in outline only. Written in Spanish with a partial English translation. Because symbols are lavishly used, much of it can be understood with only a limited knowledge of Spanish.

Guia Náutica de España. Tomo II, Costa del Azahar, Blanca and Baleares. One of a series of books featuring attractive colour pictures, some of which are out of date, and some text. Written in Spanish but an English version is sometimes available.

El Mercado Nautico (The Boat Market). A free newspaper published every two or three months and available from yacht clubs, marina offices etc. Written in Spanish, English and German it includes, amongst other things, a useful (though by no means comprehensive) listing of current marina prices.

French

Votre Livre de Bord – Méditerranée (Bloc Marine). French almanac covering the Mediterranean, including details of weather forecasts transmitted from France and Monaco. An English/French version is also published which translates some, though by no means all, the text. Published annually.

German

Spanische Gewässer, Lissabon bis Golfe du Lion, K Neumann (Delius Klasing). A seamanlike guide and semi-pilot book, which includes sketch plans of most harbours. Harbour data is limited but it contains much good general advice on sailing in this area.

Background

The Birth of Europe, Michael Andrew (BBC Books). An excellent and comprehensive work which explains in simple terms how the Mediterranean and surrounding countries developed over the ages from 3000 BC.

The First Eden, David Attenborough (William Collins). A fascinating study of 'The Mediterranean World and Man'.

The Inner Sea, Robert Fox (Sinclair-Stevenson, 1991). An account of the countries surrounding the Mediterranean and the forces which shaped them, written by a well known BBC journalist.

Sea of Seas, H Scott (van Nostrand). A half-guidebook half-storybook on the western Mediterranean. Very out of date and now out of print, but a delight to read.

III. SPANISH GLOSSARY

The following limited glossary relates to the weather, the abbreviations to be found on Spanish charts and some words likely to be useful on entering port. For a list containing many words commonly used in connection with sailing, see Webb & Manton, *Yachtsman's Ten Language Dictionary* (Adlard Coles Nautical).

Weather

On the radio, if there is a storm warning the forecast starts *aviso temporal*. If, as usual, there is no storm warning, the forecast starts no *hay temporal*. Many words are similar to the English and their meanings can be guessed. The following may be less familiar:

Viento Wind
calma calm
ventolina light air
flojito light breeze
flojo gentle breeze
bonancible moderate breeze
fresquito fresh breeze
fresco strong breeze
frescachón near gale
temporal fuerte gale
temporal duro strong gale
temporal muy duro storm
borrasca violent storm
huracán, temporal
huracanado hurricane
tempestad, borrasca thunderstorm

EL CIELO THE SKY
nube cloud
nubes altas, bajas high, low clouds
nubloso cloudy
cubierto covered, overcast
claro, despejado clear

Names of cloud types in Spanish are based on the same Latin words as the names used in English.

Visibilidad Visibility
buena good
regular moderate
mala poor
calima haze
neblina mist
bruma sea mist
niebla fog

Precipitación Precipitation
aguacero shower
llovizna drizzle
lluvia rain
aguanieve sleet
nieve snow
granizada hail

Sistemas del Tiempo Weather Systems
anticiclón anticyclone
depresión, borrasca depression
vaguada trough
cresta, dorsal ridge
cuna wedge
frente front
frio cold
cálido warm
ocluido occluded
bajando falling
subiendo rising

LIGHTS AND CHARTS – MAJOR TERMS AND ABBREVIATIONS

A	*amarilla*	yellow
Alt	*alternativa*	alternative
Ag Nv	*aguas navegables*	navigable waters
Ang	*angulo*	angle
Ant	*anterior*	anterior, earlier, forward
Apag	*apagado*	extinguished
Arrc	*arrecife*	reef
At	*atenuada*	attenuated
B	*blanca*	white
Ba	*bahía*	bay
	bajamar escorada	chart datum
Bal	*baliza*	buoy, beacon
Bal. E	*baliza elástica*	plastic (elastic) buoy
Bco	*banco*	bank
Bo	*bajo*	shoal, under, below, low
Boc	*bocina*	horn, trumpet
Br1	*babor*	port (ie. left)
C	*campana*	bell
card	*cardinal*	cardinal
Cañ	*cañon*	canyon
	boya de castillete	pillar buoy
cil	*cilíndrico*	cylindrical
C	*cabo*	cape
Cha	*chimenea*	chimney
Cno	*castillo*	castle
cón	*cónico*	conical
Ct	*centellante*	quick flashing (50-80/minute)
Ctl	*centellante interrumpida*	interrupted quick flashing
cuad	*cuadrangular*	quadrangular
D	*destello*	flash
Desap	*desaparecida*	disappeared
Dest	*destruida*	destroyed
	dique	breakwater, jetty
Dir	*direccional*	directional
DL	*destello largo*	long flash
E	*este*	east
edif	*edificio*	building
	ensenada	cove, inlet
Er	*estribor*	starboard
Est	*esférico*	spherical
Esp	*especial*	special
Est sñ	*estación de señales*	signal station
ext	*exterior*	exterior
Extr	*extremo*	end, head (of pier etc.)

F	*fija*	fixed
Fca	*fabrica*	factory
FD	*fija y destello*	fixed and flashing
FGpD	*fija y grupo de destellos*	fixed and group flashing
Flot	*flotador*	float
Fondn	*fondeadero*	anchorage
GpCt	*grupo de centellos*	group quick flashing
GpD	*grupo de destellos*	group flashing
GpOc	*grupo de ocultaciones*	group occulting
GpRp	*grupo de centellos rápidos*	group very quick flashing
hel	*helicoidales*	helicoidal
hor	*horizontal*	horizontal
Hund	*hundida*	submerged, sunk
I	*interrumpido*	interrupted
Igla	*iglesia*	church
Inf	*inferior*	inferior, lower
Intens	*intensificado*	intensified
Irreg	*irregular*	irregular
Iso	*isofase*	isophase
L	*luz*	light
La	*lateral*	lateral
	levante	eastern
M	*millas*	miles
Mte	*monte*	mountain
Mto	*monumento*	monument
N	*norte*	north
Naut	*nautófono*	foghorn
NE	*nordeste*	northeast
No	*número*	number
NW	*noroeste*	northwest
Obst	*obstrucción*	obstruction
ocas	*ocasional*	occasional
oct	*octagonal*	octagonal
oc	*oculta*	obscured
Oc	*ocultatión sectores*	obscured sectors
Pe A	*peligro aislado*	isolated danger
	poniente	western
Post	*posterior*	posterior, later
Ppal	*principal*	principal
	prohibido	prohibited
Obston	*obstrucción*	obstruction
Prov	*provisional*	provisional
prom	*prominente*	prominent, conspicuous
Pta	*punta*	point
Pto,	*puerto*	port[1]
PTO	*puerto deportivo*	yacht harbour
	puerto pesquero	fishing harbour
	puerto de Marina de Guerra	naval harbour
R	*roja*	red
Ra	*estación radar*	radar station
Ra+	*radar + suffix*	radar + suffix (Ra Ref etc.)
RC	*radiofaro circular*	non-directional radiobeacon
RD	*radiofaro dirigido*	directional radiobeacon
rect	*rectangular*	rectangular
Ra	*rocas*	rocks
Rp	*centeneallante rápida*	very quick flashing (80-160/min)
Rpl	*cent. rápida interrumpida*	interrupted very quick flashing
RW	*radiofaro giratorio*	rotating radiobeacon
s	*sugundos*	seconds
S	*sur*	south
SE	*sudeste*	southeast
sil	*silencio*	silence
Silb	*silbato*	whistle
Sincro	*sincronizda con*	syncronized with
Sir	*sirena*	siren
son	*sonido*	sound, noise, report
Sto/a	*Santo, Santa*	Saint
SW	*sudoeste*	southwest
T	*temporal*	temporary

Te	torre	tower
trans	transversal	transversal
triang	triangular	triangular
troncoc	troncocónico	truncated cone
troncop	troncopiramidal	truncated pyramid
TSH	antena de radio	radio mast
TV	antena de TV	TV mast
U	centellante ultra-rápida	ultra quick flashing (+160/min)
UI	cent. ultra-rápida interrumpido	interrupted ultra quick flashing
V	verde	green
Vis	visible	visible
	vivero	shellfish raft or bed
W	oeste	west

1. 'puerto' is applied to any landing place from a beach to a container port.

PORTS AND HARBOURS

a popa stern-to
a proa bows-to
abrigo shelter
al costado alongside
amarrar to moor
amarradero mooring
ancho breadth (see also manga)
anclar to anchor
botar to launch (a yacht)
boya de amarre mooring buoy
cabo warp, line (also cape)
calado draught
compuerta lock, basin
dársena dock, harbour
dique breakwater, jetty
escala ladder
escalera steps
esclusa lock
escollera jetty
eslora total length overall
espigón spur, spike, mole
fábrica factory
ferrocarril railway
fondear to anchor or moor
fondeadero anchorage
fondeo mooring buoy
fondo depth (bottom)
grua crane
guia mooring lazy-line (lit. guide)
nudo knot (ie. speed)
longitud length (see also eslora), longitude
lonja fish market (wholesale)
manga beam (ie. width)
muelle mole, jetty, quay
noray bollard
pantalán jetty, pontoon
parar to stop
pila estaca pile
pontón pontoon
práctico pilot (ie. pilot boat)
profundidad depth
rampa slipway
rompeolas breakwater
varadero slipway, hardstanding
varar to lift (a yacht)
vertedero (verto) spoil ground

Direction

babor port (ie. left)
estribor starboard
norte north
este east
sur south
oeste west

PHRASES USEFUL ON ARRIVAL

Donde puedo amarrar?	Where can I moor?
A donde debo ir?	Where should I go?
Que es la profundidad?	What is the depth?
Que es su eslora	
Cuantos metros?	What is your length?
Para cuantas noches?	For how many nights?

Administration and stores

aceite oil (including engine oil)
aduana customs
agua potable drinking water
aseos toilet block
astillero shipyard
capitán de puerto harbourmaster
derechos dues, rights
duchas showers
dueño, propietario owner
efectos navales chandlery
electricidad electricity
gasoleo, diesel diesel
guardia civil police
hielo (cubitos) ice (cubes)
lavandería laundry
lavandería automática launderette
luz electricity (lit. light)
manguera hosepipe
parafina, petróleo, keroseno paraffin, kerosene
patrón skipper (not owner)
gasolina petrol
título certificate
velero sailmaker (also sailing ship)

IV. CERTIFICATE OF COMPETENCE

1. Given below is a transcription of a statement made by the Counsellor for Transport at the Spanish Embassy, London in March 1996. It is directed towards citizens of the UK but doubtless the principles apply to other EU citizens. One implication is that in a particular circumstance (paragraph 2a below) a UK citizen does not need a Certificate of Competence during the first 90 days of his visit.

2. a. British citizens visiting Spain in charge of a UK registered pleasure boat flying the UK flag need only fulfil UK law.

   b. British citizens visiting Spain in charge of a Spanish registered pleasure boat flying the Spanish flag has one of two options:

   i. To obtain a Certificate of Competence issued by the Spanish authorities. See *Normas reguladore para la obtención de titulos para el gobierno de embarcaciones de recreo* issued by the Ministerio de Obras Publicas, Transportes y Medio Ambiente.

   ii. To have the Spanish equivalent of a UK certificate issued. The following equivalencies are used by the Spanish Maritime Administration:
   Yachtmaster Ocean *Capitan de Yate*
   Yachtmaster Offshore *Patron de Yate de altura*
   Coastal Skipper *Patron de Yate*
   Day Skipper *Patron de Yate embarcaciones de recreo*
   Helmsman Overseas* *Patron de embarcaciones de recreo restringido a motor*

   *The Spanish authorities have been informed that this certificate has been replaced by the International Certificate of Competence.

3. The catch to para 2(a) above is that, in common with other EU citizens, after 90 days a UK citizen is technically no longer a visitor, must apply for a *permiso de residencia* and must equip his boat to Spanish rules and licensing requirements.

In practice the requirement to apply for a permiso de residencia does not appear to be enforced in the case of cruising yachtsmen who live aboard rather than ashore and are frequently on the move. By the same token, the requirement for a British skipper in charge of a UK registered pleasure boat flying the UK flag to carry a Certificate of Competence after their first 90 days in Spanish waters also appears to be waived. Many yachtsmen have reported cruising Spanish waters for extended periods with no documentation beyond that normally carried in the UK.

4. The RYA suggests the following technique to obtain an equivalent Spanish certificate:
   a. Obtain two photocopies of your passport
   b. Have them notarised by a Spanish notary
   c. Obtain a copy of the UK Certificate of Competence and send it to the Consular Department, The Foreign and Commonwealth Office, Clive House, Petty France, London SW1H 9DH, with a request that it be stamped with the Hague Stamp (this apparently validates the document). The FCO will probably charge a fee so it would be best to call the office first ☎ 020 7270 3000.
   d. Have the stamped copy notarized by a UK notary.
   e. Send the lot to the Spanish Merchant Marine for the issue of the Spanish equivalent.

It may be both quicker and easier to take the Spanish examination.

V. CERTIFICATE OF INSURANCE

It is necessary to carry a statement regarding insurance in Spanish.

The yacht insurance broker should provide this on request.

VI. CHARTER REGULATIONS

Any EU-flag yacht applying to charter in Spanish waters must be either VAT paid or exempt (the latter most commonly due to age). Non-EU flag vessels must have a valid Temporary Import Licence and may also have to conform to other regulations.

Applying for a charter licence can be a tortuous business. Firstly the Director General de Transportes at the Conselleria d'Obres Publiques i Ordenacio del Territori must be approached with a pre-authorisation application. This obtained, the application itself is sent to the *capitanías Maritimas* together with ships' papers and proof of passenger insurance and registration as a commercial activity. A safety and seaworthiness inspection will be carried out. Finally a fiscal representative must be appointed and tax paid on revenue generated.

It will probably be simpler to make the application through one of the companies specialising in this type of work.

VII. VALUE ADDED TAX

The Spanish phrase for Value Added Tax (VAT) is Impuesto sobre el valor añadido (IVA), levied at 16% in 1996. Note that for VAT purposes the Canaries, Gibraltar, the Channel Islands and the Isle of Man are outside the EU fiscal area.

Subject to certain exceptions, vessels in EU waters are liable for VAT. One exception is a boat registered outside the EU fiscal area and owned by a non EU citizen which remains in EU waters for less than six months.

For a boat built within the EU fiscal area after 1985 the following documents taken together will show VAT status:
a. An invoice listing VAT or receipt if available
b. Registration Certificate
c. Bill of Sale

For a boat built prior to 1985 the following documentation is required:
e. Evidence of age and of ownership. The full Registration Certificate will serve but the Small Ship Registry Certificate will not.
f. Evidence that it was moored in EU fiscal waters at midnight on 31 December 1992 or, in the case of Austrian, Finnish and Swedish waters, 31 December 1994.

Any boat purchased outside the EU by an EU resident is liable for VAT on import to the EU.

EU owners of boats built within the EU, exported by them and which were outside EU fiscal waters at the cut-off date may be entitled to Returned Goods Relief. In the latter case, HM Customs and Excise may be able to issue a 'tax opinion letter'. The office has no public counter but may be approached by letter or fax. The address is: HM Customs and Excise, Dover Yacht Unit, Parcel Post Depot, Charlton Green, Dover, Kent CT16 1EH ☎ 01304 224421 *Fax* 01304 215786.

All the rules change when a yacht is used commercially – most commonly for chartering.

Note that, IVA is now charged on fuel for pleasure craft. As a result yachts cannot now obtain fuel at fishing ports and must get fuel at marina pumps (or in jerrycans from local garages).

VIII. OFFICIAL ADDRESSES

Spanish embassies and consulates
London (Embassy)
39 Chesham Place, London SW1X 8SB
   ☎ 020 7235 5555 *Fax* 020 7259 6392
   Email embespuk@mail.mae.es
London (Consulate)
20 Draycott Place, London SW3 2RZ
   ☎ 020 7589 8989 *Fax* 020 7581 7888
   Email conspalon@mail.mae.es
Manchester
Suite 1a Brook House, 70 Spring Gardens, Manchester M2 2BQ ☎ 0161 236 1262/33
Edinburgh
63 North Castle Street, Edinburgh EH2 3LJ
   ☎ 0131 220 1843 *Fax* 0131 226 4568

Washington
2375 Pennsylvania Ave DC 20037
☎ (202) 452 0100 *Fax* (202) 833 5670
New York
150 E 58th Street, New York, NY 10155
☎ 212 355 4080 *Fax* 212 644 3751
Spanish national tourist offices
London
22-23 Manchester Square, London W1M 5AP
☎ 0171 486 8077 *Fax* 0171 486 8034
www.tourspain.co.uk
New York
666 Fifth Avenue, New York, NY 10103
☎ 212 265 8822 *Fax* 212 265 8864
British and American embassies in Madrid
British Embassy
Calle de Fernando el Santo 16, 28010 Madrid
☎ (34) 91 700 8200 or 319 0200, *Fax* (34) 91 700 8210
American Embassy
Calle Serrano 75, 28006 Madrid. ☎ (34) 91 587 2200, *Fax* (34) 91 587 2303
British Consulates
Alicante
British Consulate, Plaza Calvo Sotelo
1-2, Apartado de Correas 564, 03001 Alicante
☎/*Fax* (34) 376 839 8440
Email uktiben@cyberbcn.com
Barcelona
British Consulate-General, Edificio Torre de Barcelona,
Avenida Diagonal 477-13, 08036 Barcelona
☎ (34) 93 366 6200 Fax (34) 93 366 6221
E-mail bcon@cyberbcn.com
Málaga
British Consulate, Edificio Eurocom, Bloque Sur, Calle
Mauricio Moro Pareto 2-2°, 29006 Málaga
☎ (34) 952 352 300 *Fax* (34) 952 359 211

IX. DOCUMENTATION

It has been found useful to have the following list available for registering at each port or marina to be visited:
Nombre de yate (yacht's name)
Bandiera (flag)
Lista y folio (yacht's number)
Reg. bruto (registered tonnage)
Tipo (type of vessel)
Palos (number of masts)
Motor, Marca y potencia (engine make and capacity)
Eslor total (LOA)
Maga (beam)
Calado (draft)
Puerto base (home port)
Number cabinas (number of cabins)
Seguor (insurance company)
Proprietario (skipper)
Nacionalidad (nationality)
Telefono
Pasaporte
Tripulante y pasajero (passengers on board)
1. Nombre, nacionaldid, y pasaporte
2. Nombre, nacionalidad, y pasaporte etc.

Cartagena
968 501 509

X. WAYPOINT LIST

The WPs in **bold** form a series with which one is able to steer from off Gibraltar to Dénia. All WPs are derived from electronic charts to WGS84 from source material at European Datum 50

The numerical sequence does not signify that a route may be safely selected from a coastal waypoint to harbour. Navigators must plot their own routes taking note of the numerous fish farms and other obstacles along this coastline.

Port	⊕	Lat N	Long W	
GIBRALTAR				
	1	36°08′	05°22′·5	Gibraltar Harbour approaches
	2	**36°05′·5**	**5°21′**	**Pta Europa west**
COSTA DEL SOL				
Port II	⊕	N	W	
	11	**36°05′·5**	**05°20′**	**Pta Europa east**
2	12	36°17′	05°16′·2	Puerto de Sotogrande approaches
3	13	36°21′·1	05°13′·6	Puerto de la Duquesa approaches
	14	**36°22′·5**	**05°08′**	**SE of Pta de la Doncella**
4	15	36°24′·65	05°09′·6	Estepona approaches
5	16	36°28′·9	05°57′·4	Puerto de José Banús approaches
6	17	36°30′·25	04°53′·55	Club Marbella
7	18	36°30′·3	04°52′·6	App Bajadilla
8	19	36°28′·8	04°44′·5	Cabo Pino approaches
	20	**36°29′**	**04°38′**	**Pta de Calaburras**
9	21	36°32′·6	04°36′·65	Puerto de Fuengirola approaches
11	22	36°35′·5	04°30′·5	Puerto de Benalmádena approaches
12	23	36°41′·7	04°25′·0	Puerto de Málaga approaches
	24	**36 41′**	**04°0′·5**	**Puerto de El Candado**
13	25	36°42′·8	04°20′·9	Puerto de El Candado approaches
14	26	36°44′·7	04°04′·4	Puerto Caleta de Vélez
	27	**36°42′**	**03°57′·4**	**Pta del Torrox**
III				
	28	**36°42′·5**	**03°44′**	**Pta de la Concepcion**
15	29	36°43′·7	03°43′·4	Marina del Este
16	30	36°42′·7	03°30′·7	Puerto de Motril
	31	**36°41′**	**03°28′**	**Cabo Sacratif**
17	32	36°44′·25	03°01′·0	Puerto de Adra
18	33	36°41′·65	02°48′·1	Puerto de Almerimar approaches
	34	**36°37′·5**	**02°46′**	**SSE of Pta de las Entinas**
19	35	36°45′·5	02°36′·15	Puerto de de Roquetas del Mar approaches
20	36	36°48′·7	02°33′·8	Puerto de Aguadulce approaches
21	37	36°49′·25	02°27′·75	Puerto de Almería approaches
	38	**36°46′·5**	**02°25′·5**	**S of Pta del Río**
	39	**36°41′**	**02°10′**	**Cabo de Gata**

Port	⊕	Lat N	Long W	
COSTA BLANCA				
IV				
23	50	36°45′·7	02°06′·2	Puerto de San José
	51	**36°46′**	**02°02′**	**Pta de Loma Pelada**
	52	**36°56′**	**01°52′·5**	**Pta de la Media Naranja**
24	53	36°59′·2	01°53′·5	Puerto Pescaro de Carboneras
	54	**37°10′·5**	**01°46′**	**Puerto de Garrucha**
25	55	37°10′·5	01°48′·8	Puerto de Garrucha approaches
26/27	56	37°14′·9	01°45′·7	Puerto de Esperanza approaches
28	57	37°24′	01°34′·2	Aguilas approaches
	58	**37°31′**	**01°17′·5**	**SE of Pta Negra**
29	59	37°33′·3	01°16′·3	Puerto Deportivo de Mazarrón
30	60	37°33′·9	01°15′·1	Puerto de Mazarrón approaches
31	61	37°33′·5	01°00′	Puerto de Cartagena
31	62	37°35′	00°58′·9	Puerto de Cartegena entrance
	63	**37°32′**	**00°46′**	**SE of Cabo Negrete**
33	64	37°37′·5	00°41′·8	Puerto de Cabo Palos approaches
	65	**37°40′**	**00°35′·5**	**ENE of Islas Hormigas**
34	66	37 43′·2	00°43′·0	Mar Menor approaches (S)
34	67	37°44′	00°42′·8	Mar Menor approaches (N)
34	68	37°45′	00°45′	Puerto de Tomás Maestre approaches (W)
V				
43	70	37°49′·2	00°44′·9	San Pedro del Pinatar
44	71	37°51′·8	00°45′·3	Puerto de la Horadada approaches
45	72	37°53′·8	00°44′·7	Puerto de Campoamor approaches
46	73	37°54′·6	00°43′·7	Puerto de Cabo Roig approaches
	74	**37°55′**	**00°41′**	**Cabo Roig**
47	75	37°57′·5	00°41′·1	Torrevieja approaches
48	76	38°06′·7	00°38′·0	Marina de las Dunas approaches
49	77	38°10′·7	00°33′·9	Puerto de Santa Pola
	78	**38°09′**	**00°25′**	**Off Islas de Tarbarca**
52	79	38°19′·35	00°29′·1	Puerto de Alicante
	80	**38°21′·**	**00°22′·5**	**Cabo de las Huertas**
53	81	38°21′·5	00°26′·5	Puerto de San Juan
54	82	38°25′·6	00°23′·0	Puerto de Campello
55	83	38°30′·2	00°13′·3	Puerto de Villajoyosa
56	84	38°31′·9	00°08′·2	Puerto de Benidorm
57	85	38°35′·1	00°03′·12	Puerto de Altea
60	86	38°37′·6	00°00′·3	Marina Greenwich
		N	E	
61	87	38°38′·1	00°02′·24	Puerto Blanco approaches
62	88	38°38′·12	00°03′·9	Puerto de Calpe approaches
	89	**38°37′**	**00°06′·5**	**Peñon de Ifach**
64	90	38°41′·0	00°08′·5	Puerto de Moirara approaches
	91	**38°39′·5**	**00°11′·5**	**Puerto de Moraira**
	92	**38°44′·**	**00°16′**	**Cabo de Nao**
65	93	38°47′·5	00°11′·5	Puerto de Jávea approaches
	94	**38°49′**	**00°13′**	**Cabo de San Antonio**
66	95	38°51′·4	00°08′·3	Puerto de Dénia approaches

Index